Mooi Street
and Other Moves

Mooi Street
and Other Moves

PAUL SLABOLEPSZY

WITS UNIVERSITY PRESS

Wits University Press
1 Jan Smuts Avenue
Johannesburg
2001

www.witspress.co.za

First published in 1994
Reprinted 2015
Second edition 2017

978-1-77614-159-3 (Print)
978-1-77614-160-9 (PDF)

Project managed by Hazel Cuthbertson
Cover design by Fire and Lion, South Africa
Typesetting by Fire and Lion, South Africa

PAUL SLABOLEPSZY was born in Bolton, England and emigrated to South Africa at the age of three. He grew up in the Northern Transvaal (present day Limpopo), matriculating in Pietersburg (Polokwane). He graduated from the University of Cape Town with a Bachelor of Arts in English and Drama. He was a founder member (with Athol Fugard and Yvonne Bryceland) of the Space Theatre Company in Cape Town in 1972.

A prolific playwright (as well as radio, television and film script writer), he has written 31 plays, including *Saturday Night at the Palace*, which went from Johannesburg's Market Theatre (where six of his plays have premiered) to London's Old Vic, and has been made into a successful film. His other plays are: *Renovations, The Defloration of Miles Koekemoer, Karoo Grand, Making Like America, Travelling Shots, One for the High Jump, The Eyes of their Whites* (co-written with David Kramer), *Braait Laaities, Pale Natives, My Low-Fat Almost Italian Wedding, Tickle to Fine Leg, Heel Against the Head, Once a Pirate, Going for the Jocular, Fordsburg's Finest, Planet Perth, Life's a Pitch, Crashing the Night, Running Riot, It's Just Not Cricket, Whole in One, Art of Charf, Freak Country, For Your Ears Only,* and *Suddenly the Storm.*

Paul lives in Johannesburg with his wife, Carol and their three children, Frances, Alice and Tim. His other great passion is the gentle science of cricket.

Contents

Contents

Glossary

(Largely Afrikaans slang)

Aasvoël	vulture
Abbos	derogatory name for Australian Aborigines
Affs	short for 'Africans', black people
Agterplaas	backyard
Aikona	no, no ways (isiZulu)
Akhela	name of Wolf Cub pack leader
Alles sal regkom	everything's going to come right
Atjar	vegetable pickle, relish
Bakgat	very good
Bakkie	light pick-up truck
Ballsup	mess, catastrophe
Big bok	big deal, a boaster
Blikskottel	scoundrel
Bliksem/se	cad, bastard
Boep	protruding belly
Boer maak 'n plan	farmer makes a plan
Boer/e	farmer/s
Boet/a	brother, buddy
Boggerol	bugger all
Bokdrol	buck or goat droppings
Boobs	breasts
Booze	hard liquor, strong drink
Braai	barbeque
Brak	cur, mongrel
Bredie	stew
Broek	trousers
Bult	hill, ridge
Buzz	beat, outlook, way of life
Charf	talk, chat up
Codesa-desa	negotiate
Cubs	junior version of Boy Scouts (Wolf Cubs)
Dankie	thank you
Dassie	rabbit-like wild animal
Deurmekaar	mixed up
Dingamalerie	whatjoo-macallit, thingie
Dis 'n blerrie/bladdy ...	it's a bloody ...
Dit reen	it's raining
Dof	stupid, sleepy
Doos/es	obscene term of address
Dop	drink, tot

Dorp	small town
Dronk	drunk, intoxicated
Dronklap	drunkard
Dronkverdriet	drunken self-pity
Durbs	Durban, South African seaport
Dwaal	state of confusion, absent-mindedness
Dweezil	a nerd
Eina!	ouch! (cry of pain)
Flog	sell, get rid of
Gat	hole, arsehole
Gatvol	fed up, had enough
Gemore	mess, mess up
Gooi	throw
Grease-monkey	derogatory term for motor mechanic
Groot	big, large
Hamba kahle	go well [isiZulu]
Haregat (hardegat)	miserly, tight-arse
HNP	Herstigte Nasionale Party – extreme right-wing political party
Hoer	whore
Hok	cage, pen
Houtkop	wood-head (derogatory term for a black person)
Howzit	greeting – 'how is it going?'
Hurl	throw up, vomit
Jirre	God, literally 'Here' (Afrikaans)
Jislaaik	watered-down version of 'Jesus'
Jissus/Yissus	Jesus
Jolling, jol	having a good time, partying, razzling
Jong	young man
Kaalgat	naked
Kaalpoot	bare-footed
Kaffir	unacceptable offensive word for a black person
Kak	excrement
Kak off	find oneself in deep trouble
Kakhuis	outdoor lavatory
Kakstories	rubbish
Khakibos	a type of bush weed
Khaya	dwelling, house [isiZulu]
Kip	sleep
Klaar	finished, complete, end-of-story
Klap	hit, slap, a hiding
Kleilat	children's game using flexible sticks to fling lumps of clay at an opponent
Kleinhuise	outdoor lavatory (literally, small house)
Klipdrift	brand of cheap South African brandy
Klomp	bundle, bunch

Klopdisselboom	progressing famously
Koekie	cookie, cupcake
Kommunis	communist
Kroeg	bar, public house
Kuif	quiff (hairstyle)
Kwes	short for question
Kyk	look
Laaitie	young boy
Lag	laugh
Lekker	very nice
Lomp	awkward, unsophisticated
Los	leave, as in leave it alone
Magnus Malan	Minister of Defence in the National Party government in the 1980s
Mahala	free (isiZulu)
Malgat	crazy person
Maritzburg	abbreviation of Pietermaritzburg, a city in KwaZulu-Natal
Meid	maid, housemaid
Meisie	girl
Meneer	mister, sir
Mishoop	dung heap
Moegoe/mugu	idiot
Moer	beat up, screw
Moer/sa	massive, very big
Moffie	male homosexual
Mos	just so, of course
Necklace	method of torture and murder, using a burning tyre. It was widely used, mainly against political opponents during the political unrest of the mid-1980s
Nogal	and what's more ...
Nooit	never
Oke/s	bloke/s, chap/s, guy/s
Oom	uncle, sir (polite form of address used by Afrikaans-speaking people)
Ou top	old man, father
Ou/s	bloke/s, fellow/s
Oupa	grandpa
Pap	porridge
Passela	handout, gift (isiZulu)
Pick 'n Pay	large supermarket chain
Piekniek	picnic
Piks	strikes, bites (as in snake bite)
Platteland	countryside (literally flat land), especially remote rural areas
Plug	fail (as in school exams)

Poep	fart
Poephol	arsehole
Pondok	shack, dwelling
Pooftah/poefte	a gay, a homosexual
Pozzie	place, position, turf
Pull finger	get going
Que sera sera	what will be, will be (Italian)
Robot	traffic light
Rooking	smoking (as in smoking marijuana)
Ruk 'a rol	rock 'n roll
Sasol	South African company which manufactures petrol (gasoline) from coal
Shaun Thompson	South Africa's best-known surfer
Sies/sis!	an expression of distaste, as in yeugh!
Sjambok	leather whip, quirt
Skinnering	gossiping, bitching
Skoon	clean
Skyf	cigarette (especially marijuana)
Slag	kill, slaughter
Slapgat	lazy person
Slet	slut, whore
Sluk	swallow, mouthful
Sommer	just, just because
Sowaar	truly, for sure
Split	leave, go away
Stampvol	packed full
Steek	stab
Stoep	patio, veranda
Strond	excrement
'Strue's bob	simplification of 'as true as God'
Sug	care, worry
Sussed	worked out, figured out
Sweet	sweat, perspiration
Takkies	sneakers
Tekere gaan	behave in an over-emotional, hysterical manner
Tet	nipple
Tickey-box	telephone booth
Tiekiedraai	Afrikaans folk dance
Tit	nice, pleasant, enjoyable
Toemaar	never mind, don't worry
Totsiens	goodbye
Troepie	young soldier, new recruit
Twak	rubbish, also tobacco
Umlazi	a black township outside Durban
Vasbyt, min hare, baie dae	army expressions, literally bite hard (endure), short hair, many days

Vastrap	quick-step (Afrikaans folk dance)
Vat jou good en trek	take your belongings and go away
Veld	field, plains
Veldskoen	leather lace-up outdoor shoe, especially as worn by farmers
Voël/Voëltjie	bird, small bird
Voema	vim, vigour
Voetsek	bugger-off, go away
Volksie	Volkswagen Beetle motorcar
Vrek	die
Vrot	rotten, festering
Wat ook al	whatever
Windgat	a person with a large ego, boastful
Witgat	white person
Woes	extremely angry
Wors	sausage
Woza	come here (isiZulu)
Wraggies	honestly, truthfully
Wraught	fight, battle
Zola Budd	South African Olympic runner

Introduction

ROBERT GREIG

Paul Slabolepszy is the cartographer of the white male soul facing the abyss. Better than any other South African playwright, he has depicted the dreams, hopes and insecurities, and violences of white male South Africans through the doom-laden days of apartheid's decline. Many of his plays are images of that decline: they convey uniquely the atmosphere of paralysis and paranoia of that time. More recently, in plays like *Mooi Street Moves, The Return of Elvis du Pisanie* and *Pale Natives* (1994, not included in this collection), Slabolepszy has depicted the effects of social and political change, his theatre shifting from a social to a psychological focus and, in the process, maturing.

If, as Dan Jacobson said, quoting Olive Schreiner, white South Africans are 'lower-middle-class philistines', in Slabolepszy's hands they tend to be depicted as 'lower-middle-class nihilists'. The Schreiner observation is useful, if only in indicating that the preoccupations of two writers with extensive allegiances to England are not the preoccupations of a Slabolepszy. Slabolepszy is one of a generation of post-colonial writers.

The cumulative effects of time, as well as political and cultural isolation, have made the class and cultural labels which Schreiner used and Jacobson approved seem an historical curiosity, useful only in suggesting the distance between Slabolepszy's world and that of his predecessors.

In Slabolepszy's world, 'overseas' is as remote and insubstantial as a TV sitcom, which in fact forms the images of what used to be called in South Africa 'the outside world'. In *Saturday Night at the Palace* (1982, not included in this collection), Forsie, who has never been to the sea, insists confidently that 'everyone knows Jo'burg'. He and Vince imagine overseas as Hollywood.

Throughout Slabolepszy's plays, references to the TV series, *Dallas,* occur: this, rather than the humane literacy of Bloomsbury, is the characters' reference point. To Slabolepszy, the implied comparisons which Jacobson and Schreiner make – between here and there, local and foreign, colony and parent country, province and metropolis, along with the class consciousness – are irrelevant. They are not part of his landscape yet Slabolepszy is aware of both the comedy and the pathos in the cultural references of his characters.

The Slabolepszy landscape should be described. Like others of his generation, most of Slabolepszy's life was spent under Nationalist Party rule. Anyone under the age of about fifty, without lasting experience of other countries, has lived in an atmosphere oddly blending the sensations of immobilised permanence and anxious insecurity: both of these sensations are strongly communicated in the plays. It possibly explains why the poetry of the eighties tends to be dominated by images of travelling, rootlessness and impending apocalypse, fantasies of escape and nightmares of displacement.

In Slabolepszy's landscape, the characters are stuck, their fantasies are similar and their responses are aggressive. In fact, his plays have few scene-changes: the economic constraints facing an independent writer-actor-director translate into metaphors of paralysis, immobility and degeneration.

In *Boo to the Moon,* the set is dominated by a crashed 1970s Fiat somewhere near Durban, in *Smallholding,* it is dominated by a beached caravan – an ironic allusion to a Voortrekker wagon – and littered with mechanical objects that don't work. In *Boo to the Moon,* Myrtle is haunted by nightmares of swimming-pool cleaners invading the house, while Jessica scorns her father's love affair with expensive vehicles that he can't drive properly.

The broken technological mechanisms stand for the society at large. In the hands of a Western playwright, these sets might have ushered in an indictment of mechanistic societies and perhaps a celebration of nature. Slabolepszy's characters have no such illusions: they do not celebrate nature and nature is no alternative. The characters are literally and spiritually powerless: they are stuck emotionally, morally, physically and intellectually. And being stuck, they turn to anarchic humour. On stage, many of Slabolepszy's characters are all movement and verbal pyrotechnics: it is difficult to find the core of character. Activity and action for their own sakes become modes of being, a strategy of avoiding the immobilising, oppressive atmosphere of a country which seemed to be caught between a defiled past and an uncertain future. As Spider says in *Boo to the Moon*: 'and it might be the last jol we ever have – so I'd bladdy-well enjoy it'.

The immutability which the Nationalists seemed to represent to many might have been repugnant, but at the same time, for many reasons, the alternatives seemed threatening and scary. Many South Africans therefore had and have an ambivalent relationship with their country: wanting it to change but fearing the insecurity of change, caught between the comforts of security, however stifling and morally defiling, and the unclear prospects which seem alarmingly threatening and vague. The metaphor which Slabolepszy uses in *Smallholding* is that of life with the semi-paralysed, drunken and dangerous father-figure, offering the perverse comforts of paternal authority, along with the dangers of its unpredictable exercise.

The ever-present spectre of violent, unpredictable and dangerous male authority permeates Slabolepszy's plays. At one level, these plays recognise the threat and acknowledge the fear; at another, they recognise the danger and insubstantiality of this authority. At a third, they recognise the comedy of emperors in tattered clothes. Slabolepszy's plays are an uneasy blend of different emotions and recognitions:

the comedy is anarchic, a gesture of anxious aggression. His characters do not underestimate the power of male authority and it often determines their actions: JJ, in *Smallholding*, seeks a fragile safety by 'becoming' what he fears: the violent, unpredictable killer, in much the same way that Johnny in Fugard's *Hello and Goodbye* cripples himself by ceding his own identity. Evie – ironic name – defies her father, identifying with Gideon, the black farmhand, though on stage this seems forced. These are as much responses to threat as quests for security.

A playwright like Slabolepszy grew up in another kind of insecurity, cultural insecurity. Slabolepszy was (and is) English-speaking in a country ruled by Afrikaners where the majority was black. He was born in England in 1948 and his parents emigrated to South Africa when he was three. He grew up in small Transvaal towns whose citizens were – and are – at the far right of the political spectrum. Slabolepszy was sent to the University of Cape Town to study engineering. At the end of the first term, he broke the news to his father that he had, in fact, been studying drama. To be in classes with black students was, says Slabolepszy, a shock.

He was relatively privileged, entering the theatre at a time when public funding for white theatre was munificent, though the decline of public funding for the arts in South Africa, mirroring the decline in moral and financial solvency of the apartheid state, directly affected Slabolepszy and was one reason for his putting acting in second place to the writing and production of plays, a talent he had begun to develop at school.

Slabolepszy was one of an extremely talented, university-trained generation of actors that differed from previous generations in three important respects: First, they were committed to working in South Africa and not taking the usual route out, with stars in their eyes about the West End or Broadway. Second, and relatedly, they had practical examples of South African playwrights, black and white, at work. They defined themselves as South Africans, rather than as colonials or settlers, and the emergence of examples like Athol Fugard, Barney Simon and Yvonne Bryceland, whose material was a known, rather than refracted world, was a source of strength. They had seen 'relevant' theatre at The Space with non-racial casts and felt a stronger connection to new South African work and off-off Broadway plays than to the official culture displayed by whites-only casts at the state-subsidised theatres. Third, the members of this generation tended to regard themselves as a group. They were (and are) bound by strong personal loyalties and shared ambitions and were mutually supportive. This was nothing as finite as a school or movement, but Slabolepszy's generation entered professional theatre having made a name for themselves as a particularly talented group of people, and tended to work together in the same theatres.

The Space Theatre in Cape Town was a couple of blocks away from the University of Cape Town's drama school and many of UCT's actors began working there before they left university. Since Cape Town in the seventies was a small, provincial city with relatively little professional theatre – and much of that from the politically-tainted, state-subsidised Cape Performing Arts Board (Capab) – the traditional distinctions between professional and amateur theatre were blurred. As a result, new talent could be absorbed more easily and quickly into the theatre generally. The UCT productions were reviewed and attended as professional productions and when UCT actors appeared at The Space, they were reviewed as professional actors.

Many of these actors, including Slabolepszy, moved to Johannesburg, and with the experience of working for The Space, readily slipped into the newly-formed, similar theatres in Johannesburg, like the Arena, founded by Barney Simon, which was the precursor of the famous Market Theatre. To a large extent, the generation of which Slabolepszy was a member did much to create its own opportunities: this, too, distinguished them from previous generations of university-trained actors.

Inadvertently, too, the cultural boycott helped in certain respects, though it would be a mistake to underestimate the damage it did to the intellectual life of the country. The replacement of images of Bloomsbury by images of Dallas is an example of that damage.

The cultural boycott insulated South African theatre from foreign competition and from the colonial cringe which saw imported actors getting the lead roles and local actors struggling to conceal their accents. It forced actors and writers to be self-sufficient and to follow Fugard's example by concentrating on the here and now, rather than the there and then. Most importantly, the boycott helped the theatre close what had been a yawning gap between the world of the stage and the world of the streets, the language of theatre and the language of human beings in the theatre. This closing of the gap was a source of vigour.

The concentration on the here and now is articulated in *Boo to the Moon* by Spider, probably one of Slabolepszy's most complex – and representative – characters. He is deceptive. At first blush, Spider seems like just another joller, a thicky who has failed class year after year, and is destined to spend his early adulthood writing and rewriting his matriculation exam. But there are suggestions that the character is more than this. Slabolepszy alerts us to his complexity and depth by having Spider consistently use nature imagery in his early speeches, identifying him with a wider world than the immediate. This is about as close as Slabolepszy gets to assigning a moral value to nature, as Western writers often do.

Initially, Spider seems a comic turn, a know-nothing philistine. Witness his description of Hamlet – 'Hamlet comes back from boarding school to find his mother having it off with his uncle. Because of this and also the fact that something is very rotten in the State of Denmark, he slowly but surely goes out of his mind'.

His attitude to history is crucial: 'What's history anyway? Huh? It's about a bunch of wankers trying to bullshit a bunch of even bigger wankers that such-and-such happened on such a day. Meanwhile what actually happened is something totally different. I mean, take South Africa. When the blacks take over – Jan van Riebeeck's out the window ... '.

Later, the character develops. The know-nothing-philistinism is revealed as a screen. Spider, perhaps implausibly, uses terms like 'the art of discourse' and finally indicts his goody-goody companions: 'You know when Napoleon sent a piss-willy little telegram to Bismarck but I bet you know stuff-all about what happened in Soweto on 16th a' June 1976'.

Finally, it becomes clear that Spider is not simply a Natal Jimmy Porter motivelessly ranting about the venality of the nation and his elders, with their love of emollient music and material objects. He has actually experienced political violence – a terror-bomb explosion at a supermarket. His critiques both of history and of his schoolmates' plans to join the sheep, either by emigrating or growing up 'responsibly', derive from experience of the abyss. The abyss of political violence invalidates the past and negates the future: meaning is only in the present moment.

Running through *Boo to the Moon* is a serious questioning of history, the kind of questioning that is connected not only with a sense of impending cataclysm, which will negate history, but also with a profound sense of certain histories mattering more than others. Spider suspects those, like teachers, who use history to obscure pressing realities, to muffle criticism or to infantilise. *Boo to the Moon* was, after all, written in the darkest of days – the bellicose, repressive regime of P W Botha. It reflects, obliquely, some of the intellectual debates of the time about which history mattered in South Africa, debates which helped form the fibre of anti-apartheid movements.

As the Nationalist regime began to crumble and the prospects of black rule became clearer, and as state spending on warfare absorbed more public finances, performers like Slabolepszy gradually shifted from acting to writing. In many senses, South African theatre is an actor's theatre – written by actors for actors rather than by writers for directors and actors. Economics lie behind this: the rewards and support which full-time playwrights require tend to be greater than those for full-time actors. But there's another reason: in a country where English is, at best, a second language for most citizens, the written script, as opposed to the improvised performance, can be a liability to actors.

The advantages and the disadvantages of an actor's theatre can be seen in much of Slabolepszy's work. The advantages are immediacy, actability, realistic language. The disadvantages tend to be less obvious: a certain structural formlessness, sometimes dialogue for effect rather than for thematic purpose, and sometimes considerable padding before the action of the play becomes clear. Like Fugard's white characters, Slabolepszy's often tend to live close to the dividing lines between white and black South African society. Unlike Fugard's, that dividing line is often absolute: Slabolepszy's characters seldom cross it except when impelled by enraged violence. Many of them live in a kind of depressed, urban frontier society, prickling with guns and knives, where interactions between black and white are nervous and potentially violent. Spider forces his schoolmates to cross the line by enacting the role of the violent black activist, miming a necklacing. But his action reflects fear of beyond and therefore portrays only the fearful. This contrasts with the window into familiar domestic life offered by Forsie and Vince in opening the suitcase of September, the black waiter, in *Saturday Night at the Palace*.

In Slabolepszy's plays, unlike in Fugard's, there are no blood knots. Blacks are viewed coolly from a distance and there is, in the present collection, none of the breath-taking pathos and empathy of the scene in *Saturday Night at the Palace* in which Vince raids September's suitcase, indifferently tossing out clothes intended for children September has not seen for two years.

The white characters tend to be in cul-de-sacs and, cornered, tend to attack each other, or target blacks, or self-destruct. One of the primary focuses of Slabolepszy's plays is the cornered white male and his behaviour. It is impossible to say certainly how conscious a reflection of political and social changes this is – Slabolepszy is not a cerebral playwright or a writer of ideas: his plays are as visceral as their writer's acting.

It is easier to say that Slabolepszy clearly felt a compulsion to document or reflect changes in the wider society, and this was consciously done. But in other, subtle ways, the reflection is inadvertent, but no less powerful or accurate for that. The characters act out many of the social dramas of the time; some of Slabolepszy's plays are workings out, in dramatic terms, of these changes. This occurs to the extent that the characters seem to have only social identity and role, rather than psychological or personal identities. Most successfully, especially in *Smallholding*, there is no clear dividing line: the psyche of Pa is both a personal and a political one.

Most of Slabolepszy's characters are young in terms of age and sometimes also maturity. Often, the action of the play is a loss of innocence or, at least, its qualification. During the events on stage, the characters have to grow up: Slabolepszy catches them balanced on sharp-edged hinges in their lives, between a vanishing reality and one that is vaguely threatening, though by no means apparent.

More recently (*The Return of Elvis du Pisanie* and *Mooi Street Moves* are good examples), the characters are delayed adolescents – what feminist critics of male society unkindly call 'Peter Pans', creatures of quick, scattered, disparate energy – and during the play, they confront the limitations of dreams. In Slabolepszy's scenario, facing dreams is seldom willed; it is forced and this breeds violence in those least equipped emotionally to face changes. That violence spins outwards, catching others in the whirlpool. The contagion of violence is depicted in *Saturday Night at the Palace* and *Boo to the Moon*.

There is a curious tension in Slabolepszy's works. His most arresting characters, the most energetic, are anarchists and outsiders. They also tend to be losers – the three characters in *Over the Hill* are good examples. Much of the poignancy – and comedy

– of his plays lies in watching losers comfort each other, or recognise failure in others but not in themselves. They have exaggerated estimations of their abilities; they are out of touch with the way others see them and this, in Slabolepszy's hands, is a recipe for painful comedy. When their energies are thwarted, their destructiveness can as easily turn inwards and suicidal as outwards to murder.

Hovering behind these characters is the spectre of the Sunday family murderer: authoritarian, disappointed, inarticulate, who, with a couple of beers under his belt, beats up the wife then shoots her, the children and himself. Charlie in *Over the Hill* deals with the suspicion of his wife's infidelity by fantasising violence: 'I kept my cool. All I did one night, I just casually brought out the gun ... to clean it. Made sure the kid was there too. Okay, you haven't got a kid. You got a kid, it helps. She sees you, she sees the kid, she sees the gun ... She thinks ... She doesn't try it again. [*Pause*] There's more to being the boss than making a noise'.

Eddie, in *Elvis du Pisanie* fantasises, consoling himself with the thought of being the lead character at his own funeral: 'This pathetic little bunch, all gathering around my AVBOB discount coffin and sadly shaking their heads ...'. In a long monologue, he describes in detail the acts leading up to his connecting the swimming pool cleaner hose to the exhaust of his motor car, turning on the engine and dying, anaesthetised by drink.

These fantasies are fundamentally compensatory and self-pitying. The characters are in tight corners and face the choice between turning aggression inwards or outwards. Aggression tends to be their main reaction to entrapment – aggression, or escape into derisive laughter.

In *Elvis du Pisanie,* Eddie states: 'What happens if your whole life has been one big ballsup ... from beginning to end? One big ... gemors. Well, I 'spose if that's the case, you just ... you just lag. You just ... die laughing ... !'

He does more than that. Eddie is a character who recollects, finding strength in images drawn from the past, unlike Spider. His strength is drawn from a memory of setting a trap for a pretentious, boring uncle, which involved, significantly, putting the uncle where Eddie says he himself began: in the shit. Far from being an escape, laughter becomes a permutation of the violence trap, an extension of aggression by other means.

Yet the Eddies, the Spiders, and even Pa, are immensely appealing, at least partly because they are energetic and have the child-like appeal of those who over-simplify.

By contrast, their foils seem pallid, civilised, emotionally castrated or convoluted: to an extent, especially in his earlier plays, Slabolepszy rigs the odds – nice nasties versus nasty nice guys. He tends to root for the philistines, rather the way Roy Campbell seemed to when abroad. There is something of the ebullient frontier spirit in these characters and a certain ambivalence with which Slabolepszy depicts a Pa, for example. In *Smallholding,* he is the most appealing character on stage, the character with the most weight of history and also personality. Compare him, for example, to Christiaan, the post office worker, worrying about his car radio, grotesquely obeisant to authority, or to Allie in *Boo to the Moon,* the archetypal nerd whose terror of military service is denied the dignity of desperation.

The contrast between virile pioneer and effete settler is glaringly drawn in *Under the Oaks* – between Corky, the Western Cape Boer, and Richard, the Natal Brit. These stereotypes are set deeply in the South African psyche – think, for example, of the disabled pioneers in Fugard's *Hello and Goodbye* and *People are Living There,* and their inadequate progeny. In the same period, other white writers, like Pieter-Dirk Uys, also tended to celebrate the earthiness of the Boer and deprecate the English-speaking as effete neocolonials.

Read in conjunction, *Under the Oaks* and *Smallholding* reveal much about Slabolepszy's technique and his gradual ability to develop stereotypes.

The Boer is earthy, ebullient, anarchic, living for brandy-and-Coke and the outdoors. The Brit is tight-sphinctered and overcivilised, a stranger to Newlands. Much of the comedy of the play has to do with the audience's recognition and acceptance of these stereotypes. The play has a fugitive sense of impending violence as well, related to the suggestion of conflict between the two characters, and also to one's own sense that the play surely cannot stay indefinitely with badinage: the characters have to reveal themselves and in doing so, conflict.

The conflict, when it comes, is brushed aside. It takes the form of a hesitant, undeveloped subplot featuring a relationship between the Boer's wife and the Brit. It may be asked why the play did not go further than it does – why, in fact, it hovers on the brink, ending with nothing very much actually having happened.

I don't think Slabolepszy had the technique or confidence when he wrote *Under the Oaks* to follow his material into areas of psychological conflict. He stuck to the comedy of contrast because it was easy and comfortable. Another factor is that *Under the Oaks* was a commissioned play and was written for specific actors – James Borthwick and Graham Hopkins – who conform closely to the Boer–Brit stereotypes. This may have prevented greater thematic development.

The same contrast – between a son of the soil and an overcivilised urban wimp – resurfaces in *Smallholding,* and the theme of marrying off the daughter of the son of the soil to the urban wimp becomes explicit.

Pa is an updated, live version of the father in *Hello and Goodbye,* the oldtime pioneer living on the land. The difference is that he is alive and burdensome to his children, rather than dead and burdensome. The situation, too, has changed: the smallholding of the play abuts urban sprawl; it is a dumping ground for its detritus and cast-offs. Nothing mechanical in the play really works once Pa gets hold of it: an antagonism between the historical son of the soil and the urban dweller in one person results in mechanical failure.

Nevertheless, the relationships between the characters are complex and subtle as Slabolepszy critically depicts myths and stereotypes which were taken for granted or celebrated in *Under the Oaks*. Pa may adopt the mien and style of the displaced frontiersman but his view of the frontier is largely based, not on experience, but on imported imagery drawn from urban popular culture – *Dallas,* for example. His son's violence borrows the imagery of B movies – the use of a power-saw as a weapon.

Smallholding is an extraordinarily ornate play, difficult to pin down, but haunting. One's first impression of the stage, with its beached caravan, tatty fairy lights and Roy Orbison music, recalled plays by Sam Shepard. The allusion is inescapable and, like Shepard, Slabolepszy invests the detritus of urban life with powerful poetic symbolism, while acknowledging the tattiness of that detritus. The references to *Dallas* are ironical in that they define Pa's imaginative limitations, but the definition is also sympathetic. Pa is ultimately depicted as a character living and finding life in outworn myths. For him, the myths have sustaining power, but the poignancy of the character is that those myths may sustain but they don't equip. He is literally a character subsisting rather than living. He pins his hopes on the growing of kubus (a reference to a popular scam of the early eighties) upon which Gideon urinates at the beginning of the play. One is reminded of the gods of irony in Zbigniew Herbert's poem: 'Then came the barbarians. They too valued the little god of irony. They would crush it under their heels and add it to their dishes'.

There is a marked difference in Slabolepszy's political consciousness in *Smallholding* from that in *Under the Oaks*. There is also a difference in his ability to translate that consciousness into stage images. The plot of land is haunted by the ghosts of black, dislodged people; their only trace is Gideon whose tongue was torn out by dogs belonging to the farmer. The competition for the woman, which in popular South African culture usually represents decisions about South Africa's future, is between the black and Christiaan, who is essentially another version of Richard in *Under the Oaks*.

Obliquely and sometimes directly, Slabolepszy's plays are explorations of the current dynamics of broader political change. At one level, *Smallholding* is a metaphor of broader political processes, perhaps even mechanically so. For example, it could be argued that the representation of Gideon as tongueless is an over-simple translation of votelessness.

By *Mooi Street Moves,* Slabolepszy's political consciousness has become more sophisticated. Although comic, the play is shot through with acerbic satire on the go-getting amorality of a country in a political interregnum. The setting is not rural, peri-urban or in a dorp, as it is in *Boo to the Moon, Under the Oaks, Over the Hill, Smallholding* or *The Return of Elvis du Pisanie*. It is a centre-city apartment in Hillbrow, Johannesburg, which was one of the first areas in which the demographic implications of political change were most strongly felt, as blacks occupied spaces formerly occupied by whites.

The play has another satirical dimension in its racial inversion of the stock Jim-comes-to-Jo'burg plot, the staple of both patronising white comedy and township plays. Here the country boy having to learn fast about the wiles of city life is white, and his tutor is a black spiv, Stix. Stix in turn learned from the boy's brother who was killed by cocaine. The white boy cherishes a dream of raising the money to drill for water but it is clear that this is only a dream, as nostalgic and remote and therefore as disabling in the present as Pa's get-rich-quick kubus schemes, or his hopes of a gentleman caller in a Mercedes marrying his daughter. Many of Slabolepszy's characters hope for miracles, for rescue: many of the plays are illustrations of the falsity of dreams; and much of the comedy which Slabolepszy writes gains its force from the sympathetic scorn he invites from his audiences.

Mooi Street Moves is, ultimately, a bleak play: it seems to end prematurely and with a kind of easy violence that does not seem justified by the terms of the play, but by a perception of the terms of the society about which the play is written. The violence, which depends for its effect on a confusion between shock and drama is thematically unsatisfying. Although the threat of the ruffian on the stair is established in the play, the precise motive for the killing seems unclear.

Slabolepszy's plays could, perhaps, be criticised for being too close to reality. I suspect that the pressure to earn a living through writing has sometimes denied him – and other South African writers – the freedom to reflect, to digest social material and transform it into dramatic energy. This is another way of saying that South African playwrights face – and have accepted – the responsibility to be chroniclers of their times – especially when censorship of other media transformed the stage into living newspapers. Inevitably then, their plays sometimes become a form of live reportage, a dramatic representation, in sometimes overly schematic terms, of their view of the society's dynamics. Much of the humour in Slabolepszy's plays is in the enactment of aggression – it is derisive, anarchic. It affords the audience the pleasure of watching characters say the unsayable and do the unspeakable. But the humour experienced by the audience is tempered by a sense of his characters' self-destructiveness and desperation on the one hand or, on the other, by their impotence.

Eddie in *Elvis du Pisanie* is a different matter. The play represents a new direction for Slabolepszy, formally and thematically, and for his characters.

The play is, firstly, a monologue: the character is confronting himself. It depicts Eddie drawn to the spectre of Elvis Presley and back into Eddie's own past, in which the encounter with Elvis first took place. Eddie, like other Slabolepszy characters, is trapped, and like them, has also expressed his sense of entrapment with aggression and fantasies of violence. But during the play, he faces himself, recognising the reviving force of the past and of fantasy. He does not try to become anyone else or to deny himself: he accepts and builds from there. He jokes, like most of Slabolepszy's characters, but joking is not a substitute for action or a smokescreen: his jokes tend to be self-accepting, rather than denying.

Unlike Spider's, Eddie's abyss is personal not political. He is integrated into his society: he has a past and present to which he can and will return. His survival involves tapping images of the past. These are also tacky and thin – the return of Elvis Presley and a couple of minutes of fame and acknowledgement at an Elvis impersonators' concert. But they are highly potent and energising because they involve Eddie emotionally revisiting a site of power and accomplishment, dealing with what is in his control. All Spider has is a defiled past and a violent present: he is a social being and at the mercy of social forces. One cannot imagine Spider alone; Eddie rebuilds his life by exploring his aloneness. Of all Slabolepszy's characters – excluding those in *Pale Natives* which, in many senses, have the maturity of Eddie – Eddie is the most adult and the most likely to survive.

But, unlike Spider or the gallery of frontiersmen in Slabolepszy's plays, Eddie exists within society, rather than standing outside it. He would be seen by a Spider as a sell-out and might even have been depicted by Slabolepszy earlier in his career as one of the pale, desk-bound, negligible creatures – a Christiaan, perhaps.

Elvis du Pisanie has a resonance which few of Slabolepszy's other plays have. The emotions are cooler, the monologue is without images of lacerating physical violence, the drama is psychological – and psychologically realistic and honest. In many of Slabolepszy's plays, the characters seem like stereotypes or archetypes, devoid of psychology and all impulse.

Naturally Eddie does not have the immediate, visceral appeal of Slabolepszy's outsiders. His appeal is more subtle, and so is his creator's craft.

Slabolepszy's progression as a writer has tended to mirror the development of his characters – from archetype to individual. As a playwright, he seems to be moving towards more introspective forms of realism based on close observation, not only of the way his characters speak, which he has always done superbly, but also of their emotional rhythms and tides.

Bringing Page to Stage

BOBBY HEANEY

It is every stage director's dream to be given a new play to direct – to be instrumental in shaping the play, bringing the characters to life for the first time. So, being associated either as director or producer with eleven of Paul Slabolepszy's plays has enriched my directing career immeasurably and enabled me to be a first-hand observer of the development of one of the foremost South African playwrights of this generation.

I have a very clear recollection of the day Paul brought a thin manuscript around to my house and asked me if I would like to read and perhaps direct his new play. He mentioned in passing that he had submitted the work for the Amstel Playwright of the Year award, and that two of the three characters had been written for himself and Bill Flynn to perform. I remember that the raw, powerful three-hander had been impressive enough for me to call him back the same day to tell him that I *had* to direct it, and within a week we had dates booked at the Market Theatre. *Saturday Night at the Palace* won the Amstel Award and went on to create a whole new genre of South African theatre.

For three-and-a-half exhilarating weeks I experienced for the first time the magic of a rough script being transformed, at almost miraculous speed, into a play. It was a rare privilege to be the catalyst in a process that had the unique Flynn talent challenging and sparking that of the emergent writer. We watched a myriad ideas being transformed into new pages of script each day, to be tested and honed and thrown out and added to, and finally shaped into performance. We watched the ending change again and again as we assessed and reassessed the impact of each moment. And all too soon, we were confronted by our first audience.

Two events stand out in the short period during which *Saturday Night at the Palace* previewed.

Since the play was about bikers, we thought it a good idea to invite the Hell's Angels to a performance. Only one of that night's extraordinary audience to whom I spoke had ever been inside a theatre before. With some trepidation, I sat among the smoking, whistling, drinking leather jackets as the lights went down. They talked, commented, walked across the stage to go to the toilet, and laughed and laughed. But gradually they began to listen, and grew quieter, more attentive. By the time the play took the serious turn that is a hallmark of Slabolepszy's work, the atmosphere was electric. Perhaps the evening was not as momentous as the first performance of *Waiting for Godot* in the San Quentin Penitentiary, but for us it was certainly unforgettable.

The second incident was the filming of a short excerpt from the play for publicity purposes. We filmed at a roadhouse and hoped that the television screening of the clip would help boost bookings. The day after the screening, booking for the show went through the roof and set us on the road that would take us, two years later, to Sweden, Ireland and the Old Vic Theatre in London. The two events were the first indications of something that would be borne out with each successive Slabolepszy play with which I have been associated – Paul Slabolepszy speaks to the ordinary person in South Africa. In the many months during which *Palace* was performed, we reached thousands of people who might otherwise never have set foot inside a theatre. Now, over a decade later, a new generation finds unlikely converts attracted to *The Return of Elvis du Pisanie,* and the most recent Slabolepszy play that I have directed – *Pale Natives* – and so it has been for all the others in between.

Slabolepszy's characters don't only appeal to South Africans. One of my most moving recollections is of Swedish audiences stamping their feet (their version of a standing ovation) for a deafening ten to fifteen minutes each night of the five-night run in Gothenburg. More and more of Paul's plays are being invited abroad and they have been translated into several languages.

Paul claims not to be a political animal, yet I think he has had a massive impact on the political conscience of white South Africa. The humour of his plays has seduced the unsuspecting into the stalls and there they have gained insights into many elements of life in the apartheid years.

I believe this oblique pricking of the conscience makes Slabolepszy's works more powerful than more blatant tub-thumping propaganda plays. He entertains, and the disquieted conscience is a side-effect.

It is his ability to make us laugh, combined with his rich, superbly defined characters, that make Slabolepszy such a powerful playwright. You *want* to watch his plays, even if more often than not you leave the theatre with a sense of unease. You love the characters, even if you don't admire their moral stances. You recognise yourself, and the beloved country, at every turn.

I do not think there is a South African playwright who writes finer dialogue. You only have to spend a day in rehearsal of a Slabolepszy play to realise just how easily the words translate from page to stage. The phrases are so real, the slang so natural and commonplace. And yet every play is peppered with lines so ingeniously funny or incisive that you can recall them years later.

One of the most exciting things about watching Paul develop as a playwright has been to observe the increased subtlety in his writing. *Palace* has a fairly straightforward structure, telling a simple story, but, as I worked on the later plays, I was aware that they were becoming increasingly more complex. The playlets in *Travelling Shots* are touchingly allegorical. *Smallholding* resonates far wider than the immediate family it depicts, and *Pale Natives* is much more than a play about men at a stag party.

We have had numerous discussions over the years about the 'messages' hidden in the plays, Paul fearing that they might be too obvious or that they would not be read at all. Invariably, without too much prompting from me, he gets the mix just right – they are there for the person who cares to look.

The relationship between a writer and a director is a very sensitive one when it comes to new plays – I regard my role as that of a catalyst. I think it is my duty not only to make the playwright aware of the strengths and weaknesses of the working draft, but to point out possibilities he or she may not even know exist. I have often found that Paul is unaware, at least consciously, of powerful elements that are present in his plays – I suppose in much the same way as poets are perhaps surprised by the depth of content in their work. Once discussed, these elements become cemented and are often developed.

How far must the director push the playwright ... and vice versa? I suppose it is knowing the answer to this key question that is the cornerstone of our successful writing/directing partnership. It is quite possible to destroy a new play by interfering too much in the critical pre-rehearsal and rehearsal phase of its development. By the same token, a play can be damaged by not realising the inherent potential of a virgin script.

The playwright is god – he creates his world – and the director is his chief advisor. Nothing is more exhilarating than experiencing that moment when intense discussion between playwright, director and actor suddenly causes the play to take a startling turn. That discovery has irrevocable consequences for the characters and the rest of the play. When the play is published and performed thereafter, the moment is natural and obvious – it had to happen that way – and yet, if that creative spirit had been different at the *moment critique,* perhaps a different play would have been created.

To have had the privilege of sharing in so many moments of creation is undoubtedly a highlight of my career and I hope that in some small way I contributed to the success of the plays.

Referring to *Pale Natives,* a critic wrote recently that Paul writes plays to be performed. The extraordinary thing is that this statement was intended as a criticism. Yes indeed, Paul Slabolepszy writes plays to be performed. And it is only when you start to rehearse, when you watch the characters come to life, when you watch the audiences transported by the works, that you realise just how brilliantly he does it.

Under the Oaks

A ONE-ACT PLAY

Jonathan Rands as RICHARD, and James Borthwick as CORKY.
Photograph by Ruphin Coudyzer.

Cast

CORKY (Fan Number One) ... late thirties
RICHARD (Fan Number Two) ... fortyish
BEATRICE (No Fan At All) ... mid-thirties

Newlands Cricket Ground, Cape Town, late summer

Under the Oaks was showcased at the PACT Liquifruit Pot Pourri Festival in September 1984. Corky was played by James Borthwick, Richard by Graham Hopkins and Beatrice by Jenny Sharp.

In December 1984, it was performed as part of the Oude Libertas Summer Festival in Stellenbosch, with James Borthwick as Corky, Neil McCarthy as Richard and Jenny Sharp as Beatrice.

In July 1985 it began a national tour (as part of a double-bill with *Over the Hill*) at the Grahamstown Standard Bank Festival of the Arts, with James Borthwick as Corky, Jonathan Rands as Richard and Kate Edwards as Beatrice.

In the past, I have encouraged directors/actors to update the names of the players as they change with each passing season. Now, however, the oaks have gone. They were chopped down in mid-1993 to make way for the 'new' Newlands. I suggest that future producers stick to the present text which is set before the destruction of the oaks.

Paul Slabolepszy

The Oaks. Newlands Cricket Ground.

The set comprises a section of The Oaks enclosure and should include at least four rows of benches, each higher than the one in front.

On the back-support strip of wood that runs the length of each row are numbers. It is not particularly important where they start as long as all rows end with the number 41 on the aisle (stage left), for example 36 – 37 – 38 – 39 – 40 – 41.

In front of the first row (ground level) runs a small white picket fence denoting the boundary.

The benches themselves are painted 'sports-field' green. They look well weathered and are speckled here and there with offerings from countless feathered offenders residing in the oaks above.

Before the play begins the set is bare. All we hear is the odd cry from peanut vendors, ice cream sellers and so on. Over the public address we hear a stretched tape playing military marches, old favourites and the like – the music should sound monotonous rather than stirring.

A large individual appears at the top of the aisle with much huffing, puffing and climbing. He is carrying a huge cooler bag, a garden umbrella, several cushions, a transistor radio/cassette, a small portable braai and a canvas shoulder bag (containing fuel for the fire as well as other odds and ends). Our intrepid cricket supporter makes his way down to the picket fence.

He looks straight out front and surveys what is soon to become the battlefield – the hallowed turf on which the game is to take place. Not exactly Christian Dior, he nevertheless strikes a dashing pose in his veldskoens, rugby socks, checked shorts, vertically striped shirt and ever-so-cocky straw trilby hat. By far his most prominent feature is his beer boep – a source of great pride, judging by the manner in which he ceremoniously carries it before him.

After surveying the ground, he squints up into the sky and moves back up the aisle to the fourth row. Still carrying his things, he shifts his bottom in little hops, testing each new vantage point. He shakes his head and moves to the row in front.

No place is like one's own place, and he finally settles on the aisle seat (41) in the front row. He rests the umbrella on the picket fence and begins offloading. He tests a cushion – tries two. Tries one to sit on, one to lean on. Finally settles for one plump cushion for his bottom.

He licks his lips – time for a pre-match snack? He looks down at his cooler bag, decides against it.

He pats his shirt pocket and checks that his packet of salted peanuts is still there. Satisfied, he unzips the cooler bag and takes out a plastic bag six-pack containing only two bottles of beer. He removes one dumpy and places the other back in the bag. He uncaps his beer and takes a swig ... pure bliss. He removes the packet of peanuts from his top pocket only to see the bag burst and peanuts cascade to the floor. Disgruntled, he tosses the packet down.

He digs around in his cooler bag, sniffs suspiciously at an aluminium-foil package. He replaces it and takes out a home-made hot dog. He carefully unwraps the cellophane and tucks into the food. He swigs and chews ... heaven on earth!

He looks up at the sky – it is indeed a lovely day. He rises, unbuttons his shirt, peels it off and hangs it neatly over the edge of the back rest. Resplendent in his white vest he sits down again, digs around in his canvas bag and takes out a small tin of Nivea cream. He takes off the lid and, instead of rubbing it over his whole body, simply dabs a large blob on his shiny red proboscis (nose in a cream cake effect). He puts the Nivea away, wipes his finger under the bench and resumes eating and drinking. He basks in the sun. Life is great!

The military music tails off. We hear the sound of clapping – a ripple effect (since the ground is virtually empty the applause is nothing to write home about). He hurriedly puts his food and drink down and digs in the canvas bag again. He unrolls a blue floppy hat with WP emblazoned back and front in large white letters. He swaps it with the trilby and joins in the clapping, following the progress of the players to the wicket.

CORKY: Pro – vince!

> *The clapping subsides. He sits down. Settles himself. Takes up his beer and half-eaten hot dog.*

CORKY: Hit the rubbish!

> *He watches the action.*

> SPECTATOR NUMBER TWO *arrives. He is a dapper man, scholarly in appearance, fortyish. He wears long trousers, collar, tie and blazer (or tweed sports jacket). All he carries is a newspaper (The Cape Times) and a pair of binoculars (without the case) slung over his shoulder.*

> *He looks at the rows of benches and peruses the blue ticket he holds in his hand. He seems to be having difficulty finding the right row (this is understandable since they are unmarked).*

> *He counts the rows, walking up and down the aisle. He then moves along in front of the first row, just inside the picket fence – stepping over* CORKY'S *things as he does so.*

He counts the numbers on the seats and checks his ticket. He crosses CORKY's *line of vision several times, forcing the seated man to duck this way and that in order to see the game.*

Finally it is too much.

CORKY: Hey – you work for PG Glass?
RICHARD: Oh, I *do* beg your pardon ...
CORKY [*to the players*]: Bowl him!

    Startled, RICHARD *literally jumps into the air. He turns and looks at the field of play, briefly caught up in the action.*

RICHARD: Gosh, don't tell me Pienaar's still in? [*He turns again to* CORKY, *aware of his obvious involvement, yet anxious to find his seat*] Excuse me, is this Row A?
CORKY [*attention fixed on the game*]: Hit the rubbish!
RICHARD: Excuse me ... er ...
CORKY [*watching the game*]: You'll *never* get him out like that, man!

    RICHARD *stands helpless, a spare part. He glances about, unsure of what to do next.* CORKY's *concentration, between nervous sips of beer, is intense.*

RICHARD: Marvellous day ... [*He tries again*] ... wonderful day.
CORKY: I beg yours?
RICHARD: The weather.

    CORKY *stares at him ... thinks about this.*

CORKY: Ja.
RICHARD: Absolutely superb.
CORKY: Bakgat.
RICHARD: Quite. [*Pause*] Small crowd. [*Pause*] Not many supporters.
CORKY: Final day.
RICHARD: Ah, Monday morning, that's a point. [*Pause*] Delicately poised.
CORKY: Huh?
RICHARD: Finely balanced.

    CORKY *stares at him – who is this idiot?* RICHARD *is indicating scales in equilibrium.*

RICHARD: The match ... [*He points in the direction of play*]

    CORKY, *unimpressed, turns his attention back to the action (or lack of it).*

RICHARD [*clears his throat*]: Look, I'm sorry to be such a nuisance, but could you tell me if this is Row A? [CORKY *glances at him, then back at the pitch.*] I'm actually supposed to be sitting in Row C ... See? [*He shows an uninterested* CORKY *his ticket.*] C39 ...

CORKY: So why you looking for Row A?

RICHARD: Well, I thought if this was A, then C would be ... A ... B ... C ... three rows back.

CORKY is watching the cricket.

RICHARD: See what I mean? [*Referring to his ticket*] Now you are what?

CORKY: Le Roux ...

RICHARD [*extending his hand*]: Hopcroft, how do you do?

CORKY [*his attention on the game*]: Le Roux ...

The penny drops.

RICHARD [*turning to watch*]: Ah, Garth le Roux, yes, of course.

Pause.

CORKY: Ag ... !

RICHARD: Oh, dear.

CORKY [*watching the game*]: Somebody show him those three little sticks with the bails on top ... !

RICHARD looks about him, up into the trees, taking it all in.

RICHARD: So these are the famous Oaks?

He looks along the rows of benches. He dabs at a dollop of white chalky substance on the back of the seat in front of him. He sniffs at it, looks up at the trees and back at his finger.

CORKY [*his eyes on the game*]: And those are the famous seagulls.

RICHARD leaps to his feet, checking the seat of his trousers for possible damage. He whips out a large white handkerchief and wipes the bird droppings from his finger. CORKY finds his discomfort rather amusing, and shows it.

RICHARD: Could I see your ticket, please?

CORKY: Sorry?

RICHARD: Your ticket, if I may ...

CORKY: What are you, a groundsman?

RICHARD: I'd feel a lot more comfortable if I knew where I was sitting.

CORKY [*attention on the game*]: Not on the bladdy leg stump!

RICHARD: I should hope not.

CORKY: Sorry?

RICHARD: I said I should ... never mind.

CORKY: Look, why don't you just sommer sit sommer anywhere, man?

RICHARD: Oh, no, I couldn't possibly do that. Wouldn't dream of it. I mean what if someone came along and found me sitting in their seat? Highly embarrassing ...

CORKY: Change a' bowler! [*Throwing his arms heavenwards*] Yass-like-it ... ! [*to RICHARD*] And they want to win the bladdy Currie Cup ... ?

He digs into his cooler bag for sustenance. RICHARD *is deep in thought.*

RICHARD: No, what I'll do is stay put.

CORKY cracks a hard-boiled egg on his head and begins peeling it, allowing the shells to add to the growing pile of litter at his feet.

RICHARD: I'll wait for a steward or usher or whatever they call them to wander across and sort me out ... [*to CORKY*] You don't mind, do you?

CORKY: Sorry?

RICHARD: If I sit here – you don't mind?

CORKY: Feel free.

RICHARD: Thank you.

CORKY: Egg?

RICHARD: I beg your pardon?

CORKY [*offering him an egg*]: They free-range.

RICHARD: No thank you. [*Pause*] Umbrella.

CORKY: You want my umbrella? [*Picking it up*]

RICHARD: No, no. I was simply commenting on the fact that you'd brought one.

CORKY: Just in case.

RICHARD: Changeable, is it?

CORKY [*misunderstanding him*]: No, you just use the one side.

RICHARD: I mean the weather. Is it changeable?

CORKY: Oh. [*He considers*] You never know.

RICHARD: Yes. Well. Better safe than sorry. [*Pause*] You could always use it for the seagulls.

CORKY [*swinging around*]: Sorry?

RICHARD points heavenward. CORKY *is clueless.*

RICHARD [*giving up*]: Never mind.

CORKY delves into his bag, producing a salt cellar. He liberally sprinkles salt on the egg.

RICHARD: You look like you're a regular.

CORKY [*suspiciously*]: A regular what?

RICHARD: Supporter ... Are you?

CORKY: You asking me if come here all the time?

RICHARD: Yes.

CORKY: Bladdy sure.

RICHARD: I see.

CORKY: You?

RICHARD: Me?

CORKY: Ja.

RICHARD: Oh, no ... this is my first time ... Here, that is.

CORKY: On holiday?

RICHARD: That's right.

CORKY: Out from England, hey?

RICHARD: Good gracious no. Natal, actually ...

CORKY: Natal ... !?

RICHARD: Pietermaritzburg.

CORKY: Banana Boy!

RICHARD: Hardly ...

CORKY: Bladdy Piesang Boer ...

RICHARD: Steady on, old chap ... [*Mispronouncing it*] ... 'Piesang Boer'.

> CORKY *is suddenly enjoying himself. He indicates the pitch, chuckling boyishly.*

CORKY: Pity we not playing *you* blokes, hey?

RICHARD: We don't do too badly.

CORKY: Except when you playing *us* okes.

RICHARD: That's debatable.

CORKY: That's what?

RICHARD [a *beat*]: Never mind.

CORKY [*threateningly*]: You want a debate, or shall we just talk?

RICHARD: Er ... I think I'll just watch.

CORKY: You do that.

RICHARD [*to himself*]: Healthier.

CORKY: Sorry?

RICHARD [*getting up*]: No, what I was saying was ... I think ... on second thoughts, what I think I'll do is take this as Row A ... and that being the case ... [*He moves away*] I'll go and sit back there in what must be Row C.

CORKY: Don't let me chase you away, hey.

RICHARD [*moving into the third row*]: Not at all – no.

CORKY: Got nothing against Natal, nothing at all.

RICHARD: Of course not.

CORKY: In fact, you blokes are the okes I support when we not playing you okes.

RICHARD: Ditto.

CORKY: Snap.

RICHARD [*settling down*]: Ah, yes. C39. That's better.

CORKY: We okes are what's known as Traditional Allies.

RICHARD [*feeling a lot safer now*]: Kindred Spirits. Absolutely.

CORKY: Between you and me, as far as I'm concerned a Banana Boy is always welcome here behind the Grape Curtain.

RICHARD: That's nice to know.

CORKY: Any day of the week.

RICHARD: Thank you.

CORKY: If, on the other hand, you came from that province just south of the Limpopo ... the one that shall remain nameless ... that is a different can of fish ...

RICHARD: Kettle of beans. Absolutely.

CORKY: Put it there ... [*He leans across the benches, extending his hand*] Labuschagne's the name.

RICHARD: Labba what?

CORKY: Labuschagne. Corky Labuschagne.

RICHARD [*shaking hands*]: Richard Hopcroft. How do you do?

CORKY: Hopcroft?

RICHARD: That's right.

CORKY: Pleased to meet you.

They clap at the culmination of a good over and CORKY *settles himself in his seat once more.*

RICHARD [*after a pause*]: Interesting name.

CORKY: It is, yes.

RICHARD: How would you spell it?

CORKY: Hell, now you got me ... H – O – P – P –

RICHARD: No, no. Not *my* name. Your name ... 'Labbashayn ...'

CORKY: You trying to be funny?

RICHARD: Not at all. I was simply wondering if it was of French extraction.

CORKY [*his attention back on the game*]: Ah, change of bowler. Fantastic.

RICHARD: We had this fellow at school called himself 'Labbashayn' ... what was it? Frederick Arthur Spencer Labbashayn ...

CORKY: Now watch this bloke, he's vicious.

RICHARD: Like 'champagne', is it?

CORKY: Who?

RICHARD: Champagne.

CORKY: Where?

RICHARD: Your name? Do you spell it like champagne?

CORKY: I don't know. How d'you spell champagne?

RICHARD: Gosh, now that you mention it ...

CORKY: Bowl him!

RICHARD: Depends on where you are, I suppose. The English tend to keep the 'g', same as the French, French being the original, of course.

CORKY: Take his head off ... !

RICHARD: However, I do have a sneaking suspicion the Latin countries spell it with an 'i' – Heaven knows why. You'd think people would try to keep things ...

A loud thwack reverberates around the ground. CORKY *leaps to his feet with a mixture of awe and exaltation.*

CORKY: Ei ... na ... !

RICHARD [*also rising*]: Ooooh ... !

CORKY: Eina ... la ... la ... !

RICHARD: That was a nasty one.

CORKY: Shit-a-brick!

RICHARD [*raising his binoculars*]: Thank God he was wearing a helmet.

CORKY [*beaming triumphantly*]: If you can't bowl 'em out ... knock 'em out!

RICHARD: On the head, was it?

CORKY: Side of the head.

RICHARD: Bouncer.

CORKY: Beamer.

RICHARD: Bumper.

CORKY: Wal-lop!

RICHARD: Wooph.

CORKY: Told you he was vicious.

RICHARD: Gives you the willies.

CORKY: He'll feel it tomorrow.

RICHARD: And all day the next, I should imagine.

CORKY [*a sadistic gurgle*]: And they say this is not a contact sport.

The thought of 'sport', and specifically 'contact sport' triggers something in CORKY'S *consciousness. He rises and walks up the aisle, looking off left and right.* RICHARD *squints through his binoculars.*

RICHARD: Can you spot an official?

CORKY: I'm looking for someone else.

RICHARD: They usually wear arm bands.

RICHARD scans the ground with his binoculars, CORKY *eyes the binoculars covetously.*

CORKY: Bladdy nice pair, hey.

RICHARD [*lost for a moment*]: Hmm ... ? Oh, my field glasses, yes, they are rather, aren't they?

CORKY: Flippin' expensive.

RICHARD: They weren't cheap.

CORKY sits down beside him.

CORKY: Wasn't there a famous actor called Hawkins?

RICHARD [*looking at the game through the glasses*]: Oh yes, Jack Hawkins.

CORKY: *Jack* Hawkins, that's right ... Any relation?

RICHARD: To whom?

CORKY: Hawkins.

RICHARD: My name's Hopcroft.

CORKY: Ag, sorry – Hopcroft.

RICHARD [*spelling it*]: H-O-P-C-R-O-F-T.

CORKY: Hopcroft.

RICHARD: That's right.

Pause.

CORKY: William?

RICHARD: Richard.

CORKY: Ah, Richard ... yes ... Dick.

RICHARD [*emphatically*]: Richard.

CORKY: I know. But isn't Dick short for ... ?

RICHARD: It is but my name is Richard.

CORKY: Not Dick?

RICHARD: Certainly not.

Pause.

CORKY: No-one ever call you Dick?

RICHARD: Never.

CORKY: For short?

RICHARD: Never ever.

Pause.

CORKY: Richard.

RICHARD: Richard.

Pause.

CORKY: I knew a Dick once ... Dick du Toit. Panel beater ... Ex-panel beater. Full o' bladdy sports ... a real good laugh. Sold the business and went and bought this pig farm in the Hex River Valley ... Dirty Dick, we called him ... just used to sommer jump in there with those pigs ... Didn't worry him, bugger all ... Then one day he just went into this coma, just like that ... next day he was dead ... I don't know ... they say the pigs gave him something. [*Pause*] Dirty Dick.

Pause.

RICHARD: You know, when I was in Hong Kong ...

CORKY: You been to Hong Kong?

RICHARD: Oh, yes ...

CORKY: Far East?

RICHARD: Far East, Middle East ...

CORKY: Is that right?

RICHARD: All over.

CORKY: Jet setter?

RICHARD: Business, mostly.

CORKY: You been to the Canary Islands?

RICHARD: Canary Islands?

CORKY: I got a great uncle over there. On my mother's side. His great great something or other was related to old Nelson of Trafalgar Square.

RICHARD: Is that so?

CORKY: My one great claim to fame.

RICHARD: Gosh.

CORKY: Not many people know that.

RICHARD: I don't suppose they would.

CORKY: Ja, when your name's Labuschagne and you come from Parow, a lot of people think you just spinning them a line.

RICHARD: It does seem rather a long way around.

CORKY [*attention back on the game*]: Ah, better ball! Better ball ... !

They clap for a good delivery.

CORKY: But, sorry, you were saying?

RICHARD: I was saying ... ?

CORKY: When you were in Bangkok.

RICHARD: Hang-kok – Hong Kong.

CORKY: Whatever ...

RICHARD: I was saying ... apropos of what you were saying ...

CORKY: I was saying ...

RICHARD: I met this fellow over there who'd contracted some sort of really vicious tropical disease ... Nobody knew what it was.

CORKY: They the worst.

RICHARD: He kept ... keeling over. Every so often, he'd just ... woomph .... fall over, just like that. For no apparent reason.

CORKY: What was wrong with him?

RICHARD: Nobody knew.

Pause.

CORKY: It wasn't Hong Kong Flu?

RICHARD: Definitely not.

CORKY: A tropical disease, hey?

RICHARD: Some unknown strain.

CORKY: Some kind of malaria-bilharzia type thing?

RICHARD: Something like that.

Pause.

CORKY: I had tick bite fever once.

RICHARD: [*bringing the glasses to his eyes*] You did?

CORKY: When I was twelve. [*Pause*] Whooping cough ... German measles ...

RICHARD: Chicken pox.

CORKY: You ever had the mumps?

RICHARD: Who hasn't?

CORKY: When you get them in the testicles ... !

RICHARD: Whooph!

CORKY: It happens.

RICHARD: I'm sure it does.

CORKY: You got to catch it fast.

RICHARD: Goes for most things.

CORKY: Got to catch it quick.

RICHARD: Before it catches you ... [*He is still scanning the field of play*] ... I wish someone would catch one of *these* chaps.

CORKY: Not a chance. They dug in for the day.

RICHARD: Mmm ...

Pause.

CORKY: Comes up like this ...

RICHARD: I beg your pardon?

CORKY: Scrotum ... comes up like a soccer ball.

RICHARD: Gosh.

> CORKY *turns his attention to the game. It is obviously dead. He rises disconsolately and returns to his seat down front.*

CORKY: Ag, look at these bladdy Vaalies now!

RICHARD: How long have these two been in?

CORKY: Forever.

RICHARD: Very slow.

CORKY: Makes you sick.

RICHARD: Pedestrian.

CORKY: Funereal.

RICHARD: A draw?

CORKY: Looks like it.

RICHARD: Another dull draw.

Pause.

CORKY: Of course, if they got rid of ou bladdy McBride ... new ball game.

RICHARD: Totally new. [*Pause*] Not much chance, though ... Straight bat.

CORKY: Straight arm.

RICHARD: Elbow up.

CORKY: Head down.

RICHARD: Dogged.

CORKY: Dull.

RICHARD: Dour.

CORKY: It's these sort of okes gives cricket a bad name.

RICHARD: Too true. [*Pause*] Mind you, he *is* doing his job.

CORKY: Boring the public?

RICHARD: Captain's instructions.

CORKY: I must pay ten rand for this?

RICHARD: You could do worse.

CORKY [*brightly*]: I could be at work!

RICHARD: Look at it that way.

Pause.

CORKY: My grandmother died.

RICHARD: Oh, I *am* sorry.

CORKY: That's my story.

RICHARD: Story?

CORKY: At work. That's what my boss thinks.

RICHARD: Your alibi.

CORKY [*a beat*]: Ja, that, ja ... Officially I'm at the funeral.

RICHARD: Under the Oaks.

CORKY: Under the Oaks.

Pause.

RICHARD: It's a good story.

CORKY: Great story. Except it's wearing a bit thin. It's my third grandmother this season.

RICHARD: Oh, dear ...

Pause.

RICHARD: My grandmother's still alive.

CORKY: Lucky you.

RICHARD: Rock of Gibraltar.

CORKY [*spinning around*]: God, what a place to live, hey?

RICHARD: No, no, that's what she's like. [*A beat*] She lives in Underberg.

CORKY: Aha.

RICHARD: Figure of speech.

CORKY: I got it, ja. [*His attention on the play*] Now why is he doing *that*, now?

RICHARD: No that is *not* clever.

CORKY: He doesn't need a second slip.

RICHARD: I'd send him third man.

CORKY: Where's his silly point?

RICHARD: He needs somebody deep square.

CORKY: Or backward short. [*Pause*] What would you say to a backward short leg?

RICHARD: I'd say no. Not on this pitch.

CORKY: Too dangerous?

RICHARD: Not for Jefferies.

CORKY: For Stephen ... no ways.

RICHARD: For Kuiper, perhaps.

CORKY: For Adrian, ja.

RICHARD: Or Rundle.

CORKY: Rundles, no question. [*Pause*] Ag, I dunno.

RICHARD: Oh, well.

CORKY: He's the captain.

RICHARD: He's the boss.

CORKY: He calls the shots.

RICHARD: He runs the ship.

CORKY [*looking about him, rising*]: Where the bladdy hell's the wife?

RICHARD: You expecting your wife, are you?

CORKY: I'm running out of beers here.

    He paces the aisle.

RICHARD: Still. I wouldn't complain. It's a lovely day. Marvellous company. And as for the ground ... wooph ... words fail me. I've been waiting years to visit this ground.

CORKY [*moving into RICHARD's row*]: So you heard, hey?

RICHARD: The reports ... astonishing.

CORKY [*sitting beside him*]: The view?

RICHARD: Outstanding.

CORKY [*proudly*]: So you like?

RICHARD: Very impressive. The ambience ... pure magic.

CORKY: The what?

RICHARD [*waxing lyrical*]: The atmosphere. The setting. The sheer glory of it.

CORKY: Ag, hell, yes. [*Pause*] And the cricket.

RICHARD: The cricket, of course.

CORKY [*between clenched teeth*]: When Province is winning.

RICHARD: Wonderful.

CORKY: Incredible. [*Pause*] You know, they say this is the most beautiful ground in the whole world.

RICHARD: I'm not surprised.

CORKY: So they say.

RICHARD: I second that. [*Pause*] The mountains.

CORKY: The Breweries.

> *A beat.*

RICHARD: The trees.

CORKY: What's left of the trees. [*Pointing out front, high up on the slopes*] You see up there ... ? They're cutting them all down.

> *RICHARD scans the mountain with his binoculars.*

RICHARD: Gosh.

CORKY: Soon there won't be nothing left.

RICHARD: Very sad.

> *Pause.*

CORKY: Still, if the axe doesn't get them, the bladdy acid rain will.

RICHARD: That's true.

CORKY: That's 'progress'.

RICHARD: The price we pay ... pollution.

CORKY: Corrosion ... industrial waste.

RICHARD: The legacy of Man.

CORKY: 'Specially hard on trees.

RICHARD: Acid rain?

CORKY: Eats 'em up.

RICHARD: Is that so?

CORKY: It's happening already.

RICHARD: Oh, no.

CORKY: Oh, yes. Black Forest. Germany. People's Republic of Germany.

> *A beat.*

RICHARD: You mean the Federal Republic of Germany?

CORKY: Federal's, Peoples' ... whatever.

RICHARD: Black Forest, eh?

CORKY: Black Forest, my boy. Black Forest today, Table Mountain tomorrow.

RICHARD: It's that bad?

CORKY: *Time, Scope, Huisgenoot* ... even bladdy *You* ... staring us in the face ... A world without trees!

RICHARD: Good gracious.

CORKY: A world without wood.

RICHARD: No wood?

CORKY: Not a stick.

Pause.

RICHARD: No timber.

CORKY: No logs.

RICHARD: No planks.

CORKY: Boggerol.

Pause.

RICHARD: Not much fun if you happen to be a carpenter.

Pause.

CORKY: Bloke doesn't know whether to laugh or cry.

RICHARD: Gosh.

Pause.

CORKY: No more solid three-piece suites in mahogany, kiaat or imbuia ...

RICHARD: Or teak.

CORKY: Teak.

RICHARD: Teak tables.

CORKY: Ebony armchairs.

RICHARD: Cupboards of Oregon pine.

CORKY: Sapele sideboards.

RICHARD: No sideboards of any kind whatsoever.

CORKY: Walnut.

RICHARD: Birch.

CORKY: Beech.

RICHARD: Elm.

CORKY: Poplar.

RICHARD: Cypress.

CORKY: Ash.

RICHARD: Softwood.

Pause.

CORKY: Hardwood.
RICHARD: Dogwood.
CORKY: Dagwood?
RICHARD: Dogwood.
CORKY: That's a wood?
RICHARD: A type of wood.

Pause.

CORKY: Never heard of it.
RICHARD: Oh, yes. Oh, yes. [*Beat*] Yellowwood.
CORKY: Stinkwood.
RICHARD: Cedarwood.
CORKY: Sapele.

Pause.

RICHARD: You already said that.
CORKY: I did?
RICHARD: I'm sure you did.
CORKY: OK. [*He looks up slowly*] ... Oak!
RICHARD: Oak!?

They both look above them.

CORKY: No Oaks ...
RICHARD: No Oaks enclosure.
CORKY: No wattles, no wag-'n-bietjies ...
RICHARD: No willows ...
CORKY: No bats ...
RICHARD: No what?
CORKY: No willows, no bats!
RICHARD: No *cricket* bats!
CORKY: The end of the world as we know it!

Pause.

RICHARD: Doesn't bear thinking about.
CORKY [*rising, stunned*]: You want a beer?
RICHARD: I could do with one, thank you.

   *CORKY heads for his seat. He digs into his cooler bag. RICHARD ponders, struck by
   the awesomeness of it all.*

RICHARD: The destructive power of Man ... Terrible.

CORKY: Man is a bastard, let's face it. [*He discovers to his quiet horror that he has only one beer left. He decides to push his luck*] Orange?

RICHARD: I beg your pardon?

CORKY [*holding one up*]: How about an orange?

RICHARD: You offered me a beer.

CORKY: Aha! Orange with a difference. When they ban hard liquor you got to change your tactics, boy. Ever heard of impregnation?

RICHARD: What!?

CORKY: Injection by syringe. [*He takes one orange out at a time, holding them aloft*] I got Johnny Walker, Klipdrift, Mainstay ... or if you prefer something with a *real* kick in it, may I recommend the Smirnoff.

RICHARD: A beer will suit me fine, thank you.

CORKY [*doing his best to hide his displeasure*]: Suit yourself ... [*He gives RICHARD the beer and selects an orange at random*] Cheers.

RICHARD: Cheers.

They 'clink' orange and bottle. RICHARD is hopeful that a glass may be forthcoming, but is soon disillusioned. CORKY stabs an index finger into his orange and sucks at it.

CORKY: Aaah ... Southern Comfort!

RICHARD sips. CORKY sucks, then stops.

CORKY: No oranges.

RICHARD: Sorry?

CORKY: No orange trees.

RICHARD: Orange trees.

They suck, they sip, they watch the game.

CORKY: I chopped a tree down once.

RICHARD: You did?

CORKY: Big tree. Massive tree. Front garden.

RICHARD: Fancied yourself as a lumberjack, did you?

CORKY: No, it was blocking the bladdy view. Couldn't see the Hottentots Holland when I was having a beer.

RICHARD: Ah, necessity.

CORKY: Kids couldn't play rugby on the front lawn, wife got tired of always sweeping up the leaves ...

RICHARD: Oh dear, so out came the axe?

CORKY: Out came the chopper.

RICHARD: And you've been sorry ever since?

CORKY: That's for bladdy sure. It fell on my fucken house!

RICHARD virtually chokes on his beer and is forced to mop up hastily with his trusty handkerchief. They clap at the end of a particularly good over.

RICHARD: Not wishing to sound insensitive old boy, there's a point to be learned here.

CORKY: That's for bladdy sure!

RICHARD: It's always been a personal philosophy of mine, as you sow, so shall you reap.

CORKY: No, please, I can take it, hey. As they say in the classics, that's the way the cookie crumbles. I mean once bitten, twice shy.

RICHARD: Here today, gone tomorrow.

CORKY: You scratch mine, I'll scratch yours.

RICHARD: I beg your pardon?

CORKY: I mean we all have our crosses to bear, hey ... you, me, everyone.

RICHARD: That we do. As a colleague of mine once said ... he said ... [*Lost*] Gosh, now what did he say ... ? Something about life.

CORKY: Life?

RICHARD: Life.

CORKY: If life is worth living ... ?

RICHARD: No, no, wasn't that.

CORKY: No?

RICHARD: There are some things in life ...

CORKY: Some things in life ...

RICHARD: There are those things in life ...

CORKY: Those things in life ...

RICHARD: It's right on the tip of my tongue.

CORKY: Think!

RICHARD: I am thinking! [*Beat*] Oh dear.

CORKY: Never mind. Happens to the best of us.

RICHARD is distraught, clearly upset that he cannot remember something so profound.

RICHARD: Gosh. Oh, well. Anyway what I'm basically trying to say is ... is ... that's life.

CORKY: That's life?

RICHARD: That's life.

CORKY [*ecstatic*]: But that's what I've always said!

RICHARD: You have?

CORKY: Always.

RICHARD: Well, there you are, you see.

CORKY: That makes two of us.

RICHARD: Both of us.

CORKY: Great minds, and all that ...

RICHARD: Yes. Take it as it comes.

CORKY: Life?

RICHARD: Life.

CORKY: Exactly.

RICHARD: The ups and the downs.

CORKY: Ups and the downs ...

RICHARD: With equal ...

CORKY: With equal ... whatever.

RICHARD: Exactly.

CORKY: Never pays to get upset.

RICHARD: Never.

CORKY: Only hurt yourself.

RICHARD: Nobody else.

CORKY: I mean why should we get upset because they can't get rid of ou bladdy McBride.

RICHARD: No reason for it.

CORKY: Let him bat all day.

RICHARD: All day, if he wants to ...

CORKY: Okay, so we lose the match.

RICHARD: What's a match?

CORKY: What's a match in the grand scheme of things?

RICHARD: What's a match when millions are starving in Ethiopia?

CORKY: When thousands are being slaughtered in Siberia.

RICHARD: Every day.

CORKY: Every day.

RICHARD: Nothing.

CORKY: Bugger all.

Newlands erupts with the combined cacophony of eleven male voices screaming HOWWWWZZATTT! in unison.

CORKY [*leaping to his feet*]: Howzat!?

RICHARD [*following suit*]: Howzat!?

Pause.

CORKY: You heard that?

RICHARD: I heard it.

CORKY: Everybody heard it!

RICHARD: He touched it.

CORKY: He snicked it. He's out! [*Incredulous*] So why isn't he walking?

RICHARD: He's not out.

CORKY: Not out?

RICHARD: Could've brushed the pad.

CORKY: Brushed the pad? [*Turning on him*] Are you mad?

RICHARD: You can't be sure.

CORKY [*holding an earlobe*]: You think I don't know the difference between a bat and
    a pad? Walk McBride, walk. Pienaar, tell him to walk.

RICHARD: The umpire obviously thought ...

CORKY: The umpire's obviously paid ... ! [*Getting really worked up*] ... it's bribery and
    bladdy corruption, that's what it is!

RICHARD: Now hang on, old chap ...

CORKY: What d'you mean 'hang on'? You think I don't know what's going on here?
    It's a bladdy bottle of whisky before the game, that's what it is! You kiss my arse,
    I kiss yours. I sit here every day, man ... Bit of this, bit of that ... I see it all the
    time. Where the hell you think that umpire comes from, hey!? I give you three
    guesses ... don't say it, we know it! You think he wants us to win? No ways! He's
    out there making bladdy sure we don't win. [*Shouting*] Hey, umpire, how much
    they pay you!?

RICHARD has long since sat down and buried his head in his newspaper. CORKY
continues, half to himself, half to anyone who may care to listen.

CORKY [*indicating the field*]: I don't know why I put up with all this ... I don't know
    why I subject myself to this day after day ... I don't need this in my life. I mean,
    shit, man, a man's life is hard enough. [*He begins setting up his portable braai,*
    punctuating each stage with a fresh comment.] It's a bladdy racket. A cooking
    of books. A greasing of palms ... ! [*He takes some old newspapers from his*
    canvas bag.] That's the problem in the world today ... no decency ... no honesty.
    'Specially honesty ... [*A supermarket packet is opened to reveal his wood,*
    carefully placed atop balls of paper.] If you haven't got honesty, you haven't
    got nothing. That's what my father always said ... can still hear him saying it.
    [*Pausing to deliver the immortal words*] Cornelius, he used to say ... he never
    called me Corky, only my mates called me Corky ... Cornelius, he used to say,
    you can go out into this world, you can climb to the top of the bladdy tree, Cock
    of the Walk, but if you not honest, if you not a honest man, you bugger all.
    [*He rearranges the wood, places a final piece of wood on the braai and deftly slides*
    the grilling frame into place. He fashions a paper taper by pulling a corner of the

newspaper halfway through the grill. The braai is ready.] His very words. *He…he* was a honest man, boy. OK, he might have been a bastard, but he was a honest bastard. And anyone who tells me you can't be honest and still be a bastard is a bladdy bastard himself … that's all I got to say … [*Looking around*] Now where my bladdy matches …?

RICHARD [*attention on the game*]: Now that's a mistake …

CORKY: 'Cause we talking decency here …

RICHARD: Not Kuiper!?

CORKY: Not crookery … Where?

He looks up, shocked. RICHARD *is viewing play through his binoculars.*

RICHARD: They're bringing him on.

CORKY: That's a bladdy joke! He's blown it. He's left it too late. [*Pointing out front*] Look at this poephol [*With total disdain*] Three! He scores three! Give me a bat, send me out, *I* could score three!

RICHARD: He did score a hundred last week.

CORKY: That was *last* week. As far as I'm concerned, you only as good as your last score, and his last score was three! [*Cupping his hands, shouting*] Kuiper, go back to Bishops!!

Pause.

RICHARD: I think he went to Rondebosch.

CORKY: Go back to Rondebosch!!

RICHARD: Or was it Wynberg?

CORKY [*tersely*]: Make up your bladdy mind. [*He goes on searching for his matches, getting more and more frustrated.*] Where my bladdy matches now … !?

RICHARD: Henry Fotheringham went to Michaelhouse.

CORKY: Big deal. I went to Durbanville.

RICHARD: I only mention it because we happen to share the same Alma Mater.

CORKY: Same ouma-what?

RICHARD: We went to the same school.

CORKY: So what does that make you? [*Under his breath*] Bladdy windgat.
[*Offering him a meat stick*] You want some wors?

RICHARD: No thanks. I'm skipping lunch.

CORKY: You what?

RICHARD: Now and again I skip lunch.

CORKY eyes him suspiciously. RICHARD *reads his paper.*

CORKY [*suspiciously*]: You not one of those vegetarian monkeys?

RICHARD: Oh, good gracious, no.

CORKY: I was just going to say ... [*Biting into his wors, still searching for the matches*] ... Windgat school, windgat diet, next thing you tell me you a bladdy moffie.

RICHARD: No, it's just that I have this doctor who believes that as a species the Caucasian male has a propensity to overindulge.

CORKY [*a beat*]: He's definitely a moffie. [*At last he finds his matches, they are in the canvas bag.*] Ah, matches ... fantastic ...

He takes out a match and bends over the braai. RICHARD *has spotted an officer of the law and clears his throat.*

RICHARD: I wouldn't light that.

CORKY [*striking a match*]: Huh?

RICHARD: Policeman. That policeman's watching you.

CORKY: Where?

RICHARD: He's pointing at the sign.

CORKY: What sign?

RICHARD: NO BARBECUES – see it? [*Pointing*] Over there – big letters ... NO BARBECUES.

CORKY: *This* is a braaivleis.

RICHARD: He's signalling something behind the grandstand ... I think he means you have to go there.

CORKY: Bull. I don't want to go behind the grandstand. I'm here to watch the cricket. How can I watch the cricket if I'm stuck behind the bladdy grandstand!?

He strikes another match. RICHARD's *eyes are fixed on the distant policeman.*

RICHARD: I think he means it.

They both watch the policeman. CORKY *blows out the match with a great deal of venom. He hurls the matchbox to the ground.*

CORKY: Shit! Free Country!? I mean this is supposed to be a free country! It's a police state. It's nothing less than a full blown, honest-to-God bliksemse bloody police state.

RICHARD: He's going.

CORKY: A man can't even cook his own meat!

RICHARD: He's gone.

CORKY: That's it! I'm going to Australia. I'm packing up, I'm pushing off, I'm pulling out! I'm going to bladdy Australia. Got a mate in Sydney ... What you can't do in Sydney! Nothing you can't do there ... the booze ... the gambling ...

RICHARD [*reading from the scoreboard*]: Two-twenty-six ...

CORKY: In Sydney you can sit down and watch a strip-show while you having your lunch, man. Your *lunch!* Twelve o'clock. Midday! You don't have to drive nearly two-thousand kays to bladdy Bophuthatswana ... ! [*RICHARD scans the field, hiding his embarrassment behind his binoculars.*] And as for the cricket, it's *real* cricket! Not this second-class rubbish! [*Shouting*] Hit the rubbish!

Pause.

CORKY: March ... June ... after my annual leave ... !

Pause.

RICHARD: My brother tried Australia. Came back after eight months.

CORKY: He did?

RICHARD: No jobs.

CORKY: Is that right?

RICHARD: Unions ...

CORKY: Trade unions?

RICHARD: Closed shop. Unemployment ... heavy recession ... not to mention the flies.

CORKY: Flies!?

RICHARD: All over the place.

CORKY: Flies too, hey?

RICHARD: Too terrible ... epidemic proportions.

Pause.

CORKY: Well, stuff it, I go to New Zealand. [*Pause*] Or Canada. There's a country, Canada! The Rockies! Rocky Mountain High ... Colorado ... !

RICHARD: That's the United States.

CORKY: Same thing. I'm buggering off. I've had enough. [*He kicks at the legs of his portable braai. It crashes to the ground. He makes no attempt to tidy it up. RICHARD goes back to hiding behind his binoculars. CORKY digs into his cooler bag, seeking solace in drink.*] Shit, man, no more beers! [*Getting up and pacing the aisle*] Where the hell is she? That's it. Divorce. She's had it. Eleven o'clock, I said. Eleven o'clock, she says. She'll probably rock up here eleven o'clock tonight! No, I tell you something, my boy, Canada will suit me fine. Alaska! The further away the better.

He plonks himself down in his seat. RICHARD, still peering through his binoculars, attempts to defuse the situation by discussing matters cricket.

RICHARD: Where's Omar Henry?

CORKY: [*muttering*] Niagra Falls ... !

RICHARD: Matthews's looking worried.

CORKY looks up, his interest aroused.

CORKY: Can't I have a squizz through those things?

RICHARD [*lowering the glasses*]: I beg your pardon?

CORKY: Could I take a quick look?

RICHARD is not at all keen on the idea.

RICHARD: How are your hands?

CORKY: Hands? They great hands. I work with my hands ...

RICHARD: No, I meant ...

He rubs his fingers together and pulls an appropriate distasteful expression.

CORKY: Aha ... yes ... [*He wipes his greasy paws on his shorts. RICHARD passes him the binoculars with some trepidation.*] Thanks. [*CORKY almost drops them, causing RICHARD's heart to skip a beat. CORKY scans the field of play.*] Hell ... ! Ou Gooch has got a walrus.

RICHARD: I think it rather becomes him.

CORKY: Viva Zapata!!

RICHARD [*a beat*]: That was Marlon Brando, wasn't it?

CORKY follows events with the help of the glasses.

CORKY: He's moving his long leg ... *Square* leg – that's better.

RICHARD: Kitchener had one of those handle-bar things ... like Errol Flynn ... or, wait a minute, Errol Flynn had a Clark Gable, that's right, a ... whatdo-you-callit? ... pencil.

CORKY's gaze has been moving across the field and onto the crowd. Inevitably, he hits the sun worshippers on the grass embankment in front of the main grandstand. He lets out a gigantic wolf whistle, his fingers fiddling frantically with the focus knobs.

CORKY: Will you look at *that!* Now that's flaunting it. I mean that is really flaunting it. [*Holding up the glasses for RICHARD*] Take a check through these things. Main stand ... grass in front ... [*RICHARD refocuses the glasses*] The one in the toga.

RICHARD: Toga?

CORKY: Toga ... Tandem ... Whatever ...

RICHARD [*spotting the person in question*]: Ah ... Tanga.

CORKY: Tanga! There's it. Same thing.

RICHARD does not really approve but tries to sound as though he is impressed.

RICHARD: Hm. Very well endowed.

CORKY: Endowed ... ? [*Taking back the glasses*] I bet she needs a bally endowment policy just to hold them up!

CORKY brings the binoculars to his eyes, feverishly finding focus. RICHARD, a trifle peeved and totally unimpressed that his glasses are being used for something other than cricket, returns to his seat.

Unnoticed by CORKY (and, initially by RICHARD) a woman appears at the rear – on the opposite side to that of the two men. BEATRICE, a rather buxom bottle blonde, is a couple of years younger than CORKY. She wears outsize sunglasses, a hideous wide brimmed hat, turquoise slacks (several sizes to tight) and a loud top. Her high heeled sandals are totally inappropriate for the occasion. She carries a large sling bag and a You magazine. She scans the ground, the stands and so on.

CORKY [*positively drooling*]: They shouldn't allow it ... there should be a law against coming to a cricket match dressed like that. Never mind distracting, it's downright bladdy disgusting. [*BEATRICE, having spotted her husband, moves along the back of the benches. RICHARD sees her and knows instinctively who she is.*] What a pair! What a Class-A pair ... ! [*BEATRICE moves down the aisle and squints into the distance, trying to see what CORKY finds so interesting.*] Not that I'm a tit man but hell, ou Dolly Parton lies down next to her, you got instant Drakensberg, the Swiss bladdy Alps ... and whose for a bit of mountain climbing now and then? Whose for conquering a few peaks when the time is ripe ... ? Whoah! If that isn't topless, I dunno what is...! [*He gurgles lecherously. BEATRICE stands above him brandishing her rolled up magazine. RICHARD is powerless, unable to warn CORKY. The action is getting to him.*] Ooh, that's it ... move, move, baby move, keep moving ... roll over, yes, that's it. Yes. Oooh, this is painful ... this is sheer bladdy agony! [*CORKY squirms with delight. RICHARD cringes. BEATRICE boils, her knuckles tightening around the magazine.*] Oh the pain! I wonder if she gives head? [*BEATRICE steps across his line of vision, forcing CORKY to blink, move the glasses. He looks up taking the binoculars from his eyes. He is startled and horrified.*]: Beatrice ... !?

She thwacks him across the head with her magazine.

BEATRICE: You wonder if who gives what!?
CORKY: Hello, darling.
BEATRICE: What you looking at through those?
CORKY [*all innocence*]: These ... ?
BEATRICE: I thought you come here to watch cricket?
CORKY: Beatrice, I'd like you to meet a friend of mine – Hoppy Hopkins ... my wife ...
RICHARD: Hopcroft.
CORKY: Hopcroft – my mistake.
RICHARD [*standing*]: Richard Hopcroft, how do you do?

BEATRICE: Hello there. [*Handing him the binoculars*] If these are yours, I'd hang onto them. [*Glaring at* CORKY] Bladdy nonsense. [*She flops down beside her husband.*] Phew! Have I been led a merry dance.

CORKY: Where's my beers?

BEATRICE: Your what?

CORKY: Where the hell you been?

BEATRICE: Don't talk to me.

CORKY: I am talking to you.

BEATRICE: I couldn't find the Oaks.

CORKY: What d'you mean you couldn't find the Oaks. You ask anyone around here where's the Oaks, they tell you.

BEATRICE: I did. I asked a policeman where's the Oaks, he introduces me to these two okes from Grabouw.

CORKY: You trying to be funny?

BEATRICE: Am I laughing?

CORKY: Two okes from Grabouw?

BEATRICE: You didn't tell me they were *trees!*

CORKY [*to* RICHARD *scoffing*]: I didn't tell her they were trees ...

BEATRICE: You didn't say nothing about trees.

CORKY [*with infinite patience*]: 'Beatrice', I said, 'you'll find me under the Oaks'. Isn't that what I said? 'You'll find me under the Oaks'. 'I'll be sitting *under* the Oaks'!

BEATRICE: Well, how must I know what you get up to at your cricket? I haven't been to a cricket match in my whole life.

CORKY: Beatrice, what do you take me for?

BEATRICE: Don't ask me! I'm always hearing about these long legs and short legs.

CORKY [*sighing*]: Beatrice ...

BEATRICE: Middle legs.

RICHARD [*butting in*]: Middle-and-leg.

BEATRICE: Beg your pardon?

RICHARD: Middle-and-leg.

CORKY: You tell her, Hoppy.

RICHARD: Hopcroft. When you're taking guard, you ask for middle-and-leg.

BEATRICE: Sounds obscene.

CORKY: Ja, well! You don't like it you shouldn't be here.

BEATRICE: I don't want to be here. Rather be at Clifton, Cavendish Square. Anywhere.

CORKY: So what you doing here?

BEATRICE: You asked me to come, remember?

CORKY: Oh no, I didn't.

BEATRICE: Oh yes, you did.

CORKY: *Oh,* no.

BEATRICE: *Oh,* yes.

CORKY: You said to me ...

BEATRICE: I said to you ...

CORKY: 'Corky', you said ...

BEATRICE: 'I want to see the cricket'.

CORKY: You want to see the cricket. That's right.

BEATRICE: And then you said to me ...

CORKY: I said to you ....

BEATRICE: Come along.

CORKY: 'It's up to you'.

BEATRICE: 'Come along', you said.

CORKY: 'It's up to you', I said.

BEATRICE: No you didn't.

CORKY: Yes I did.

BEATRICE: No you didn't.

CORKY: Yes I did.

BEATRICE: You said to come along.

CORKY: I said to come along it's up to you.

BEATRICE: Well ... ?

CORKY: ... or it's up to you come along – something like that.

BEATRICE: Same thing.

CORKY: No it isn't.

BEATRICE: Yes it is.

CORKY: Up to you was the crux of the matter.

BEATRICE: Come along is what I heard.

CORKY: You only hear what you want to hear.

BEATRICE: Listen who's talking.

CORKY: I mean what I say.

BEATRICE: Maybe you should say what you mean.

CORKY: What do you mean?

BEATRICE: You know what I mean.

CORKY: Meaning what?

BEATRICE: Exactly that.

CORKY: Exactly what?

BEATRICE: What I say.

CORKY: And what do you say?

BEATRICE: What?

CORKY: What do you say?

BEATRICE: Say when?

CORKY: When?

BEATRICE: Hey?

CORKY: Hey? [*They stare at each other.*] What the hell we talking here, man!?

BEATRICE: Who were you looking at through those binoculars?

CORKY: Where's my beers?

BEATRICE: I forgot them.

CORKY: You forgot them! How the hell can you forget my bladdy beers, man?

BEATRICE: Same way you forgot who you were looking at.

CORKY [*turning to RICHARD*]: What a man has to put up with, hey?

BEATRICE: Actually I lie ... I gave them to those two okes from Grabouw.

CORKY: You married Hoppy?

RICHARD: Hopcroft.

BEATRICE: Had a party. Drank the lot.

CORKY: Cling to your freedom, pal.

BEATRICE: Had a whale of a time.

CORKY: Cherish it. Guard it. Because when you take that so-called plunge – that's exactly what it is, and it's all the way to the bottom. You never come up again.

BEATRICE: Maybe you should tell Mr Hapcraft that it works both ways.

RICHARD: Hopcroft.

BEATRICE: Who?

RICHARD: Call me Richard, please.

BEATRICE: Richard?

RICHARD: A lot easier.

BEATRICE [*a beat*]: We knew a Richard, didn't we darling? Richard du Toit ... except we called him Dick.

CORKY: He knows.

BEATRICE: Dick du Toit ...

CORKY: I already told him.

BEATRICE: He had this pig farm in Tulbach.

CORKY: I already *told* him.

BEATRICE: You already told him?

CORKY: Yes.

BEATRICE: About Dick du Toit?

CORKY: Yes.

BEATRICE: You tell him *all* about Dick du Toit?

RICHARD: Yes!

BEATRICE [*a beat*]: Did you tell him about Dick du Toit's wife?

CORKY: He doesn't want to know about Dick du Toit's wife.

BEATRICE: How do you know?

CORKY: Because he doesn't.

BEATRICE: Have you asked him?

CORKY: Beatrice, please, man!

BEATRICE: Because that woman went through hell.

CORKY: I'm sure she did.

BEATRICE: How do you know? You weren't even there. It was *my* shoulder she cried on.

CORKY: Good for you, Beatrice.

BEATRICE [*to RICHARD*]: Do you know that after Dick died, poor ol' Dolly didn't get nothing. Not a brass farthing!

CORKY: Beatrice, we've come to watch the cricket, now do you mind?

BEATRICE: Cricket! What cricket! I don't see no cricket.

CORKY [*to RICHARD*]: Now you know why they don't let women in the Long Room.

BEATRICE: When's the bladdy kick-off?

CORKY: See what I mean?

RICHARD: No, no, no! You don't kick off in cricket.

CORKY: You tell her, Hoppers.

RICHARD: Hopcroft.

BEATRICE: Knock-off.

CORKY: Try again.

BEATRICE: Whatever you do in this silly game.

CORKY: Beatrice, they already started. They been playing half a hour already.

BEATRICE: They playing *cricket*?

CORKY: No, they playing ice hockey!

BEATRICE [*a beat*]: They seem to do a heck of a lot of strolling around.

CORKY [*gritting his teeth*]: That's because it's between overs.

BEATRICE: What's overs?

CORKY: Our marriage, if you don't shut up now!

Pause.

BEATRICE: Well, if this is supposed to be cricket, I honestly can't see what all the fuss is about.

CORKY: Beatrice, you've only just arrived.

BEATRICE: And nothing's happened yet.

CORKY: Look, why don't you just go buy us a coupla' beers, there's a good girl.

BEATRICE: I want to watch. I want to see what it is that keeps you glued to the television all summer like it's going to run away. [*Nodding in the direction of the pitch*] For a start. Why are there *two* men with racquets?

CORKY: They bats.

BEATRICE: They must be to play *this* game.

CORKY *bites the bullet.* RICHARD *is unable to remain silent.*

RICHARD: No, no. You see those two are the batsmen who are at bat for the team that is batting.
BEATRICE: Batting?
RICHARD: That's right.
BEATRICE: Those two?
RICHARD: Correct.
BEATRICE [*a beat*]: How can two people bat at once?
RICHARD: They don't. They cross over.
BEATRICE: What for?
CORKY [*sarcastically*]: To get to the other side.

> RICHARD *leans forward, ever eager to enlighten the uninitiated about the finer points of the game.*

RICHARD: It's all quite simple, really when you analyse it ... the rules and regulations.
CORKY: Nothing to it.
RICHARD: Quite straightforward.
CORKY: Piece a' cake.
RICHARD: [*warming to his task*] You see, you have two sides ...
BEATRICE: Two sides ...
RICHARD: Two teams ...
CORKY: That's obvious.
RICHARD: Goes without saying.
CORKY: Two opposing sides.
RICHARD: One out in the field and one in.
BEATRICE: One in?
RICHARD: Correct. Now. Each chap that's in the side that's in goes out and when *he's* out, he comes in ...
CORKY: And the next bloke goes in until he's out ...
RICHARD: He's out ...
BEATRICE: He's out ...
RICHARD: Correct. Now. When they are all out, the side that's out comes in, and the side that's been in goes out ...
CORKY: Goes out and tries to get the side that's coming in out ...
RICHARD: In, out ...
CORKY: In, out ...
RICHARD: Correct. Am I right?
CORKY: Dead right.
RICHARD: Good. Now, when both sides have been in and out ...
CORKY: In and out ...
RICHARD: Both sides ...

CORKY: The two teams ...

RICHARD: Including the not outs ...

CORKY: Including them, yes ...

RICHARD: That's the end of the game.

CORKY: HOWZAT!

Pause.

BEATRICE: Come again?

RICHARD: Nothing to it.

CORKY: Piece of cake.

BEATRICE [*a beat*]: How many beers did you say you want?

RICHARD: Now the one-day game on the other hand is somewhat different.

CORKY: Totally different.

RICHARD: All about runs.

CORKY: Chasing runs.

RICHARD: Scoring runs.

BEATRICE [*half to herself*]: I'm just going to run away.

RICHARD: It's still cricket ...

CORKY: ... still cricket ...

RICHARD: But a faster version.

CORKY: All action ... [*She has risen and is moving away.*] Where you going?

BEATRICE: Home.

CORKY: Home!? I thought you wanted to know what's going on here? [*She is halfway up the aisle.*] Me and ou Richie's just hotting up here.

RICHARD: Richard!

CORKY: Richard.

RICHARD: That's my name.

CORKY: *I know that.*

BEATRICE: You called him Ricky.

CORKY: Who asked you?

RICHARD is on his feet, almost at the end of his tether.

RICHARD: How many times do I have to say it? I'm not Richie, I'm not Ricky, I'm not Dick, nor am I Hoppy, Hoppers, or ... or ... Hopsy ...

CORKY: Hopsy! I like that.

RICHARD: If you can't call me by my proper name don't call me anything at all!

CORKY [*to BEATRICE*]: How's this oke, hey?

RICHARD: I'm sorry, but that's the way I feel. It's simply a matter of ... common courtesy ...

CORKY: Shit-a-brick!

RICHARD: Call it what you will.

CORKY is unable to hide his displeasure

CORKY: Well, fuckit if you can't take a joke ...

BEATRICE [*horrified*]: Corky!!

CORKY: Corky – you hear that? Corky! Do I get upset when okes call me Corky?

RICHARD: I've never called you Corky.

CORKY: You can call me whatever you like, I'm not proud.

BEATRICE: With a name like Cornelius, I'm not surprised.

CORKY: I wouldn't talk ... Be-at-rass!.

RICHARD: There's no need to be rude.

CORKY: Who asked you?

RICHARD: I think Beatrice is a beautiful name.

CORKY: You would.

BEATRICE [*to RICHARD*]: Thank you.

RICHARD: It has grace.

BEATRICE: Grace?

RICHARD: Bearing.

BEATRICE: Ooh. That's nice.

RICHARD beams broadly, grateful for this opportunity to scatter a few pearls of wisdom.

RICHARD: It comes from the Latin. It means 'she who brings joy'.

BEATRICE: Joy? Well, I do that. I bring joy. [*to CORKY*] I bring quite a lot of joy now and again, don't I, darling?

CORKY [*quietly*]: Pity you don't bring the beers.

RICHARD: [*Italian accent*] Bea-tri-chay!

She sits down beside RICHARD, warming to him.

BEATRICE: My second name is Lydia.

RICHARD: Lydia ...

There is an almighty roar from the pitch as eleven players go up in unison.

PLAYERS [*off stage*]: HOWWW-ZATTT!!

CORKY [*leaping to his feet*]: HOWW-WOZ-HEEE!!?

BEATRICE [*startled*]: What's happened?

RICHARD [*raising his binoculars*]: He's L-B.

BEATRICE: What's ell-bee?

RICHARD: Leg before.

CORKY is glaring at the distant umpire with growing incredulity, his hackles rising.

CORKY: Where's his finger?

BEATRICE: His finger?

CORKY: Where's his bladdy finger?

BEATRICE [*to* RICHARD]: I thought you said leg?

RICHARD: The umpire's finger. He's supposed to put it up.

BEATRICE: Up? Up where?

CORKY [*a cold, slow, awesome fury*]: That's it. Beautiful. The end of a lovely friendship. The honeymoon, as they say in the classics, is over. [*He looks for his shirt.*] If they can't beat a bunch of so-called professional poeftes from across the Vaal, they not worth the time, nor the effort. Finish and klaar.

He buttons up his shirt with burning deliberation.

BEATRICE [*sensing his mood*]: Corky!

CORKY *pulls a blue season ticket from his top pocket and holds it aloft.*

CORKY: Anyone for a second-hand season ticket? Two hundred and fifty rand going for nothing. No? No takers? Not bladdy surprised. [*He flashes it around*] Going once, going twice ... gone. [*He rips the ticket into four neat squares and hurls it to the ground.* BEATRICE *covers her face with her hands.*] Province ... this is for you!

He throws a gloriously bold V-sign in the direction of play, turns on his heel and heads up the aisle.

BEATRICE [*tremulously*]: It's only a game, darling.

He stops and turns, throwing a final barb.

CORKY: And Kuiper ... I am *never* coming back!!

He is gone. There is a stunned silence.

BEATRICE [*half to herself*]: O, my Gaawd!

RICHARD: What was all that about?

BEATRICE: That's the last you'll see of him.

RICHARD: You don't mean ... ? But he's left all his things.

BEATRICE: That's the least of my worries! It's what comes next that frightens me. What I call Labuschagne's Lament.

RICHARD: Labba-what's what?

BEATRICE: Goes on for weeks. Like when those All Blacks were here. The Wimblebeys.

RICHARD: Wallabies ....

The two of them stare at CORKY's *empty seat.*

BEATRICE: Like a bear with a sore head. Until we win again. All in the name of sport.

RICHARD considers this.

RICHARD: Of course, you do know what George Bernard Shaw said about the True Fan, don't you?

BEATRICE: Who?

RICHARD: Shaw.

BEATRICE: Shaw?

RICHARD: George Bernard.

BEATRICE [*rising*]: Sure, I'd love to but I better get all this stuff home.

RICHARD: Oh.

BEATRICE: Just look at this mess.

RICHARD: Here, let me help you.

They begin picking things up.

BEATRICE: Now to get all this onto the bus.

RICHARD: You don't mean … ? Surely he doesn't expect … ?

BEATRICE: Please! What my husband doesn't expect … !?

RICHARD: You must allow me to take you home.

BEATRICE: Ag, we live too far away, man.

RICHARD: No, no, I insist.

BEATRICE [*a beat*]: Thank you, Mr Hopcroft.

RICHARD: Call me Richard.

BEATRICE: Richard. Thank you Richard. You know Richard, there are times when I say to myself 'is it worth it?'

RICHARD [*gathering the braai and so on*]: Don't we all.

BEATRICE: Call me Beatrice.

RICHARD [*a beat*]: Yes.

BEATRICE: No, I mean … seriously. The other day I woke up, I put on my dressing gown, I went into the bathroom, I looked in the mirror, I said … 'ag no, man' … [*RICHARD picks up CORKY's tatty cushion, revealing a smart, though garish cushion beneath it.*] Ag no, man! [*Picking it up*] How many times do I have to tell him *not* to take my bally lounge cushions to the cricket!? That's it. I've had it. He can wash it himself. I'll tell him he can wash it himself or I'm leaving. In fact I'm leaving anyway … him and his bally nonsense …

RICHARD: Well, if ever you're up in Pietermaritzburg …

BEATRICE: Very kind of you.

RICHARD: I'm quite serious. All above board, of course.

BEATRICE: Thank you, Richard.

They begin moving up the aisle, laden with gear.

RICHARD: I've got a guest cottage down at Toti.

BEATRICE: Toti?

RICHARD: Amanzimtoti.

BEATRICE: I like Port Shepstone.

RICHARD: You do?

BEATRICE: Umbogentwini. You ever been there?

RICHARD: Not lately, no.

BEATRICE: Nor've I but we've got some friends who go there every year. The Wilkinsons. They never miss. They always telling us if you haven't been there you haven't been anywhere ... [*She ad-libs on until she is stopped by the sight of CORKY who re-enters, carrying a six pack of beers (one of which he is already drinking). BEATRICE and RICHARD stand transfixed as he barges between then, grabbing his favourite cushion as he does so.*] I thought you gone home!?

He moves to his place in the front row and plonks himself down on the cushion.

CORKY: When you *look* for beer, you can *get* a beer!

BEATRICE: I thought you gone home!?

CORKY: Cheers!

BEATRICE: Corky, what did I say about my bally lounge cushions?

CORKY [*his eyes on the game*]: I don't want chicken again tonight, hey.

BEATRICE: I'm leaving.

CORKY [*shouting*]: Hey, Kuipsy, you want a beer?

BEATRICE: You hear what I'm saying?

CORKY: Hit the rubbish!

BEATRICE: Richard is being so kind as to give me a lift.

RICHARD: We thought you were ... what I mean is ...

BEATRICE: We're thinking of popping up to his little place in 'Twini.

RICHARD: It's Toti, actually, but ... um ... that's not quite what I had in mind ...

CORKY: [*eyes on the game*] Take his head off!

BEATRICE: Corky!

CORKY: Pro – vince!

BEATRICE: Corky!!

CORKY: Put some bladdy effort into it now, man!

BEATRICE: Ag, come on, Richard, I'm wasted on this one.

With a defiant toss of her head, she is gone. RICHARD is left betwixt and between, holding an armful of gear.

RICHARD [*to CORKY*]: Look ... er ... now that you're back, surely you can ... er ...

BEATRICE [*off*]: Ri – chard!!

RICHARD: Oh dear ... well, not much point in asking you to look after my seat. Not that anyone's going to want to sit there at this late stage ... [*He looks at the field*]

Ooh, look – change of bowler. Who is it?

He lifts his binoculars to his eyes, or tries to, but is rudely interrupted by
BEATRICE's shrill voice off.

BEATRICE: [*off*] Richard!!

RICHARD: Well, er, cheerio. Nice meeting you and all that ... and if ever you're in
Maritzburg ... Toti ... whatever [*Not wanting to leave at all*] Oh, dear ... this is
totally ridiculous ... [*He dithers for a fraction, seems to be leaving, but suddenly
stops and turns around.* CORKY's *attention all the while remains firmly fixed on
the cricket.*]

RICHARD [*brightly*]: Oh, I've just remembered what that friend of mine said about
Life. Well, it wasn't about Life, really ... suppose it was ... just not in so many
words ... [*Proclaiming*] 'The moving finger writes ... and having writ moves on ...
Nor all thy piety nor all thy wit, can cancel half a line of it ... Omar Khayyam ...

BEATRICE: [*off*] Ri – chard!!

RICHARD: The Fitzgerald translation ... hmm ... hm ...

He exits, baffled and bemused, leaving CORKY *alone (at last).*

CORKY *looks right and left and carefully picks up his shredded season ticket,*
placing it lovingly in his shirt pocket. With a beer in his hand, his team on the
field and all distractions removed, he is as happy as the proverbial pig in shit.

CORKY: Ah ... better ball ... better ball ...

The lights fade to blackout.

Over the Hill

A ONE-ACT PLAY

Jonathan Rands as STEVE.
Photograph by Ruphin Coudyzer.

Cast

STEVE (a flyhalf) ... twenty-four
CHARLIE (a tight-head prop) ... thirty-six
LYNETTE (an ex-Citrus Queen) ... late twenties.

A rugby dressing room, Nelspruit, late winter.

Over the Hill was first performed at the Standard Bank Grahamstown Festival of the Arts, in July 1985, as part of a double bill with *Under the Oaks,* after which it toured nationally. Jonathan Rands played Steve, James Borthwick, Charlie, and Kate Edwards, Lynette.

This version of the script first appeared in *South Africa Plays,* edited by Stephen Gray and published in London by Nick Hern Books and in South Africa by Heinemann-Centaur.

A rugby dressing room after a 'Sport Pienaar' (provincial sub-section) game.

It is like any dressing room anywhere in the world except, being Nelspruit, there are perhaps more orange peels on the floor than there would be if this were, say, Cardiff Arms Park.

Empty beer cans, cigarette stubs and other bits of rubbish, litter the floor. A low massage table stands in the centre of the room. Against the stage left wall stands a wicker kit-skip (dirty jerseys, shorts, socks hanging out). High above the skip is a long narrow window (which overlooks the car park behind the stadium). Along the back and stage right walls is a single row of slatted benches above which are located clothes hooks – twenty-odd, evenly spaced. The entrance to the dressing room (from a corridor) is located in the stage right wall, while the archway to the showers and loos (marked 'Shower/Stortbad') is in the back wall, stage left. A lone rugby ball is situated near the shower exit, beneath the benches.

Under the only hook supporting any clothing, alone and sipping at a beer, sits STEVE *'Sophie' Sofianek, a twenty-four-year-old flyhalf. His bruised face suggests the game has been a hard one and the togs he still wears positively steam with the sweat of battle.*

In another part of the stadium – high, distant and quite muted, a long-winded congratulatory speech is coming to an end. The manager or coach of STEVE'*s team is trying to speak above the din and heckle of the players.*

MANAGER [*off*]: Okay, okay, I don't know what it's going to be like not having your ugly dial around anymore, but what the hell ... [*We hear assorted boos and groans from the players as the Boss continues*] As they say where I come from 'what you lose on the roundabouts, you get back on the swings'. [*More boos, whistling and heckling. The Boss raises his voice above this.*] Let's have the man himself.

The 'man himself', however, is unable to start speaking because he is bombarded with broken snatches of 'For he's a jolly good fellow', 'Why was he born so beautiful', and so on, ending with the famous South African drinking number, 'Here's to Charlie he's so blue, he's a drunkard through and through, he's a bastard so they say, tried to go to Heaven but he went the other way. Drink it down ... two ... three ... four ... five ... six ...' and so on.

The drinking song is itself drowned by laughter, and 'party music' of the Platteland kind takes over (this music – an interesting selection – continues throughout the play. It should, however, drop to a level which allows the audience to become almost totally unaware of it, a distant buzz, nothing more).

Throughout the above, STEVE *has been sitting quietly, sipping his beer. At one point he ambles slowly to the door to the passage and gazes out and up. His face shows no particular emotion. He kicks at the odd bit of rubbish. He finishes the beer at about the same time as party music begins and tosses the empty can into a corner. He moves to where several plastic beer packets lie. Digging through them he becomes more and more frustrated, finally slapping the empty packets with a curse. He at last finds an unopened beer beneath another bench.*

He is busy drinking it, back at his spot beneath his clothes hook, when CHARLIE THERON *enters. Thirty-six years old and sporting a fresh white plaster above one eye, he wears a team blazer (dark, with a distinctive gold blesbok-head badge. Below the head, is a gold blaze with 'Blesbokke' on it). He is wearing a matching tie, grey slacks and black shoes. He carries a Scotch in one hand and a large, ornate 'golden' clock in the other. He is in a state of considerable agitation.*

CHARLIE [*shouting off down the passage*]: Bugger off, man ... ja, ja ... and the same to you with brass bladdy knobs on it! Jislaaik-it ... ! [*to* STEVE, *calmer*] How's this, hey? Oke outside here's looking for autographs. Comes up to me, asks if I'm Charlie Theron. I say, who do I look like? He says, Charlie Theron. I say, right. I'm about to sign his bladdy book – he takes it back. He says no, he doesn't want Charlie Theron ... Prick! [*Placing the clock on the massage table*] How d'you like? [STEVE *doesn't respond.* CHARLIE *moves to the door, then back again, still mildly agitated.*] Bladdy wankers. Should do what Paul Newman does. You know what Paul Newman does? Tells them to stuff off. Straight. They come up to him – stuff off! He really lets them know where they can get off. Like that famous golfer, whatsisname? Tall bloke. Instead of signing his name, he writes 'Up Yours'. Oke comes up to him, he says sure, takes the book [*Miming a signature*] 'Up Yours'. Soon puts them right. Wankers. [*Indicating the clock*] So – what d'you say?

STEVE: Hey?

CHARLIE: It's original. I'll give them that.

STEVE sips his beer in silence, in no mood to communicate.

CHARLIE [*smiling wryly*]: Huh. To think there are some blokes work their whole lives for one of these. My Uncle Dup in Krugersdorp. Thirty-seven years with the PA – clocking in, clocking out. What does he get for his troubles ... ? A whacking great clock. [*They stare at the clock.*] I wonder if it's gold? I mean a gold clock should be gold, right? [*Considers this*] Maybe I can melt it down.

STEVE: Huh?

CHARLIE: Hey, come on – snap out of it, man. I'm asking you about this clock. You reckon it's genuine?

STEVE: Genuine?

CHARLIE: Genuine? Kosher? Halaal ... ?

STEVE: How must I know?

CHARLIE: Soon find out. [*He goes over to it and picks it up. Looks at it. Listens to it. Shakes it. Hits it. Listens again.*] Doesn't even work. Can you believe it?

STEVE: Would help if you wound it first.

CHARLIE [*a beat*]: That's also true. [*He locates the key at the back of the clock and winds it up. He checks his watch. It has stopped. He smacks it, shakes it, holds it to his ear. Looks again.*] Dammit. What's the time?

STEVE: Time we buggered off.

CHARLIE: Let's call it ... ag, what the hell ... [*He moves the hands to an approximate time*] More or less ... [*Replacing the clock carefully on the table*] There. How's that? [*He steps back to admire it*] It'll look great on my mantelpiece. [*Pause*] Nine years faithful service. [*Pause*] You should've heard the Boss. The oke was really laying it on, hey. [*Dropping his voice in mock seriousness*] 'The Blesbokke won't be the Blesbokke without ou Charlie Theron ...' [*Pause*] For that, they give me a clock.

They sit in silence, the party continuing unabated upstairs. CHARLIE looks up, listening to the distant sounds of merriment.

CHARLIE: Sounds like it's becoming quite a party up there.

STEVE: So what you doing down here?

CHARLIE: I was going to ask you the same question.

STEVE [*sharply*]: If you come to look for me you can forget it.

CHARLIE [*indicating the clock*]: To tell you the truth – I was going to quietly flush this thing down the bog. [STEVE *is unamused*] Ha-ha. That's a joke. You allowed to laugh. [STEVE *looks away*] Hey ... don't take it so serious. You win some, you lose some.

STEVE [*unconvinced*]: Ja.

CHARLIE watches him a long time before turning to look at the clock.

CHARLIE: You know, what they actually should've given me was one of those massive great cuckoo clocks. One of those things that jump out at you in the middle of the night. You tiptoeing down a passage two o'clock in the morning – you got past the cat without standing on the damn thing and suddenly – KOE-KOEK! – bang goes a lovely evening. [*He smiles at the memory*] When I was a kid we had one in the front hall. I always used to try grab the little voeltjie – just as he popped out. The clock was a cock up. Bladdy cuckoo used to come out whenever he felt like it – and even then he only came out once – KOE-KOEK – back inside. Sometimes you sit there three hours and then all of a sudden – KOE-KOEK – gone, missed him again. [*Pause*] But I got it right eventually ...

Bliksemmed the bladdy bird with a baseball bat. [*Pause*] Should've seen what it did to the clock.

STEVE: Listen, Charlie, why don't you just do me a favour and piss off. You got something to say to me – say it – don't mess me around.

CHARLIE: You telling me to piss off?

STEVE: Just leave me alone, okay?

CHARLIE [*a beat, then angrily*]: You reckon you're the only bloke who ever lost a match? Hey? You know how many matches *I* lost? I lost so many bladdy matches I get Christmas cards from all the other provinces. [*He allows this to sink in*] It's history, man. You punched him so you punched him so it's finish. It's over. End of story.

Pause.

STEVE: Right in front of the bladdy poles.

CHARLIE: That's rugby. Rugby, you want to hit a bloke, you hit him so the ref can't see; otherwise you wait 'til the final whistle. That way you can kick him in the balls.

STEVE: And that's rugby?

CHARLIE: That's rugby.

STEVE lifts his jersey to reveal wicked stud marks in his rib area. The flesh is torn and bleeding.

STEVE: This rugby too?

CHARLIE [*unimpressed*]: That's bugger all.

STEVE: Oh, yes?

CHARLIE lifts one trouser leg, revealing a long scar on his shin.

CHARLIE: 1976. South Western Districts. Eighteen stitches.

STEVE: Big deal.

CHARLIE: No injection.

STEVE: Big flippin' deal.

CHARLIE: That's right, my friend. It's all part of paying your dues. And until you've done that – you'd do better to keep your mouth shut. [*Pause*] Let me tell you something right now, my boy. You got one *helluva* problem. It's called attitude.

STEVE: Attitude?

CHARLIE: Attitude.

STEVE: I'll remember that.

CHARLIE: I mean what kind of idiot comes off the pitch and tells the Boss to get stuffed?

STEVE: I told him to suck eggs.

CHARLIE: Same thing. You don't do it. Not to the Boss.

He moves to the door, restless, peering out down the corridor.

STEVE: You know what he tunes me?

CHARLIE: Doesn't matter what he tunes you.

STEVE: He tunes me I should've gone blind that last scrum of the match. A two-man overlap and I should've gone blind.

CHARLIE: If the Boss says you should've gone blind, you should've gone blind.

STEVE: With a two-man overlap!?

CHARLIE: Ten-man overlap – makes no difference.

STEVE: You would've gone blind?

CHARLIE: I don't know what I would've done.

STEVE: *You* would've gone blind?

CHARLIE: The point is – you don't argue.

STEVE: The point is – I was right!

CHARLIE: You see? Attitude.

STEVE: Stuff attitude! I'm the one who's out there with his bladdy chop on the block.

CHARLIE [*looking towards the door*]: Shhh!

STEVE: If I had've gone blind, the stupid turd would've told me I had a two-man flippin' overlap ... !

CHARLIE: Shhh ... okay, okay, point taken – shhh!

STEVE: What you shushing?

CHARLIE: It's okay – l thought I heard something. [*STEVE kicks the bench in frustration.*] I'm not trying to put you down here. I just don't want you to look like a poephol.

STEVE: I am a poephol.

CHARLIE: I'm not *saying* you a poephol.

STEVE: I'm a poephol. Say it. I'm a poephol.

Pause.

CHARLIE: You a poephol.

Pause.

CHARLIE: Look, they not going to drop a oke after his first game, so don't worry. [*STEVE looks up at him, not so sure.*] Come on, Sophie. Go shower – get dressed – we go get pissed. [*Brightly*] Hey. You must see. They got these chicks outside here, they lining them up. Looks like they hauled in every little boeremeisie from Piet Retief to Phalaborwa. [*Chuckling*] Hey, this is the place they pick the Orange Queen. Who knows, maybe there's a Grapefruit Queen lurking about here as well ... ? A Quince Queen ... ?

STEVE: I'm sorry, Charlie. I let the okes down.

CHARLIE moves to STEVE's kitbag and opens it.

CHARLIE: Bull. Where's your towel?

STEVE [*angry with himself*]: Just one bladdy punch, man.

He wanders into the shower area. disappearing off left. CHARLIE goes through his things, tossing out spare shorts. underwear and so on.

CHARLIE: Jeez, what's all this shit you keep in here? [*Taking out a large pack of condoms*] Hey, hey, hey ... ! [*Reading*] 'Lubricated with Sensatol'. [*Shouting off in the direction of the showers*] Who packs your bag ... the wife?

STEVE comes back out of the shower area.

STEVE [*pointing into the showers*]: How these bust windows through here?

CHARLIE: What did you expect? Loftus bladdy Versveld? Southern fucken Suns?

STEVE moves to the skip. inspecting CHARLIE's clock.

CHARLIE [*taking out a bottle of aftershave*]. What's this? [*Sniffing, then reading the label*]: 'Macho'.

STEVE [*correcting him*]: Macco.

CHARLIE: Says Macho.

STEVE: It's Macco.

CHARLIE [*spelling*]: M – A – C – H – O.

STEVE: That's how you say it.

CHARLIE: Says who?

STEVE: Says the oke in the shop.

CHARLIE [*a beat*]: You may be Macco, baby – I'm Macho.

STEVE: You're just a bladdy pleb.

CHARLIE has the top off and is splashing on the aftershave.

CHARLIE: What's it like?

STEVE: Hey! Take it easy there. [*He goes to grab it. CHARLIE pulls away.*] You going to honk like a moffie, man.

CHARLIE: What ... with Macho!?

CHARLIE jumps up onto the benches, lifting his belt and splashing into his underpants. STEVE goes to grab the bottle and CHARLIE jumps down and runs to the massage table.

STEVE: Stuff you, Charlie – it's sixteen bucks a bottle, man.

CHARLIE yanks the massage table into the centre, darting behind it.

CHARLIE: Come on, Sophie – smile. Smile for your Uncle Charlie.

STEVE [*picking up the clock*]: I'll smash this thing, s'true's God.

CHARLIE: Hell, please! Do me a favour – be my guest, man. [*STEVE places the clock on the bench and gives chase, only to have CHARLIE dart around the massage table, using it as a shield between himself and the youngster.*] Brom-brom-brom, die Blesbokke kom ... Come on, man. Who are – who are – who are we ... ? Come on.

STEVE: Give here.

CHARLIE [*keeping him at bay*]: Come on. War cry. Who are – who are – who are we ... ? Come on ... we are – we are – ...

STEVE: Bugger off now, Charlie – give here.

CHARLIE [*enjoying this*]: You coming right now. I wanna see you smile. Now come on ... war cry.

STEVE: Don't be a moegoe, man.

CHARLIE continues with the mocking chant, all the while running this way and that, constantly keeping the massage table between them. He tips the bottle.

CHARLIE: Who are – who are – who are we ... ?

STEVE [*quickly, before any is spilt*]: We are – we are – can't you see ... ?

CHARLIE [*pointing to STEVE*]: B –

STEVE: B –?

CHARLIE: L –

STEVE: What?

CHARLIE: Come on. Come on, man ... B –

CHARLIE points to STEVE.

STEVE: B –

To himself.

CHARLIE: L –

STEVE: E –

CHARLIE: S –

STEVE: K –

CHARLIE: K ... !? What d'you mean 'K'? Again. B –

Pointing at STEVE.

STEVE: B –

CHARLIE: L –

STEVE: E -

CHARLIE: S –

STEVE: K –

CHARLIE: What!?

STEVE: O –? B –? Shit, man! I dunno. What we spelling here?

CHARLIE: Jislaaik ... !

STEVE: I don't want to play this crap.

CHARLIE: No wonder we can't win a game. Can't even spell our own bladdy name right!

STEVE: Cocks this now, man.

CHARLIE: Who are we? We bladdy Blesbokke, man. How many years you been shouting for the Blesbokke.

STEVE: Ja, Charlie.

CHARLIE: From the top.

STEVE: No, Charlie.

CHARLIE: From the top! Who are – who are – who are we ...

CHARLIE and STEVE: We are – we are – can't you see ... ?

CHARLIE points to STEVE.

STEVE: B –

CHARLIE: L –

STEVE: E –

CHARLIE: S –

STEVE [*a beat*]: B –

CHARLIE: O –

STEVE: K –

CHARLIE: Now it's 'K ... K –

STEVE: E –

CHARLIE and STEVE: Blesbokke!!

CHARLIE still withholds the bottle of aftershave.

CHARLIE: You okay now?

STEVE: Ja.

CHARLIE: You fixed up now?

STEVE: Ja.

CHARLIE: Twenty press-ups.

STEVE: What?

CHARLIE: Twenty press-ups.

STEVE: Ah, no – come on, Charlie, man, for ....

CHARLIE: Nothing like a bit a' sweat to get the head right [*Keeping the bottle from him*] Down ...

STEVE: I'm okay now, I swear ...

CHARLIE [*shoving him down*]: Down you go. One – two ...

STEVE [*down but still protesting*]: Charlie ...

CHARLIE: *One – two – three – four –* [STEVE *reluctantly begins to do press-ups.*] *five – six – when you pissed off you do press-ups ... gets it out of the system ... eight – nine – ten – sheesh, you bladdy unfit, hey?*

STEVE [*not stopping*]: Just played a bladdy game, man.

CHARLIE: ... twelve – thirteen – fourteen –

STEVE: Count right, man.

CHARLIE: Shaddap! This is what they call 'therapy' – faster ... sixteen – seventeen – eighteen – nineteen – five more ...

STEVE: Bull!

CHARLIE [*fetching STEVE's half empty beer and putting down the aftershave*]: Five more. Twenty-one – twenty-two – twenty-three – twenty-four – twenty-five ...

As STEVE reaches the final press-up, CHARLIE pours a stream of beer onto his head. STEVE leaps to his feet and CHARLIE escapes by running around the massage table. CHARLIE shakes the can all the while, working up some pressure.

He lets the youngster have a jet and leaps up onto the skip. STEVE pelts him with empty beer cans. The 'game' stops when CHARLIE spots something through the window above the skip.

CHARLIE: Stick around. Wait. Wait!

STEVE [*still hurling junk*]: Stuff you, boy.

CHARLIE: No, give it up, man. Come check here – quick!

STEVE [*staying where he is*]: Bull ... dust.

CHARLIE: No, swear to God – quickly man.

STEVE is wary, but CHARLIE's bubbling enthusiasm seems too sincere to be acted. He gets up onto the skip and together they crane their necks, as if trying to see something through the window in a downstage direction.

CHARLIE: You see?

STEVE: I see.

CHARLIE: What I tell you?

STEVE: Like you said.

CHARLIE [*socked between the eyes*]: Check. Check!

STEVE: I check. The one with the ... ?

CHARLIE: The one with the ... ja.

STEVE [*impressed*]: Ja.

CHARLIE: Hey?

STEVE: Ja.

CHARLIE: On a plate, my mate.

STEVE [*taking his beer from CHARLIE and jumping down*]: Nurses.

CHARLIE [*still ogling*]: Hey?

STEVE: Nurses.

CHARLIE: What do you mean 'nurses'?

STEVE: Nurses – you know – Morning Doctor – Morning Nurse ...

CHARLIE: What the bladdy hell's wrong with nurses?

STEVE: Nothing. You got a skyf?

CHARLIE [*shaking his head*]: Poephol.

STEVE puts his beer down.

STEVE: This thing's flat. You owe me one.

CHARLIE is looking through the window again. STEVE picks up his aftershave, moves to his kitbag and starts going through it.

CHARLIE: How do you know they're nurses?

STEVE: I dunno. Maybe they a bus load of Troepies in drag.

CHARLIE [*middle finger*]: This is for you.

STEVE: Save it for the nurses. [*STEVE laughs and turns his attention to his kitbag once more. He digs around in it.*] What you do with my soap, now?

CHARLIE: [*jumping down*]: Come on, stop faffing around now. Bliksem!

He advances on STEVE in mock aggression.

STEVE: *I'm* a bliksem?

They grab each other and begin wrestling. A typical dressing room fight ensues. It is (in some eyes) childish, ridiculous; but it is the traditional manner in which gladiators 'kiss and make up'. In the middle of it all, LYNETTE MCALLISTER appears in the doorway. She is on the wrong side of twenty-five, an ex-beauty queen, single and still on the make. Her attempt to appear 'with-it' in her style of dress immediately endears her to us – the platteland notion of high chic made even more off-key because she has gone a little to seed. She stands watching the players roll this way and that, totally oblivious to the attentions of their silent observer. Finally, they become aware of her presence and, highly embarrassed, get to their feet and dust themselves off.

CHARLIE: Oh. Hi. Lynette. Sorry. Er ... Steve, this is Lynette. Lynette ... Steve.

STEVE: Hi.

LYNETTE: What happened?

CHARLIE [*misunderstanding her*]: No, he punched me over here, so I just ...

STEVE: Bullsh ... bulldust, ou!

They are about to launch into their argument again when LYNETTE interrupts, addressing CHARLIE.

LYNETTE: No, I mean upstairs ... upstairs. One minute you were there – the next you were ... I been looking for you everywhere.

CHARLIE: Oh, ja ... er ... [*Indicating* STEVE] I came to look for this idiot.

LYNETTE: Are you going to take this photo now or what you want me to do?

CHARLIE: Oh, yes – picture. Dammit. Steve, where's the camera?

STEVE: What camera?

CHARLIE: Camera, man. Click-click. Thing that takes pictures.

STEVE: Cam ... ? Er ... [*Covering for him*] Must be upstairs.

CHARLIE [*really busking now*]: Must be upstairs.

LYNETTE: Someone's getting me that tape if you want to hear it.

CHARLIE: Great! Fantastic!

LYNETTE: You still want to hear it, don't you!

CHARLIE: For sure. Guaranteed. Look ... er ... we'll be with you in a minute. Why don't you go get us a dop in the meantime ... Two dops. Steve ... ? Three dops ... we'll be right there. [*She hovers in the doorway, unsure of the territory.*] Swear to God. We right there.

LYNETTE: Don't be long, hey?

CHARLIE: No, we there.

She lingers briefly then makes her way down the corridor. STEVE *sniggers, on to* CHARLIE'*s game.*

STEVE: Camera ... ? I mean, jissus ...

CHARLIE: Shhh. Listen, do us a favour. You going to have to bail me out here.

STEVE: What d' you mean?

CHARLIE: Ag, long bladdy story, man. My own fault. Last time we played here, I told her I run this modelling agency in Alberton.

STEVE: You what!?

CHARLIE: Don't laugh. I had a bet with Van der Westhuizen – six bottles of J & B I scored the Orange Queen.

STEVE: She's a Orange Queen?

CHARLIE: Ex-Orange Queen.

STEVE: You obviously cracked it.

CHARLIE: Please! Where from?

STEVE: I thought it was supposed to be a piece of cake with these platteland chicks?

CHARLIE: Ja, you smile at them – they hear wedding bells. Only problem is – they got to see the ring on their finger first. [STEVE *cannot stop laughing.* CHARLIE *moves to the door, looking off down the passage.*] Shit, I was hoping she'd bugger off. No such bladdy luck.

STEVE: What's this about a tape?

CHARLIE: Ag, she's got some tape, man. Wants to play me a tape – show me what she can do.

STEVE: Rather you than me, ou.

CHARLIE: That's why it pays to cover up your tracks, my boy. Come on. Pull finger.

Let's get the hell out of here. We go grab us a coupla nurses – jol back to the hotel.

STEVE's mood changes abruptly.

STEVE: Ja, look – you go ahead.

CHARLIE [*sitting near the door*]: Come on, I'll wait for you.

STEVE picks up a rugby ball and begins toying with it.

STEVE: No – look – forget it. I'm not messing around anymore.

CHARLIE: You're not messing around anymore? You ... ! The biggest razzler in the business!?

STEVE: Ja, I'm ... taking it easy for a while. I'm cooling it.

CHARLIE stares at him, incredulous.

CHARLIE: Hey ... forget about the wife, you on tour now, man. [*STEVE looks away*] She giving you grief again, or what ... ? [*Still no response*] Look, I've told you before – first year of marriage is always the worst.

STEVE: Ja, if it lasts that long.

This is news to CHARLIE.

CHARLIE: Bullshit.

STEVE: Swear to God. Now all of a sudden she wants to bugger off.

CHARLIE: Estelle? Since when?

STEVE: I'm telling you. Last week already. I come home one night – Wednesday – Thursday – whatever. Late practice – you know – the usual. I walk in the door – I wasn't even lousy to her. I just said what's for supper?

CHARLIE: What's for supper?

STEVE: What's for supper. She says we finish. Just like that.

CHARLIE: That's what she says?

STEVE: Straight. We finish.

CHARLIE: Ei – na!

STEVE: That's what I thought.

CHARLIE: Who wouldn't.

STEVE: The way she said it. To my face. No stuffing about – no nothing. We finish. So now I'm thinking – now what's this now? Normally she gives me uphill I just laugh, you know – grip her arse, slap her around ...

CHARLIE: The usual.

STEVE: That's right. Only this time I can't because she's changed – it's not Estelle. I mean there's this woman standing in front of me but it's not Estelle.

CHARLIE: She's different.

STEVE: She's otherwise. These eyes – bladdy lasers.

CHARLIE: So you tune her ...

STEVE: So I'm standing there. S'posed to have been at late practice, but I's with, ah, shit – what's her name?

CHARLIE: Janet?

STEVE: Naah, man – the other one ...

CHARLIE: Anyway ...

STEVE: Anyway. I been at her place. So I'm standing there, hey. A real arsehole. My dirty togs in one hand, bunch of flowers in the other; and now I'm trying to hold them behind my back so she can't see them ...

CHARLIE: Women are crazy.

STEVE: Mad, man. Anyway – so it's aftershave, mint imperials, the works, and I'm praying like hell she can't smell anything else and all of a sudden I'm thinking, oh nice, some little groupie's phoned her up. Or some bastard's been shooting his mouth off ...

CHARLIE: I know the type.

STEVE: Some big talker, you know. So I say is it me? Something I've done? She says no, it's not you – meaning me.

CHARLIE: So what do you do?

STEVE: What can I do?

CHARLIE: You give her the flowers.

STEVE: How can I give her the flowers?

CHARLIE: They not *her* flowers?

STEVE: Of course they her flowers, man. But how can I give her the bladdy flowers ... ? She tells me she's leaving I give her this massive great bunch of carnations!

CHARLIE: Okay, okay, so what happened?

STEVE: Bugger all. She goes to her room, locks the door and that's that. Twenty minutes later she's back in the lounge and it's all okay. She's sorry, she didn't mean it.

CHARLIE: That's all?

STEVE: That's all. Except this long face ever since.

CHARLIE: Women are mad, man.

STEVE: Crazy.

CHARLIE: Temporary insanity – hits them now and again.

STEVE: What the hell you do?

CHARLIE: You get her right, boy – but quick. You find out what's her buzz.

STEVE: She won't tell me.

CHARLIE: Where's your balls, man? You must listen to your Uncle Charlie here. I know what I'm talking about.

STEVE stares at the older man, shocked by his directness.

CHARLIE: Charmaine tried the same trick on me. Three weeks she doesn't talk to me. All of a sudden she's going to pottery classes. Pottery classes, huh! When I ask to see her pots there's no pots because it turns out there's no classes either. We both at home – the phone rings – I pick it up, there's no-one there. All that kind of crap.

STEVE: You think she was having a bit of a ... ?

CHARLIE: How must I know?

STEVE: You didn't ask her?

CHARLIE [*smirking*]: Fuck that! I must sink so low?

STEVE: So what you do?

CHARLIE: I kept my cool. All I did was, one night, I just casually brought out the gun ... to clean it. Made sure the kid was there too. Okay, you haven't got a kid. You got a kid, it helps. She sees you, she sees the kid, she sees the gun ... She thinks ... She doesn't try it again. [*Pause*] There's more to being the boss than making a noise. [*STEVE simply stares at him.*] Come on. Into that shower. We going to get you arseholes tonight, boy – but totally.

He grabs STEVE's bag and tosses it to him. He moves to the small mirror near the door to the passage and whips out a comb. STEVE watches him as he runs the comb through his thinning hair.

STEVE: You wouldn't really do it, would you?

CHARLIE [*preoccupied with his hair*]: Ag no, dammit man ... just look at these ... grey hairs. Gets to the stage you stop bladdy counting them.

STEVE: Charlie ... ?

CHARLIE: Shit, go like this ...

He lifts his hair off his forehead.

STEVE: Huh?

CHARLIE [*indicating that STEVE should do it*]: Go like this.

STEVE: What for?

CHARLIE: Just lift your hair, man. [*STEVE complies.*] Ja, you see, you too.

STEVE: Bullshit.

CHARLIE: Two – three years. You watch.

STEVE: You wouldn't *really* use it, would you?

CHARLIE: Bald as a coot in five years ... Use what?

STEVE: The gun?

CHARLIE: You think I'm crazy or something?

STEVE: I dunno.

CHARLIE [*still into the mirror*]: I might shoot a burglar ... but the wife! I mean that's going too far ... [*Suddenly, horrified*] Shit, I don't believe it ... !

STEVE: What?

CHARLIE [*holding out the comb*]: More on the comb than on my bladdy head. Still. I should complain? Ou Moerdyk's getting himself a hairpiece next week. As long as he doesn't play in the damn thing. Oke gives him a high tackle – he's left with a fur-burger in his hand. [*He goes on combing his hair, adding the finishing touches.* STEVE *digs around in his bag, then unzips a side panel.*] No, I'm telling you. [*Admiring the finished product*] In this life it all comes down to balls, that's all. A question of balls. Whose got the balls.

STEVE *takes his soap and a plastic miniature Donald Duck from the side panel.*

STEVE: Here, Ballsey, this is for you.
CHARLIE [*catching it*]: What's this?
STEVE: Donald Duck.
CHARLIE [*throwing it back*]: Fuck Donald Duck. I got a Donald Duck.
STEVE: What must *I* do with it?
CHARLIE: Don't ask me!
STEVE: Thanks a lot. I graze a whole box of corn flakes for this.
CHARLIE: I *told* you. I *got* a Donald Duck. I got a Donald Duck, a Mickey Mouse, a Goofy and a Porky Pig. It's *Pluto* I want. I get a Pluto I got the whole set.
STEVE [*about to put it back*]: Oh, well. Stuff you then.
CHARLIE: No, no. Give here. I'll swop it.
STEVE [*giving it to him*]: Jissis, why you got to waste your time with the kid's stuff ... ?
CHARLIE: Kid's stuff!?
STEVE: I mean how's your bladdy head with all that?
CHARLIE: Please! Woman next door won herself a flippin' deep freeze. Fourteen cubic foot!
STEVE [*removing his boots and socks*]: All my life ...
CHARLIE [*fired up now*]: I'm telling you! How's this, hey? She comes to me two weeks ago, she asks me if I got a Mickey Mouse. I say okay. I give her my spare Mickey Mouse – she already had a Pluto, the bitch. Fuck me if she doesn't win a bladdy deep freeze. [*Pause.* STEVE *is inspecting his toes.*] What I couldn't do with a deep freeze. [STEVE *gets up and goes to his bag, digging around in it.*] Mincer-mixer-shredder-liquidiser ...
STEVE: You got any nail clippers?
CHARLIE: I mean just the other day this bloke down the road wins one of those big outside swings ... [STEVE *finds an emery board and begins working on a toe nail.*] One of those huge couch swing things for the garden – two-tone blue and white, tassels round the side ... okay, it's not a deep freeze but who's complaining? I mean, hell. I could use a bladdy outside swing. Stick it outside. Middle of the lawn. Look fantastic the middle of my lawn.
STEVE [*filing his toenails*]: You haven't got a lawn.

CHARLIE: I know. But if I had a swing I'd flippin' grow one, wouldn't I? [*STEVE blows at the emery board, tosses it and his boots into his kitbag.*] Ag, I dunno. It's just not fair, man. Friday I buy eight packets. Eight! I get seven Porky Pigs and one Goofy. There's no bladdy justice in the world.

STEVE: Where's my soap?

CHARLIE: I didn't touch your soap.

STEVE looks down at his jersey, reluctant to take it off. CHARLIE toys with the Donald Duck.

CHARLIE: Why is it that every man must always try screw the next man? You know I'm willing to bet that for every five thousand Porky Pigs, Donald Ducks and Mickey Mouses they only got about half a dozen Plutos.

STEVE: Mickey Mice.

CHARLIE: Hey?

STEVE: Mickey Mice. One mouse – two mice.

CHARLIE: You think I'm joking?

STEVE: No, I'm with you. Those okes know what they're on about. It's what they call consumer incentive – the big carrot.

CHARLIE: Carrots ... ? What shit you talking now?

STEVE: Carrot on the stick. Oldest trick in the book.

CHARLIE: Why don't you just stop talking shit and go shower? Before you know it, that bladdy Quince Queen's going to be down here again, man. [*STEVE pulls his jersey over his head but stops short of taking it off completely. He stands with his arms still in the sleeves, staring down at it. CHARLIE thinks he is looking at his muscles.*] Boy-oh-boy, check the Tarzan here. Looks to me you need to get back on weights, my friend.

STEVE [*pre-occupied*]: I haven't stopped.

CHARLIE: What you pumping? Toothpicks? [*In a single motion STEVE has pulled his jersey back on again. CHARLIE half suspects the young player's motives.*] What the bladdy hell's your case now? [*STEVE shrugs, embarrassed. Unsure of what to do next.*] Don't tell me. You want to kip in the damn thing?

STEVE: Laugh, my friend – you were probably the same.

CHARLIE: You bladdy right, yes. Okes had to tear it off my back. [*Pause*] Well, come on. You can't sit here all bladdy night.

STEVE: I wonder if I should kiss the collar?

CHARLIE: What for?

STEVE: When I played school's rugby I always kissed the collar before I took it off.

CHARLIE [*sceptical*]: You reckon that did the trick?

STEVE: I never got dropped.

STEVE looks at the jersey.

CHARLIE looks at STEVE.

CHARLIE: So? What you waiting for? Kiss the damn thing.

STEVE: I dunno, man.

CHARLIE: What's the problem?

STEVE: 'S different.

CHARLIE: Different?

STEVE: Different. Different team – different ... you know ...

CHARLIE: Christ, you're worse than the bladdy Irish.

STEVE: I'm serious.

CHARLIE: You ever been into a Irish dressing room? Got to be seen to be believed. Okes are outa their minds, man – spitting on their boots, hitting their heads against the wall ...

STEVE: It's not funny.

CHARLIE: There was this one poephol played for Shamrocks had to walk on the ceiling before he went onto the pitch.

Pause. STEVE looks up.

STEVE: How the hell he do that?

CHARLIE: Don't ask me. Okes had to stand on the table. Hold him upside down.

Pause.

STEVE: Now that's crazy.

CHARLIE: That's what I'm saying. [*Pause*] So what's it going to be? Spit? Kiss? Fart?

STEVE [*he has the ball again*]: How d'you like my dummy scissors just before half-time?

CHARLIE: What dummy scissors?

STEVE: Just before half-time, man ... [*Demonstrating*] Half-gap ... held onto it ... little grubber through ... [*Leaping up on to the bench*] That much further ... *That* much further, ou Pinky would've been over.

CHARLIE: Ja.

STEVE: You didn't think I'd crack it, hey? That first time I jolled into Old Boy's – that practice – you didn't think I'd crack it ... ?

CHARLIE: I always knew you'd crack it.

STEVE [*indicating the emblem on his chest*]: North-Easterns, my mate ... [*He wanders along the bench, squatting near the clock. He points to it.*] Been a long time for you already, hey?

CHARLIE: Bladdy sure. Fourteen years. Seems like yesterday.

STEVE: They give everybody a clock?

CHARLIE: Depends. Some okes get nothing. On the other hand three years ago they gave ou Wally Joubert a dinner service. Bone china. Bladdy wankers.

STEVE: You feel shit about it?

CHARLIE: About the clock?

STEVE: About retiring.

CHARLIE: Ah, what the fuck.

   Pause.

STEVE: I'll never forget. First time I saw you was against those South Americans at the Pam Brink. You scored two tries and the blokes carried you off.

CHARLIE: You were there?

STEVE [*demonstrating*]: I was so high.

CHARLIE: You never told me you were there.

STEVE: *That* was the game I first said to myself I'm going to be a Blesbok.

CHARLIE [*bitterly*]: Two tries. And then for that Gazelle game they went and picked that bladdy poephol from South West.

STEVE: It was always going to be different. I was always going to score a couple of tries. Maybe put over a drop ... One thing's for sure – I was never gonna lose us the game.

CHARLIE: Lesson Number One in this kind of rugby – it means bugger all. You play like a champion you find out afterwards they been watching somebody else. [*Pause*] You mustn't take it to kop. This game can bladdy kill you.

   Pause.

STEVE: How you reckon I played today?

CHARLIE [*not relishing this*]: Today?

STEVE: Ja.

CHARLIE [*a beat*]: Okay. You were okay.

STEVE: Sort of okay or quite okay or what?

CHARLIE: For a first game, you were bladdy okay.

STEVE: No, but I mean not counting first game. Just taking it as a game. Any old game ...

CHARLIE: What do you want me to say, Sophie?

STEVE: I want you to say what you think.

CHARLIE: I told you what I think. I think you were great.

STEVE: You mean that?

CHARLIE: Listen, are you coming upstairs or not?

STEVE: I want to *know* Charlie. I want to know from you – not from the other okes, or from the papers, or some stupid arsehole in the street ... I want to hear it from somebody who knows what I can do.

   Pause. There is no avoiding it.

CHARLIE: You played like a first class prick.

Pause.

STEVE: Thanks.

CHARLIE: In fact you were worse than that.

STEVE: Okay, okay ...

CHARLIE [*shrugging*]: You wanted to know.

STEVE: Well, fuck you.

CHARLIE: Fuck you too.

STEVE: *You* played like an arsehole.

CHARLIE: Oh, ja?

STEVE: Arsehole-de-luxe.

CHARLIE: Well after a hundred and thirty-four games for this province I can afford to, can't I?

STEVE: Stick your bladdy province, man!

CHARLIE: Don't get pissed off with *me* now.

STEVE: You said I was great.

CHARLIE: I said you were okay.

STEVE: And now you telling me I'm shit.

CHARLIE: You're not at school anymore, man. This isn't the first fucken fifteen.

STEVE: What's that supposed to mean?

CHARLIE: Listen, Sunshine, why they pick you for this game?

STEVE: Because I'm fucken good.

CHARLIE [*exploding*]: Don't talk shit to me now, I'm being serious!

STEVE: Because De Waal's injured.

CHARLIE: Okay, De Waal's injured. But why they pick *you* not somebody else?

STEVE: I dunno – they fucked in the head.

CHARLIE: Because you kick, poephol. You're a kicker. Everybody knows we got the worst backline in ten years, so they pick someone who's going to play the forwards – right?

STEVE: Right.

CHARLIE: A flyhalf who's going to kick – right? [*STEVE remains silent*] Right. So what do you do? You're letting it out behind your own bladdy tryline, for fuck's sake.

STEVE: What else could I do?

CHARLIE: You play safe, poephol. You kick, and you kick, and keep on bladdy kicking.

STEVE: But the oke was on top of me.

CHARLIE [*pacing about*]: Where these beers? Don't tell me you drank all these beers? Look at this mess.

STEVE: You can't kick *all* the time.

CHARLIE: Now you know why these places stink like a beer hall. Come on, let's get out of here, man. Sis!

STEVE: So you reckon that's it, hey?

CHARLIE: You know I came into a dressing room once. It was in Durban. Kings Park. There were these wankers pissing up the wall, seeing who could piss the highest.

STEVE: Charlie ... ? You reckon I'm out?

CHARLIE: Whole bladdy team – slashing up the walls ... [*Pause*] Animals ... pigs.

STEVE: You know what Danie Craven said to me?

CHARLIE: Disgusting.

Pause.

STEVE: You know what Danie Craven said to me ... ?

CHARLIE: I know what Danie Craven said to you.

STEVE: How can you? I've never told you.

CHARLIE: Danie Craven said a lot of things to a lot of people.

STEVE: He told me to come to Stellenbosch.

CHARLIE: Is that so? He said the same thing to me eighteen years ago. [*STEVE stares at CHARLIE. He has hit rock bottom.*] There's a lot of fish in this little pond, my boy ... fucken lot of fish.[*Slowly STEVE peels off his jersey and allows it to drop to the floor. They sit in silence for a while. The party upstairs continues unabated.*] You didn't kiss the collar.

STEVE: Hey?

CHARLIE: Collar. You didn't ... you know.

STEVE [*unconcerned*]: Ja.

Suddenly CHARLIE gets to his feet, heading for the door.

CHARLIE: I don't know about you, but I gotta have a dop. I tell you what. I'll slip back to the hotel maybe score us some chicks. By the time you rock up I'll have them ticking, how's that? Even better you can take your pick – first choice.

STEVE [*unamused*]: Always the joker, hey?

CHARLIE: Got to take your chances, boy. Chances is chances. Grab them while you can – you catch? [*STEVE looks away, hassled, preoccupied.*] Okay. You want it straight. Fine. They probably going to drop you. In fact they *are* going to drop you ... You're out on your arse. How's that?

STEVE [*beyond it now*]: Let's just los it, okay?

CHARLIE: What do you want from this game? You want to play rugby or you want a clock? You want a clock – you can have this one with pleasure.

STEVE: Talk crap, man.

CHARLIE: Then what is it? What's the big deal? I mean where the bladdy hell you come from, man? You mope around this dressing room worrying if and when you going to wear that jersey again – you're what? You're twenty-three!

STEVE: Twenty-four.

CHARLIE: You know how old I am?

STEVE: It's enough, okay?

CHARLIE: I said do you know how old I am? Tonight's supposed to be my bladdy farewell in case you'd forgotten.

STEVE: I hadn't forgotten.

CHARLIE: Ja, well maybe I'm feeling a bit shit too. Maybe right now I'd like to be getting pissed out of my mind, trying to forget I've played my last bladdy game for the Blesbokke.

STEVE: Ja, but for you it's okay – you've had a good go of it. And if you wanted to, you could always come back.

CHARLIE: That simple, hey?

STEVE: For sure. You got a couple more years – at least!

CHARLIE: Says who?

STEVE: Ah come on man, you're ... I mean you're Charlie Theron.

CHARLIE: Oh yes? You know what the Boss says to Charlie Theron half-way through the season ... ? Hey ... ? You really want to know ... ? [STEVE *stares at the older man. Way out of his depth now.*] You know bugger all about this game, do you? You think it's a matter of choice. Am I going to play or am I not going to play? Choice never comes into it, sunshine. It's politics. [STEVE *is silent.* CHARLIE *points to the clock.*] That clock's not just a farewell gift. It's part of a deal. It's like a medal they give to a foot-soldier who's had his bladdy legs blown off. [*There is a long silence.* STEVE *knows that for* CHARLIE *there is no going back.*] You think *you've* been cheated? Remind me to tell you some time.

He heads for the door.

STEVE: Charlie.

CHARLIE: Ja.

STEVE: I'm sorry.

CHARLIE: What for?

STEVE: I didn't know it was like that, I swear.

CHARLIE: It's okay.

STEVE: I didn't really mean it just now when I said you played like an arsehole.

CHARLIE: Forget it. How *I* play doesn't matter anymore.

STEVE [*passionately*]: But it *does.* You got to show them. You got to prove it to them.

CHARLIE: Prove what?

STEVE: That you're still the best.

CHARLIE: What for ... ? [STEVE *stares at him nonplussed.*] I'm sick of this game. I've had it up to here. For years already. The busted kneecaps – the dislocated shoulders. And as for the newspapers – Christ, the crap they write about you in the newspapers!

STEVE [*a picture of utter confusion*]: I don't understand ...

CHARLIE: I know, I know – it's crazy – it's madness. I want to play and I don't want to play. But what else is there? When you're me? When rugby's the only thing you know? Half the reason I'm not upstairs is because I'm too shit scared to face up to it. Wondering what the bladdy hell I'm going to do. I mean where do I go from here? What happens to me now?

STEVE has to search for this.

STEVE: What happens to anyone?

CHARLIE [*not letting him off the hook*]: No. I'm not talking about anyone. I'm talking about me. About Charlie Theron. Two – three years down the line. Sixty years old. Hanging around the clubhouse bar 'til they kick me out at closing time.

STEVE: Like ou Fats Vorster.

CHARLIE: Ja ...

STEVE: Fats is a joke, man.

CHARLIE: That's exactly what I mean. [*He smiles suddenly, remembering something.*] Huh. A coupla weeks ago I go in for this interview ... new job ... hopefully. This bloke asks me what experience I got. I tell him playing rugby and selling jock-straps.

STEVE: There's no crime in that.

CHARLIE: Bloke says to me, occupation. How's this, hey? He's filling out this form. He says to me, occupation. I say to him tight-head prop. Just as a joke. He looks at me. He's never heard of a tight-head prop. Can you believe it? A fully grown, so-called educated man – he's never heard of a tight-head prop!

STEVE [*quietly*]: Jesus.

Pause.

CHARLIE: Ag, what the hell .... [*He moves to the door.*] Look, if I spot you, I spot you, okay?

He exits. STEVE, moved by the older man's plight calls after him.

STEVE: Charlie ... ?

CHARLIE [*stopping some distance down the passage*]: Ja?

STEVE: Charlie ... ? [*CHARLIE ambles back to the dressing room door. He pops his head in.*] Cha ... ? Hey, Charlie ... go order the dops, man. Let's get out of our bladdy minds.

CHARLIE [*beaming*]: Now you talking, ou.

He leaves. He has barely disappeared when he comes bursting back in, catching STEVE in the process of removing his shorts and jock-strap

CHARLIE: Shit, I don't believe it! Get decent. Here she comes!

STEVE [*pulling on his shorts*]: What's up?

CHARLIE has whipped STEVE's blazer off the clothes hook and is thrusting it into his hands.

CHARLIE: Listen, you haven't seen me, okay? [*He heads for the shower arch.*] I'm going to get out through the window in the shower.

STEVE [*bewildered at the frenzy*]: What?

CHARLIE [*pointing off*]: I'm getting out the window here ...

STEVE: Talk junk, man. Stick around ...

CHARLIE: Just give me enough time to get my stuff upstairs and bugger off.

STEVE [*his blazer on now*]: Wait a minute. What am I going to tell her ... ?

CHARLIE: Tell her anything. Just give me enough time to get away.

STEVE: Bull. This is your bladdy stuff up, not mine ...

CHARLIE notices he has forgotten the clock. He darts back to fetch it.

CHARLIE: Give a guy a break, man. I'd do the same for you.

As he whips up the clock, LYNETTE, wine glass in hand, sticks her head in the door.

LYNETTE: Coo-ee ... Hello there.

CHARLIE [*changing gear rapidly*]: Hi, Lynette. I was just coming to find you.

He replaces the clock.

She holds up a tatty portable tape recorder.

LYNETTE: I've got the tape.

CHARLIE: Wonderful. Let's hear it. Come inside.

LYNETTE: Thanks. It's getting a bit wild up there. I don't know why it is that rugby players must always stand on the tables.

CHARLIE: Ja, well better on top than underneath, hey?

LYNETTE: There some there too.

She has had a couple of drinks and is very slightly tipsy. CHARLIE indicates her glass.

CHARLIE: I see you're fixed up.

LYNETTE: Oh, this – ja. I should of brought a bottle down, hey?

CHARLIE: Never mind. I'll go get some.

He turns to go.

STEVE: Where you going?

CHARLIE: To get a dop.

STEVE: You coming back?

CHARLIE: Of course I'm coming back. What're you having? It's okay, I know what you're having. Lynette, same again?

About to leave, he spots the clock and moves to fetch it.

STEVE: Charlie ... What am I going to ... ?

CHARLIE shrugs him off; gratefully whipping up the clock and heading out.

STEVE is in a state of panic.

CHARLIE: It's okay, it's okay – don't panic.

STEVE is left alone with LYNETTE. There is an awkward silence.

LYNETTE: God, I'm so nervous. You think he'll take me?

STEVE: Hey?

LYNETTE: Weren't you also playing today?

STEVE: How did you guess?

LYNETTE: No, I'm sorry, I didn't say anything earlier – I thought everyone who was playing was supposed to be at the party.

STEVE: When I'm allowed to have a shower, I might eventually get up there.

LYNETTE: Ag, hell – forgive me. I didn't mean to interrupt.

STEVE: It's okay. It's not serious.

Pause.

LYNETTE [*looking around and giggling girlishly*]: This is my first time in a dressing room. I mean in a proper sort of men's dressing room. I've been in a dressing room before, but not this kind of a dressing room, if you know what I mean ... you know what I mean ... ? [*STEVE stares at her.*] Ag, I'm being stupid now. [*She touches her cheek.*] Are my cheeks red?

STEVE: Not that I can notice.

LYNETTE: Whenever I've had too much wine my cheeks go red and people think I'm blushing. Not that I'm not blushing, but it looks like I'm blushing all the time ... which I'm not. [*She slaps her cheek.*] Ag, shut up, Lynette, you talking rubbish now, man.

Pause.

STEVE: Charlie tells me you were the Quince Queen.

LYNETTE: The what?

STEVE: Sorry – Orange Queen.

LYNETTE [*smiling*]: You mean the Citrus Queen.

STEVE: Citrus Queen.

LYNETTE: I *was* the Citrus Queen

STEVE: What I mean, ja.

LYNETTE: Ja. Long time ago. [*Pause*] How did you know?

STEVE: Charlie told me.

LYNETTE: Oh, ja ... I thought maybe you recognised me.

STEVE: No, no ...

LYNETTE: No. No such luck, hey?

STEVE: No.

Pause.

LYNETTE: Ja. Nineteen eighty-two.

STEVE: Eighty-two. That was a good year.

LYNETTE: People say that, ja.

STEVE [*cracking a joke*]: Good year for wines too. Not to mention orange juice.

His weak joke falls flat, wasted on her at this point.

LYNETTE: I've still got my sash.

STEVE: Is it?

LYNETTE: Ja, my big orange sash with gold writing on it. I've got it hanging above my bed. My mother thinks it's vain but, like they say in that ad for the perfume – when you've got it, flaunt it.

STEVE: For sure.

STEVE gets up and goes to the door. He looks down the passage and turns back to the room.

LYNETTE: Weren't you playing fullback?

STEVE: Me ... ?

LYNETTE: Wait a minute – wing? You were wing ...

STEVE: How about lock?

LYNETTE: Was that you. *That* wasn't you.

STEVE: Says a lot for my game, hey?

LYNETTE: Ag, don't tease now, man.

STEVE: I was flyhalf.

LYNETTE: Is it? [*She knows her rugby*]. You and Naas Botha.

STEVE: Please! All my life!

LYNETTE: You know I almost nearly met him once. It's true. In Pretoria. He was opening this new Checkers in Sunnyside ... or was it Menlo Park? Pick 'n Pay – that was it! If I put my hand out, I could of actually touched him. [*She gives another girlish giggle.*] I was still quite silly in those days.

STEVE: Listen, you haven't perhaps got a smoke, have you?

LYNETTE [*opening her handbag*]: I'm afraid they're not Camel.

STEVE: What makes you think I smoke Camel?

LYNETTE: All rugby players smoke Camel.

STEVE: Is that so ... ? [*She produces the pack.* STEVE *changes his mind as she reveals the name – Craven A menthols (the long ones).*] On second thoughts, forget it.

LYNETTE: You sure? You don't mind if I do?

STEVE: Go ahead.

He returns to the door, rapidly losing hope that CHARLIE *will ever come back. She lights up a smoke.*

LYNETTE [*sipping at her wine, loosening* up]: Ag no – you know, the night I was crowned they were all there ... *Sarie – Rooi Rose – Darling.* They even took some pictures of me for the *Farmer's Weekly.* Cover story. The Girl with the Bubbly Personality. I mean – me! I nearly died. Some of my friends at the building society laughed because I was half hidden by this cow, but I didn't mind. Anyway, they were just jealous. None of them ever got *into* a magazine, forget about the *cover.* And inside. Inside there was this big colour picture of me on my own in a swimming costume holding a bowl of oranges and it said 'Quo Vadis, Lynette McAllister'. [*Pause*] Where to now, Lynette McAllister.

STEVE: Oh.

LYNETTE: Ja. I had it all worked out. I can still remember the adjudicator – one of the judges – he was that Deputy something-or-other of Transport Affairs. Not the one with the moustache – the other one. He also picks the Cherry Queen in Ficksburg. Anyway. Him. He said to me I must go to Jo'burg. He said in Jo'burg a girl like me can go far. But I didn't. Like a fool I stayed here. Now what have I got to show for it ... ? [*She reads the name tag on* STEVE's *kitbag*] Steve Sofi-who ... ?

STEVE [*at the door*]: Sorry?

LYNETTE [*indicating the tag*]: Your name? Steve Sofi-what?

STEVE: Sofianek.

LYNETTE: Is that Jewish?

STEVE: It's Czech.

LYNETTE: Check ... ?

STEVE: My old man was Czech.

LYNETTE: What's that? Like Hindu or something?

STEVE: No, no – Czechoslovakia – the country.

LYNETTE: Oh, ja – you mean like Russian?

STEVE: Ja. I mean, no. I mean Russia's up there, Czechoslovakia's down here.

LYNETTE: Oh, I see – ja.

STEVE: Also the Russians are Commies ... We Commies too, but there are Commies and Commies ...

LYNETTE [*reading the name tag*]: So-fi-a-nek.

STEVE: That's right.

Pause.

LYNETTE: No prizes for guessing what they call you for short, hey?

STEVE smiles thinly.

LYNETTE: Ja. My ancestors also come from overseas ... Scotland. [*Pause*] God, I'm so nervous I could die. [*She indicates the tape recorder.*] Listen, you don't mine if I just quickly go through my steps, do you? If I practise my routine?

She fetches the recorder and takes it to the massage table.

STEVE: What, you want to ... !

LYNETTE: I just want to play the tape – quick.

STEVE [*not too happy about this*]: Look – er ...

She sets the machine up, rewinding it.

LYNETTE: Do you know anything about ramp?

STEVE: Ramp ... ?

LYNETTE: Ramp work. It's the art form of the future as far as modelling's concerned. That's what they all say, anyway. I know I've got the height and all that, but I read in a magazine somewhere the model of tomorrow doesn't only have to look good – she must be able to sing, dance, act, sparkle – everything. [*She is chuffed with herself.*] Now that I've said bye-bye to the building society, I must take it seriously.

STEVE: You what?

LYNETTE: Ja. Quite a big step, hey?

STEVE: You left your job?

LYNETTE: You are looking at a full time model – TA-RAAAM!. [*She strikes a 'model' pose.*] That is if Charlie takes me. He could hardly believe his ears when I told him I took his advice. [*STEVE stares at her in disbelief.*] It's true. Last time he was here he said to me if ever I decided to take up modelling full time, I must come to him. So about three months ago, when I finally bust up with my ex, I said to myself – come on, McAllister, what've you got to lose ... So here I am with this tape. Marcia de Bruyn thinks it's okay, but then what does she know? She only takes the local kids for ballet.

STEVE: Look, er – Lynette ... I don't want to sort of ... throw a spanner in the works here, but ...

LYNETTE: Look, if you don't want to listen, you must just say so. I mean, I don't want to force you.

STEVE [*doing his best to be tactful*]: No, no – it's just that between you and me I think you might be just sort of ... wasting your time sort of thing.

LYNETTE: You mean you don't think he'll take me ... ?

STEVE: No, no ... What I mean is – he's taking a long time. Maybe he's sort of ... not coming back.

LYNETTE: You mean like right now, you mean?

STEVE: Maybe he's got sidetracked.

LYNETTE: No, he's probably looking for a camera. Prolly gone to fetch a Poly. He told me he needed a head-and-shoulders and, like a fool, ol' Dizzy Dora here loses the only new pic she's got ... [*She doesn't give him a chance to answer.*] Look, all I want you to do is just sort of tell me if it's sort of okay – okay ... ? [*STEVE stares at her, helpless in the face of her blinkered enthusiasm.*] Am I being a pain? If I'm being a pain, you must just say so, hey. [*She carries on regardless.*] Now this is not sort of professional or anything, it's just sort of well – let me show you and then ... [*She starts the tape. A series of odd noises issues forth before the actual music begins.*] Ag, that's a lorry outside. Had to do it at home ... [*to the tape*] Come on, come on ... ! [*A dog starts barking ... harsh, incessant.*] Bladdy brak next door ... there millions of dogs in our neighbourhood – one starts, they all go off ... [*From the tape comes the sound of a number of dogs barking while she goes on describing the format.*] This isn't me singing. It's just a demo. I sort of mouth the words while ... [*The music begins, throwing her. She is forced to break off and stop the tape.*] Dammit. Took me by surprise. This always happens. [*The song she has recorded is Tina Turner's 'Private Dancer'.* LYNETTE *has 'learnt' a dance routine which she endeavours to perform, while at the same time mouthing the words a la Sun City Extravaganza.*] God, imagine if Charlie'd seen that? He'd of died.

STEVE can take this lot no longer.

STEVE: Look, Lynette – maybe you should just practise so long and I'll go hop in the shower.

LYNETTE: It won't take long.

He moves to his hook, grabs the remainder of his clothes, kitbag, shoes and so on and heads for the showers.

STEVE: No, you go ahead. Carry on.

LYNETTE: I had to record it holding the microphone in front of the speaker because I didn't have one of those ... one of those ... what do you call those little plug things?

STEVE: Jack.

LYNETTE: Jack – that's right. [*STEVE slinks out through the shower arch. She is preoccupied with her machine.*] Of course, if my boyfriend was still around he'd of fixed it in no time. He knew all about recording. He had tapes of everything

– Bobby Angel, you name it ... [*She pushes the play button. The music resumes where it left off – the opening bars of 'Private Dancer'. The music underscores her speech.*] Ja. The first time I went to Jo'burg was with my ex. School holidays – Standard Nine. We came in on the Heidelberg Road and there was this drive-in on top of a mine dump with the biggest neon sign I'd ever seen ... I thought – My God – I've arrived ... [*She spots the mirror.*] It was like New York ... [*She moves to the mirror and fiddles with her hair.*] My boyfriend hated it. He just wanted to get back home. I'm sure that's why we broke up in the end. He wanted me just to sommer settle down and be a housewife. He was so lomp ... like everyone else in this dump ... I was lomp before I met Charlie ... [*She becomes aware that Tina Turner has started on the words 'I'm your Private Dancer' and, cross with herself, runs across to the tape recorder, snapping it off. She shouts off to where she imagines STEVE to be.*] It's just as well I'm trying this out. You forget so quick if you've had a couple of sips of wine ... Do you think this music's okay? Tina Turner? Or d'you think I should try something more 'showbizzy' ... ? Steve ... ? Steve ... !?

There is no answer from the shower area. She stands in the archway, perplexed, yet unable to go in and look. She calls his name again and then goes to the door to the dressing room, looking out down the passage. Not giving it much further thought, she returns to her tape recorder and snaps it on. Tina Turner's voice comes through singing 'I'm Your Private Dancer' for the second time. LYNETTE begins her routine. It is sad, almost pathetic. The steps she has learnt are her own. As the music swells she really gets into it. The sounds of crowds cheering and whistling melt into the soundtrack, creating the sensation that she is appearing onstage at some concert. Isolated in a pool of purple light – the crowds still cheering and Tina belting out the song – she lives out her fantasy as we fade to blackout.

Boo to the Moon

A ONE-ACT PLAY

Minnaloushe creeps through the grass. Alone, important and wise,
And lifts to the changing moon. His changing eyes.

W B YEATS ('The Cat and the Moon').

Director Bobby Heaney (right) and the 1986 cast of the PACT production of *Boo to the Moon* (left to right), Anna-Mart van der Merwe as MYRTLE, Bruce Alexander as COXIE, Susan Danford as JESSICA, Stephen Jennings as SPIDER and Glenn Swart as ALLIE.
Photograph by Bob Martin.

Cast

SPIDER, the oldest – a dismal school record reflected in his behaviour and dress (totally inappropriate for something as formal as a Matric Farewell). He wears a casual jacket, its lapels covered in badges. He also wears a school cap.

JESSICA, a school prefect with a mind of her own. She knows the rules, but still plays the game her own way.

COXIE, head boy and rugby star – the only one wearing a 'tux'.

MYRTLE, the youngest – she has made her 'Pamela Ewing' dress herself and is very proud of the fact.

ALLIE, bespectacled, the class boffin. His 'straight' suit is worn in a way that suggests a total ignorance of hip, as does his body language.

The time is 1986.

Boo to the Moon was first performed by NAPAC's Loft Theatre Company in the Loft Theatre (Natal Playhouse) on 12 November 1986. Greg Melvill Smith played Spider, Judy Broderick, Jessica, Christopher Wells, Coxie, Simon Heale, Allie, and Annie Harvey, Myrtle. The production was directed by Paul Slabolepszy.

The play was subsequently performed throughout 1987 by PACT who toured it nationally. The production opened at Johannesburg's Windybrow Theatre in May 1987, with Stephen Jennings as Spider, Susan Danford as Jessica, Bruce Alexander as Coxie, Glenn Swart as Allie, and Anna-Mart van der Merwe as Myrtle. The production was directed by Bobby Heaney.

The entire play takes place in and around a crashed medium-to-small saloon car – mid to late seventies vintage (a four-door Fiat 128?). The wreck, mildly battered and with a flat rear wheel, stands at an angle on an open patch of veld. We are to imagine that the vehicle has tumbled from the Durban–South Coast highway (off stage and up a steep incline).

Since the actual accident only happens in the first beat of the play, it is important that the incoming audience does not see the car. Where there is no proscenium arch, the vehicle should be covered with a tarpaulin or stage cloth. As the auditorium lights dim and the theatre becomes totally dark, we hear the all encompassing cacophony of a motor accident. With a squealing of brakes, a crunching of metal and smashing of glass, a car rolls over and over again, finally coming to a halt. The sound of heavy rock music gives way to Robin Alexander and Radio Orion as the cassette tape ejects from the tape player.

As the stage lights slowly fade up, we are confronted with the sight of the battered vehicle in the pale light of the moon. Upstage left is a rusty steel canopy frame (perhaps from a burnt-out Bedford truck). Down right is a battered, halfsquashed forty-four-gallon drum.

A tiny jet of steam oozes from under the bonnet. The car boasts ND (Durban) number plates and one of them hangs from a bumper, swinging gently to and fro. Robin Alexander continues his mindless chatter, a mocking counterpoint to the eerie post-crash atmosphere. For a while nothing happens.

A girl's voice (MYRTLE) pierces the still night air. She screams unashamedly. This is a cue for general pandemonium. There are shrieks and shouts – a mixture of tipsy euphoria and genuine fear. A sense of a roller-coaster ride gone wrong. It is almost as if the whole thing has been (or still is) some kind of weird dream. Since all we see at this stage are silhouettes, it does not matter that we do not know who is speaking or how many people there are in the car. In fact, this should make the opening scene (until the interior cab light is switched on) both bizarre and slightly comic.

COXIE: Shut up!

MYRTLE whimpers.

ALLIE: Ei-na!
SPIDER: Fuck a duck.
JESSICA: Oh, my God. What happened? Where are we?
COXIE: It's okay.

MYRTLE whimpers.

ALLIE: Ei-na.

COXIE: Allie?

SPIDER: Shit a brick.

COXIE: Allie?

ALLIE: Hello.

COXIE: You okay?

ALLIE: My arm.

COXIE: For God-sake, Spider!

SPIDER: What?

MYRTLE whimpers.

JESSICA: Myrtle?

COXIE: How's Myrtle?

JESSICA: You okay, Myrtle?

COXIE struggles with the overhead light. SPIDER at last switches off Radio Orion as a rubbishy song begins.

COXIE: Shit, where's the light?

MYRTLE whimpers.

JESSICA: Oh, my God, I don't believe it.

COXIE: What?

JESSICA: She swallowed her brace.

COXIE: Her brace?

SPIDER: Swallowed her what?

ALLIE: Must be in her mouth.

COXIE: Check her mouth.

JESSICA: No, it's not.

MYRTLE: I haven't got it.

COXIE: Look on the floor.

SPIDER: Hit her on her back.

COXIE [*angrily*]: Stuff this light!

SPIDER [*feeling for the light*]: Move your hand, man.

ALLIE: I can't find it on the floor.

MYRTLE: I haven't got it.

COXIE: Hit her on the back, man.

MYRTLE: I haven't got it. I wasn't wearing my brace.

COXIE: Are you sure?

MYRTLE [*starting to cry*]: I took it out for the dance.

COXIE: Okay, Myrtle, okay.

JESSICA: Don't cry, Myrt.

The overhead light snaps on. (For theatrical purposes the light is more powerful than normal and though it does not actually flood the interior of the car with light, we are at least able to distinguish the occupants.) COXIE *and* SPIDER *are up front – the latter behind the wheel.* MYRTLE *is sandwiched between* JESSICA *and* ALLIE *in the back.*

SPIDER [*as the light comes on*]: Fat Cat!

ALLIE: That's better.

MYRTLE whimpers.

JESSICA: Myrtle?

COXIE: Is she hurt?

ALLIE: Are you hurt?

SPIDER: I'm not hurt.

COXIE: No one asked you! Jessie?

JESSICA: What happened to the road?

SPIDER: We took a detour. Cross country.

COXIE: Shut your face, man!

SPIDER: What's up with you?

COXIE: What the hell you do?

SPIDER: What d'you mean what the hell I do? You saw what I did.

JESSICA: Shh ...

COXIE: You roll a' bladdy car!

SPIDER: Don't look at me.

COXIE: Who the hell's behind the wheel ... !?

JESSICA: Shht ... !

SPIDER: You didn't see it?

COXIE: See what?

SPIDER: Don't tell me you didn't see it!?

COXIE: Talk shit, man – you fall asleep ...

SPIDER: Right in the middle of the bladdy road ...

JESSICA: Oh, shut up now, man!

SPIDER: Who you telling to shut up?

JESSICA: We been in an accident here ...

SPIDER: You shut up yourself, my girl ...

COXIE: Don't you tell my chick to shut up ...

They argue.

ALLIE: Leave it, Coxie!

MYRTLE [*hysterical, stopping them*]: Shut up the lot of you!

For a moment there is absolute silence.

COXIE [*under his breath*]: Jislaaik! We've actually rolled the flippin' car.
SPIDER: Look on the bright side. We could be upside down.
JESSICA: Oh, my God.

Pause.

ALLIE: Maybe we're all dead and this is Heaven.
JESSICA: That's not funny.
ALLIE: Sorry.
JESSICA: This is no time to be cracking jokes.
ALLIE: I said – I'm sorry.
SPIDER [*sniffs the air*]: Shut up.
COXIE: What's the matter?
SPIDER: You smell that?
COXIE: Smell what?
SPIDER: Can't you smell?

They all sniff the air.

COXIE: Petrol?
SPIDER: Petrol.
JESSICA: Petrol!
MYRTLE: Petrol?
ALLIE: Petrol?

There is a frantic scramble as they all try to open the nearest door. Some are stuck, causing further panic, cries of, 'We're going to blow up!', and so on. Finally, with much shoving, shouting and general chaos, they all climb safely out of the car. They seem relatively unscathed considering their ordeal. But for ruffled party gear, they appear to be in good shape. ALLIE rubs a sore shoulder as he inspects the damage, while MYRTLE displays a small cut on her forehead.

ALLIE: Shit – just look at this!
JESSICA: Oh, my God.
COXIE: Jeez, check where the road is.
JESSICA: Oh, my God.
COXIE: Bladdy genius, Spider – you know that?
SPIDER: It was a dassie, man.
COXIE: Rubbish!
SPIDER: I'm telling you.
COXIE: You don't get dassies in Durbs.

SPIDER: How d'you know?

COXIE: 'Cause you don't.

MYRTLE: We could have all been killed.

SPIDER: So what makes you such an expert on dassies?

JESSICA: Spider, shut up!

SPIDER [*still on at* COXIE]: You a zoologist or something? You a social bladdy anthropologist?

ALLIE circles the car, devastated. JESSICA *has spotted* MYRTLE'*s bleeding forehead.*

COXIE. Dassies are rock-rabbits, man. They confined to rocky outcrops, to high-lying areas. Not the bladdy seaside!

ALLIE: Will you look at this car ...

JESSICA [*to* MYRTLE]: You're bleeding.

MYRTLE: Hey?

SPIDER [*pursuing his point*]: So maybe the dassies are moving? They jolling down to the coast. Maybe some dassies dig the surf? Shaun Thompson Dassie? How do you know?

MYRTLE [*as* JESSICA *dabs at her cut*]: Ow!

JESSICA: Sore?

SPIDER: Prick!

ALLIE: What am I going to tell my folks?

COXIE [*to* ALLIE]: How's your arm?

SPIDER: Let me tell you something Professor Know-all, the sooner you bugger off to Australia, the better.

COXIE: Shut up. [*to* ALLIE.] Is it okay?

ALLIE [*rubbing his shoulder*]: Ja.

SPIDER: Bladdy chicken. Like all the rest.

COXIE: Look, you shut up about Australia, okay?

SPIDER: They won't let you in, mate. Rule number one – no pooftahs!

COXIE: Who's your pooftah?

SPIDER: Fader.

ALLIE is still preoccupied with the car.

ALLIE: What am I going to tell my folks?

COXIE [*irritated*]: Ag, tell 'em anything, man.

ALLIE: My mom's gonna be really charmed.

COXIE: Your mom!?

ALLIE: It's her car.

COXIE: You told us it was yours!?

ALLIE: I only said that to impress everybody.

SPIDER: You trying to tell me this is someone else's car?

ALLIE: Why did you have to crash the damn thing?

COXIE [*clutching his head*]: Alli – ie ...

SPIDER: You didn't tell us! It's your fault!

JESSICA [*finishes tending to MYRTLE's cut*]: That's better.

MYRTLE: Thanks, Jess.

JESSICA: Hey, what happened to your shoe?

The boys are circling the car, a maudlin ALLIE at the head.

ALLIE: This is it. I'm finished.

SPIDER: Crap, man. It's just a bit a' panel-beating.

He kicks the front bumper. It drops off.

ALLIE: Oh, yes?

COXIE: Like hell.

SPIDER: They can do miracles these days. I got a mate who's got a mate.

COXIE: After tonight you gonna have no mates.

ALLIE: Fantastic. What a way to finish Matric!

Pause.

MYRTLE: What're we going to do now?

COXIE leans into the car, going for the ignition.

JESSICA: What's happening?

MYRTLE: We going now, or what? Hey? I gotta get home. Hey?

COXIE turns the ignition key – nothing. MYRTLE gets into the car to fetch her shoe.

COXIE: Great.

JESSICA: What?

COXIE: Dead.

JESSICA: Dead?

MYRTLE: Dead! What d'you mean – dead?

COXIE: Zed. Zero. Bugger all.

JESSICA: Brill. That's really brill.

MYRTLE: Does that mean we stuck?

COXIE moves to the front of the car, removing his jacket and opening the bonnet.

COXIE: Allie – you got some tools?

ALLIE: In the boot.

MYRTLE: Are we stuck now, or what? Hey? Are we stuck?

SPIDER: Myrtle – shut up!

MYRTLE: I want to know what's happening.

SPIDER: Nothing's happening.

MYRTLE: So what's Coxie doing?

SPIDER: He's fixing the Rocket Booster so we can blast into hyperspace. Now, piss off!

JESSICA: Leave her alone, man.

SPIDER: Tell her to stop whining.

JESSICA: She wants to go home.

SPIDER: Starting to grate me something chronic here.

ALLJE has opened the boot, and is digging out a tool bag. He brings it across to COXIE, taking out the torch.

ALLIE [*pointing at the engine*]: I hope you can get it going.

COXIE: So do I.

ALLIE tries to click the torch on. He switches it on in his own face, giving him a small fright. He shines the torch in a semicircle over the audience – beams the light in JESSICA's face.

JESSICA: Ah, voetsek Allie, man.

ALLIE walks downstage flicking the torch on and off.

ALLIE: Hey, any of you chaps know Morse?

COXIE [*over the engine*]: Morse who?

ALLIE: SOS. We learnt it in cubs.

SPIDER [*stands to one side, addresses them all*]: Hey, listen – okes I'm sorry, hey.

ALLIE [*chanting*]: Akhela, we'll dib-dib-dib.

SPIDER: I said I'm sorry.

ALLIE: We'll dob-dob-dob.

SPIDER [*turning away*]: To hell with you too. See if I care.

ALLIE still plays with the torch beam. COXIE tinkers with the engine.

ALLIE: Dot – dot – dash. Dash – dash – three longs, three shorts ... [*Turns and moves.*] I got my knots, my pathfinders.

COXIE: Hey, where's that torch, man?

ALLIE: One badge I could never get was the fire lighting. Could never make a flame.

COXIE: Shoulda used a Bic. Now gimme that torch.

JESSICA: Shhht ... !

ALLIE: Maybe the wood was wet.

JESSICA: Shht! [*Pause.*] You hear that?

MYRTLE: What?

They listen.

ALLIE: It's the beetles.

SPIDER: Ringo Starr.

JESSICA: Shht.

ALLIE: Christmas beetles.

They listen, then relax. ALLIE goes behind the car.

ALLIE: They make that noise by banging their legs together.

COXIE: They don't bang them, they rub them – now give here.

ALLIE: That's what I'm saying – friction.

COXIE: Just give here ...

ALLIE [*looking into the engine*]: My Dad usually just kicks it.

COXIE: Shut up.

ALLIE: A hard one. In the front.

COXIE: Shut up!

SPIDER: He's right, man. Kick the bladdy thing.

JESSICA: Ah, shut up, man!

SPIDER [*indicating COXIE*]: At least we can thank our lucky stars we got a grease
     monkey among us.

COXIE: Only bladdy monkey around here is you. Drink 'n bloody drive.

SPIDER: You can talk.

COXIE: I wasn't driving, was I?

SPIDER: How many times must I tell you? I swerved for a bladdy dassie, man!

COXIE: What colour was it – pink?

MYRTLE [*clutching her midriff*]: Ugh – my stomach!

SPIDER: Allie – you see that dassie?

ALLIE: Huh?

MYRTLE: I want to be sick.

COXIE: Pink dassies.

SPIDER: Jessie – how about you?

JESSICA [*indicating MYRTLE*]: She's going to be sick.

MYRTLE: Ugh.

COXIE: You wanna hurl, Myrt?

SPIDER: Myrtle?

MYRTLE: Ughh ...

COXIE: You wanna hurl, go hurl by the trees.

SPIDER [*giving up*]: Great. No one sees the dassie.

ALLIE: Lie down in the back.

SPIDER: Fine. Wonderful. I'm blind. I dreamt it ...

MYRTLE: I'm okay.

SPIDER: I'm a stuff up.

JESSICA: What sort of person swerves for a dassie anyway?

SPIDER: You ever hit a dassie?

COXIE: Not with a two-ton truck, no.

SPIDER [*stares at* COXIE *in mock disbelief*]: Listen to it! Ou Cliffie van Rensburg hit that goat in the Transkei. Six weeks in hospital.

COXIE: That was a goat.

SPIDER: Six weeks. Umtata General.

ALLIE [*circling the car*]: My Dad's going to murder me.

SPIDER sits astride the forty-four-gallon drum.

SPIDER: I mean, shit – I knew a bloke who drove over a snake in the Kruger National Park. You know what happened to him?

COXIE: I believe you, okay?

SPIDER: No, this oke. He thinks he's a Big Bok. He drives over this snake. He thinks – ah, snake, what-the-hell I'm in my car. Next morning. Gets home. Opens the bonnet. Bladdy snake's curled up on the radiator. Piks him in the neck. Dead. Finish. Sat.

COXIE: Ja.

SPIDER: The highways and byways, my friend. Fraught with hidden dangers.

COXIE [*rolling up his sleeves*]: Hey, Allie – you got a number twelve?

ALLIE: What's a number twelve?

COXIE: It's your IQ, poephol.

He tosses a spanner to ALLIE who swaps it for another.

SPIDER: I mean what you want me to do? You ous want me to walk a line? Here. Make me a line. I'll walk it ... You want me to stand on one leg?

They all ignore him.

COXIE [*moving to MYRTLE*]: You okay, Myrt?

JESSICA: What're we going to do, Michael?

COXIE: Don't worry about it.

SPIDER [*apart, peeved*]: Hell, that's gratitude for you, hey? I save half my classmates from total bladdy extinction and all I get is uphill.

JESSICA [*almost to herself*]: You drink too much, man.

SPIDER [*picking this up*]: You telling me I'm drunk?

JESSICA: You never know when to stop.

SPIDER: Is it my fault they decide to have the Matric Farewell in Margate?

MYRTLE: How far we still got to go?

JESSICA: Heaven knows.

SPIDER: Durbs is just over the hill here, man.

COXIE: Bullshit. We miles away.

ALLIE [*still preoccupied with the car*]: Somebody tell me this is not happening.

SPIDER: Shit. That's the last time I stick my neck out to help somebody. I could've been home already. Could've caught a ride with Freddy and the boys.

JESSICA: Well, why didn't you?

SPIDER: Because I'm the poephol with the licence, remember? I bailed you out, man. I'm doing you one helluva favour just being here.

MYRTLE: Thanks for nothing.

COXIE: Hey, Allie – we got ourselves a saint here.

JESSICA: Some saint.

COXIE: Moses and the Promised Land.

SPIDER: You laugh?

COXIE [*meaning the accelerator*]: Someone is gonna have to help me just now.

SPIDER: Okay. Take Moses. When Moses led the Israelites across the desert, it was no picnic. For a start – they walked. Think about that.

COXIE [*over the engine*]: I got enough to think about, okay?

SPIDER: Hundreds of miles across a burning desert. You don't know how lucky you are.

ALLIE: If this is lucky, I'd hate to land in the shit.

SPIDER: I mean what's the furthest you ever walk?

COXIE: Check a' fan belt ...

SPIDER: Use a stocking. How far you walk? Furthest?

COXIE: They never walked anyway.

SPIDER: Who? The Israelites!?

COXIE: No ways.

SPIDER [*to the rest*]: How's this? [*Back to* COXIE.] So how they do it? Hey? Red Sea? Mount Sinai? How they do it?

COXIE [*still tinkering*]: I dunno. Camels.

SPIDER [*a beat*]: What d'you mean – camels?

COXIE: Those things with the humps. Some got one, some got ...

SPIDER: I know what a camel is, you cunt.

COXIE: Well, then ...

JESSICA: Shut up.

SPIDER: I'm asking you where they get them?

COXIE: How must I know? Pharaoh.

SPIDER: Pharaoh ... !?

JESSICA: Shut up.

SPIDER: Ou Pharaoh's gonna give them camels – just like that?

COXIE: Why not?

JESSICA: I said shut up! You give me a pain. The both of you.

SPIDER [*to JESSICA*]: How can you hang around with this arsehole?

ALLIE: Where's the booze?

SPIDER: In the front. [*Declaiming.*] Hey, Moses – wanna few camels? [*Changing his voice.*] Sure thing, Pharaoh – what you got?

ALLIE: Where in the front?

SPIDER: Cubby-hole. Underneath. I mean where in the Bible does it say anything about camels? Tell me that.

MYRTLE: Anybody got the time?

SPIDER: You know what a camel was in those days? Bladdy Cadillac! Ou Pharaoh's gonna give away a fleet a' Cadillacs, just like that!

COXIE [*indicating SPIDER*]: Hey, can someone pull the plug on this racket here?

SPIDER: Doesn't make sense, man. Economics. Pure and simple.

ALLIE [*from inside the car*]: Hell's Teeth – what's all this.

ALLIE has pulled a flat cardboard box from under the front seat. In it are several unopened bottles of Southern Comfort.

SPIDER: Hey, leave those alone! [*He grabs the box from ALLIE.*]

The boys follow him to the rear of the car.

ALLIE: We were allowed one per table

SPIDER: The school got them free, man.

ALLIE: How many bottles you got here?

COXIE: I'll have a coupla those.

SPIDER: Are you a collector?

COXIE: I'm a liquor lover.

There is a light-hearted scramble for the bottles. JESSICA and MYRTLE are unamused at the goings-on.

SPIDER: Cocks you, sweetness!

COXIE: Give here.

ALLIE: I want some.

JESSICA: When you guys have quite finished.

COXIE [*takes a packet of cigarettes from the booze box*]: Hey, what's this?

SPIDER: School's over. [*Wrestling with COXIE.*] You still owe me a packet a' smokes, hey?

COXIE: Where from?

SPIDER: Three Gunstons, four Chesterfields, and half a pack a' Camels.

COXIE: I gave the Camels to Pharaoh.

SPIDER: Haa-haa I'm still waiting, friend.

JESSICA: Listen, I hate to break up the party, but don't you guys think we should be doing something about getting us home?

MYRTLE: Ja.

SPIDER: Never fear – Coxie's here.

JESSICA: I'm not joking, Spider.

SPIDER: Who's laughing?

He moves around the car, taking his box back to the front seat.

JESSICA: It's all very well to play the fool, but you can count yourself damn lucky no one was killed.

SPIDER: Stick around okes – here comes a lecture from the Girl Guides.

COXIE [*moving to the engine*]: She's right, Spider. Let's do something to get this bladdy show on the road.

JESSICA: Who votes we try to get a lift?

ALLIE: At this time a' night?

MYRTLE: My mother said I have to be home by midnight.

SPIDER [*looking at his watch*]: Well, you blown it, Cinderella – it's nearly one o'clock.

COXIE is once more tinkering with the engine. SPIDER is slumped in the front passenger seat. ALLIE sits on the drum, perusing his bottle, JESSICA beside him. SPIDER pushes the tape (the one we heard at the beginning of the play) back into the deck. Heavy rock explodes from the speakers (Cory Hart's 'Komrade Kiev').

COXIE [*over the noise*]: Switch it off, man.

MYRTLE: Spider!

COXIE: Your sucking power – turn it off!

MYRTLE: Spider, man!

SPIDER grooves to the music a while before JESSICA snaps it off. SPIDER grabs at her inside the car. She slaps him.

COXIE: Thank you.

SPIDER [*to COXIE*]: Wanker. You gonna kak off next week when you got no teachers to suck up to, hey? No more tea and biscuits in the staff canteen.

MYRTLE [*to COXIE*]: You want me to hold the torch?

COXIE: It's okay.

JESSICA: How long is it going to take you to fix it?

COXIE: I don't even know what's the problem yet.

MYRTLE: I knew it. We never going to get out of here.

SPIDER: Shame, hey? Just think a' that. No one's gonna check you in that lekker Sue Ellen outfit again. [*Smirking wickedly.*] Oh, sorry – or was it Pamela?

MYRTLE: Drop dead, man.

SPIDER: So who won the look alike? Hey? Which one a' the lovely ladies cracked it?

MYRTLE and JESSICA do their best to ignore him.

JESSICA [*bending over the engine alongside* COXIE]: What's an alternator?

COXIE: It's not the alternator.

SPIDER [*to* ALLIE]: Can you believe these chicks? Hey? Pamela Ewing Look Alike Competition! [*Pause.*] Some a' them would done better trying for the Hulk.

JESSICA: Very funny, Spider.

SPIDER: Orraight, so which one a' you Dallas-crazy dooses did it?

COXIE: Give it a break now, for pete-sake?

SPIDER: Whoa – Ray Krebbs to the rescue.

He is beginning to really enjoy this.

MYRTLE: I'd like to know who would've been laughing if one of us had won the trip to Mauritius?

SPIDER: I would, sweetheart. In fact I'd of hosed myself. The thought of any a' you two bats trying to windsurf on Mauritius would be enough to break me up for a week. [MYRTLE *walks away.*] Mauritius. At this rate none of us are even gonna get back to Durbs. [*Looking about.*] We stuck here for life. Death by starvation. Slowly. Painfully. [*Glancing up at the distant road.*] Either that or the Comrades are gonna come down and give us all the necklace.

MYRTLE: Sis, man.

JESSICA: I think that's in very bad taste.

SPIDER: You're such an uptight bitch, everything's in bad taste.

COXIE [*holding up the distributor cap and handing it to* JESSICA]: Just hold this. [*She does so.*] Thanks.

MYRTLE [*drifts some distance*]: Maybe there's a house nearby here somewhere?

SPIDER: Why is everybody in such a bladdy hurry to get home, man? We should be celebrating. [*Singing.*] 'Pappa was a Rolling Stone ...' Hey? Don't you okes realise this is our last jol together? I mean this is it, man.

ALLIE: What?

SPIDER [*raising a fist*]: End of school! Freedom! Liberation!

ALLIE [*back to his bottle*]: Oh.

SPIDER: Next year we all bugger off into the wild blue yonder and it's bye-bye forever. Jessie's down at Rhodes ... Coxie's doing the chicken run ...

ALLIE: Lucky him.

SPIDER: Allie's in the Army.

ALLIE: Not if I can help it.

SPIDER: You got no choice, buster.

He puts a finger to his temple.

ALLIE: Ag, stop it, man!

He punches SPIDER *who rolls over in mock agony.*

SPIDER: And Myrtle. What'll Myrt be doing?

He hums the Wedding March and mimes walking down the aisle.

MYRTLE: I know what *you'll* be doing. Everybody knows.

JESSICA: Oldest matric at Excelsior High.

SPIDER: No ways.

MYRTLE: You wanna bet?

COXIE: You plug once more, the school's gonna give you a medal for long service.

SPIDER: Bull.

ALLIE: 2001 – A Spider Matric!

SPIDER: First class pass. Three distinctions.

COXIE: You wish.

JESSICA: For a guy who didn't even read *Hamlet* – you got helluva high hopes.

SPIDER: I must waste my time with Shakespeare?

MYRTLE: How else do you expect to write the exam?

SPIDER: Ou Allie gave me a crash course the night before. Not so, Allie?

ALLIE: Ja, just as well. He was under the impression Polonius's daughter was Othello.

They all laugh.

COXIE: Now *that's* what I call First Class.

SPIDER: Okay. So what? Minor detail. It's the overall picture that counts.

COXIE: I wouldn't flog my blazer, my friend.

SPIDER: I passed, man. Guaranteed. Allie put me right.

JESSICA [*to MYRTLE*]: He probably thinks an Oedipus Complex is the place they building the new Pick 'n Pay.

SPIDER: Ha-haa!

JESSICA: Okay, so what is it?

SPIDER: What is this – an oral?

JESSICA: You see.

SPIDER: It's a hang up, man. Oke's got the hots for his mother.

JESSICA: Is that what you wrote?

SPIDER [*a beat*]: Okay. Okay. Franco–Prussian War. Ask me the date.

JESSICA: We talking *Hamlet*.

SPIDER: Ask me the date.

JESSICA: Why change the subject?

SPIDER: You see. You scared.

JESSICA: *I'm* scared?

SPIDER: You too scared to ask me the date.

JESSICA: So what? So you know it. So big deal.

SPIDER: So don't talk to me.

MYRTLE: 19th of July, 1870. Big deal.

SPIDER: 13th.

JESSICA: What?

SPIDER [*smiles a smile of triumph*]: Allie. Tell them.

ALLIE [*a beat*]: It was the 19th, Spider.

SPIDER: Talk shit.

COXIE: The 13th was the telegram, ou.

SPIDER: What telegram?

JESSICA: The Ems telegram. From William the First to Bismarck.

SPIDER [*to ALLIE*]: You didn't tell me about this.

ALLIE: I didn't?

SPIDER: You told me stuff all about a telegram.

MYRTLE: On the 13th of July, 1870, William the First sent a telegram to Bismarck.

JESSICA: Which Bismarck changed to suit his needs.

MYRTLE: That's right. Then he went and published it in the newspaper.

JESSICA: This had the desired effect of a 'red rag upon the Gallic bull', and a few days later – on the 19th of July – Napoleon the Third officially declared war on Prussia.

MYRTLE: So weh!

The girls, flushed with their success, grin like Cheshire cats. COXIE is doing his best to stifle his laughter, head buried deep in the engine. ALLIE stares at SPIDER whose brow is well and truly furrowed.

SPIDER: You see. This is what pisses me off. The teachers tell you one thing – bladdy books tell you something else. I take you a bet half the okes in those days didn't even know what a bliksemse telegram was!

COXIE: Don't try get out of it, ou.

SPIDER: It's a fact, man. What's history, anyway? Huh? It's a bunch of wankers trying to bullshit a bunch a' even bigger wankers that such-and-such happened on such-and-such a day. Meanwhile what actually happened is something totally different. I mean, take South Africa. You watch – when the blacks take over – Jan van Riebeeck's out the window. Bye-bye Piet Retief. I mean don't even talk about the Great Trek.

JESSICA: Who's talking the Great Trek. We're talking about someone who writes an exam without reading *Hamlet*.

SPIDER: Please! You wanna know the story a' *Hamlet*?

COXIE: No thanks!

SPIDER: C'mon you okes think I plugged.

MYRTLE: No, we don't.

JESSICA: You've convinced us.

SPIDER [*rattling it off*]: Hamlet comes back from boarding school to find his mother having it off with his uncle. Because of this and also the fact that something is very rotten in the State of Denmark – he slowly but surely goes out of his mind. [*Pause.*] How's that?

JESSICA [*a beat*]: Actually that's not bad.

SPIDER [*chuffed*]: You see. All you got to know is the general outline and the rest is waffle. Padding. Bullshit baffles brains. I learnt that a long time ago.

COXIE: Pity it didn't work in Standard 8, hey?

SPIDER: It didn't work in Standard 8 because ol' Zombie had it in for me.

COXJE: Come off it, man.

SPIDER: Swear to God. The oke's a potential rapist. Serial honker. First degree.

JESSICA: Mr van der Vyver?

SPIDER: I caught him with his hand up Cornelia Snyman's dress. The oke never forgave me.

COXIE: Bull.

JESSICA: Mr van der Vyver?

COXIE: When was this?

SPIDER: One day in class. I left my smokes in my desk – went back to fetch them. There he was, feeling her up.

JESSICA: Hell, but you can cook up some rubbish.

MYRTLE: It's the truth, Jessie.

SPIDER: Thanks, Myrtle – you tell them.

MYRTLE: He tried the same thing with me.

JESSICA: Mr van der Vyver?

SPIDER: What did I tell you?

MYRTLE: He was always trying something.

COXIE: Like what?

MYRTLE: Like – you know.

COXIE: No, I don't.

JESSICA: Michael –

COXIE: He tried to grip you?

MYRTLE: Well ... [*She hesitates.*]

COXIE: Talk? Sexy talk? Suggestions?

MYRTLE: Sort of.

ALLIE: Rude ones?

SPIDER: What a kwes, man.

COXIE: Very rude or quite rude or what?

MYRTLE: Rude-rude.

ALLIE: Oh, ja?

COXIE: How rude is that?

JESSICA: Stop it. I think it's disgusting.

COXIE: No, she says rude-rude. I wanna know how rude that is.

MYRTLE: I can't tell you.

ALLIE: Ah, come on, man.

MYRTLE: I'll start blushing.

COXIE: You blushing already.

SPIDER: He ask you to sit on his face, or what?

JESSICA: Sis, Spider!

She whacks him with her handbag.

SPIDER: Well – what did he say?

JESSIE chases SPIDER, belting him.

COXIE: Is that what he said?

JESSICA: God, but you're so crude!

Belting him again.

SPIDER: I'm trying to find out what he said, man.

JESSIE [*to MYRTLE*]: Why didn't you just go and tell Mr Cartwright about him, Myrtle?

SPIDER: Bloubal!?

COXIE: What's the point in telling Bloubal?

SPIDER: Bloubal wouldn't do anything about it, dofburger!

JESSICA: Of course he would. He's the headmaster.

SPIDER: Ah, jeez – someone get this chick to wake up.

COXIE: Cartwright's got his own problems. The teachers have got him there.

He presses a thumb on his palm.

SPIDER: School prefect – she knows nothing.

JESSICA: What?

COXIE: He's one a' those ous, man.

JESSICA: Huh?

COXIE minces about.

SPIDER: He's a moffie, man.

JESSICA: A *what?*

COXIE: He's not married.

JESSICA: So what does that prove?

SPIDER: He's fifty-two years old.

JESSICA: So? Next birthday he'll be fifty-three.

SPIDER [*a beat*]: You Berea chicks are all the same. You walk around with your bladdy heads in the sand.

JESSICA: I want to know what makes you such an expert on Mr Cartwright?

SPIDER [*to* COXIE, *sotto voce*]: Tell her what he said to you.

COXIE: Huh?

SPIDER: C'mon. Tell her.

COXIE: That time in the gym?

SPIDER: That time he came up to you. After PT.

COXIE: You tell her.

SPIDER: He said it to you. [*Pause.*] This oke's in the gym, hey. He's in his shorts. Ou Bloubal comes up to him ... [*to* COXIE.] What did he say to you?

COXIE: He said – he just said ... [*Turning to* SPIDER *for support, then back to* JESSIE.] He said I got nice thighs for rugby.

ALLIE [*horrified*]: Jislaaik!!

JESSICA: So?

SPIDER: Nice thighs for rugby!?

JESSICA: It's perfectly true.

SPIDER: That's not the point. The point is that okes don't say that to other okes. Real okes.

JESSICA: Huh?

SPIDER: Proper okes.

Slight pause.

JESSICA: What on earth are you talking about?

COXIE: Look, man – guys don't say that sort of thing to each other.

JESSICA stares at COXIE.

MYRTLE: What *do* guys say to each other?

COXIE [*momentarily thrown*]: I dunno. Spider?

SPIDER: I dunno – anything. You got a good build for rugby, that sorta thing.

ALLIE [*nodding*]: Ja ... !

COXIE: Ja ... !

ALLIE: A good build for rugby ... !

COXIE: That's right. That what you'd say ...

SPIDER: Thighs have got bugger all to do with it ...

COXIE: Thighs never come into it.

JESSICA: God – you guys are pathetic.

COXIE: When you talk about rugby, you just don't talk about thighs.

MYRTLE: So that makes Mr Cartwright a homosexual?

SPIDER: No question.

ALLIE: Hey, listen, there's nothing basically wrong with being homosexual, hey?

SPIDER: Did I say there was?

JESSICA: You're just like the HNP – every black man's a terrorist.

SPIDER: Listen, man. Open your eyes. Just think about it for a second. [*A beat.*] Okay. Look. It's like me saying to you – you got a nice arse for horse riding.

JESSICA [*stares at him – then leaves, abruptly, heading toward the highway*]: Thank you very much.

SPIDER: Hey, where you going?

COXIE: Subtle, Spider. Subtle. [*Follows JESSICA.*]

SPIDER: What's the matter?

MYRTLE: You should be ashamed of yourself

She leaves too.

SPIDER: What did I do now? [*Shouting after them.*] Hey, come back here, man!

SPIDER and ALLIE watch the trio as they head towards the road. SPIDER is genuinely nonplussed as to what could have caused the mass exodus.

ALLIE [*after a pause*]: You shouldn't have said that.

SPIDER: Why not?

ALLIE: She's got a thing about her bum.

SPIDER: Thing?

ALLIE: She's sort of – you know – sensitive.

SPIDER: What's she got to be sensitive about?

ALLIE: She thinks it's too big.

SPIDER: Too big?

ALLIE: You can make fun of her boobs – but just don't laugh about her bum.

SPIDER [*eyes on the distant JESSICA*]: I think she's got a great bum.

ALLIE: Ja-well Maybe you should go tell her that.

SPIDER: You reckon?

ALLIE: On second thoughts, forget it. You'll probably only make it worse.

They stare off.

SPIDER: You see? That's chicks for you! Can't even have a decent conversation. You talking lekker. You make a perfectly innocent statement – they suddenly get all emotional. And then they still blame you 'cause you don't wanna talk. It's a dead loss, man. You can't win. [*Patting his pockets.*] Where my smokes? [*He moves towards the car door.*] Chicks! [*Eventually finds some cigarettes.*] The world is made of two types a' people, Allie. Those who can take it – and those who can't. If you belong to the second group, my friend – the world can be one helluva shit place to live in.

Slight pause.

ALLIE: How do you know?

SPIDER: I know because I know.

ALLIE: No, I mean how do you know which group you belong to?

SPIDER: You can't tell?

ALLIE: Sometimes it's quite hard.

SPIDER: It's easier than you think.

ALLIE: How's that?

SPIDER: The traffic-light test. My own invention.

ALLIE: Traffic-light test?

SPIDER: Sorts out the men from the boys.

ALLIE: How does it go?

SPIDER: You don't wanna know.

ALLIE: Try me.

SPIDER: You sure?

ALLIE: Try me.

SPIDER [*lights up a smoke. A beat*]: You burning along in your car, okay? You coming towards the robot. It's green. It suddenly turns orange. What do you do?

ALLIE: I don't drive.

SPIDER: I'm not asking if you drive. I'm asking what you'd do?

ALLIE: When the light turns orange?

SPIDER: When the light turns orange.

ALLIE: Is this a trick question?

SPIDER: The light's turned orange, man – quick! What do you do?

ALLIE: You slow down.

SPIDER: That's it for you.

ALLIE: What do you mean?

SPCDER: You're a loser. You failed the test.

ALLIE: A loser? But that's the law!

SPIDER: The law says red is stop and green is go. When it's orange, you put foot, man. You hit the gas.

ALLIE: That's not what I was taught.

SPIDER: That's what I mean when I say it's a simple test.

ALLIE: I think it's a stupid test.

SPIDER: Ja, well you would, you see. It's psychological. You know you a dweezil so you think it's stupid. Myself, I think it's brilliant. Where's the chips?

ALLIE is destroyed, unable to cope with the fact that such a simple test can at the same time be so brutal. SPIDER is searching the car.

ALLIE: But wait a minute – didn't you learn that song when you were small?

SPIDER: Where's the chips, man?

113

ALLIE: Spider, listen to me.

SPIDER: Didn't we bring some graze along?

ALLIE: That song, man? When we were kids.

SPIDER [*finds the chips in the boot*]: Ah, great. [*He sits in the front seat.*]

ALLIE: That song everybody learns in nursery school, man. About robots. [*Singing*] 'Green means go, yellow means slow, red – means – stop!' [*Pause.*] 'Stop says the red light, go says the green. Be careful says the yellow light, blinking in between'. That's one a' the first things you learn about road safety. Step number one in the rules of the road.

SPIDER [*stares at* ALLIE, *stops munching*]: If you gonna let something you learned in nursery school dictate the pattern of your life-you in big trouble, my friend. Very big trouble. [*Tosses the chips to* ALLIE.] Here.

ALLIE is still clutching his bottle. He looks down at it. COXIE comes back to the car. He reaches onto the back seat for the girls' handbags, shawls, and so on. He has to step around ALLIE at the rear door.

COXIE: Excuse me, Allie.

SPIDER: What you doing?

COXIE: We gonna try hitching. Go wait up on the road.

SPIDER: How's ou bum-face?

COXIE: You guys corning?

SPIDER: Fader.

COXIE: Allie?

ALLIE: It's okay.

COXIE: What d'you mean – it's okay?

ALLIE: Don't worry about me.

COXIE: But we going now.

ALLIE: I can't go home.

COXIE: Talk junk, man. You gotta come home.

ALLIE: Ja? And what? 'Hi, Ma – I lost your car'. [*Slight pause.*]

COXIE: So what you gonna do?

ALLIE: I dunno. Go try my luck in Swaziland.

COXIE: It was a bladdy accident, man.

ALLIE: Tell that to my dad. He doesn't even know I got the damn thing. [*He looks from one to the other.*] I'm telling you! I told my ma Mr Stopforth was gonna be driving. She said it was fine.

SPIDER: You told your ma ou Death Breath was gonna take us to Margate?

ALLIE: She wouldn't have let me use it otherwise.

Pause.

COXIE: Fantastic.

SPIDER: You could try cyanide. It's painful – but it's bladdy effective.

Stalemate. Nobody moves.

COXIE: Ja-well, look – the girls are waiting. [*Begins to move off.*]

SPIDER: Fader. [*COXIE ignores him.*] Chicken.

COXIE [*stops and turns to* ALLIE]: What do I tell your folks?

ALLIE: Don't tell them anything.

COXIE: I got to tell them something.

SPIDER: Why don't you tell them about Australia, Bruce?

ALLIE [*sensing aggro*]: I'll phone them.

SPIDER [*trying an Aussie accent*]: Tell 'em why you running away.

COXIE: Don't push me, Spider.

SPIDER [*squatting on the front seat, holding the door, ready to shut it should* COXIE *make his move*]: Hey, Allie – here's a good one. How do you pick out the ex-South African in a pub full a' Aussies?

COXIE [*under his breath*]: Jissus ... !

SPIDER: He's the one going – pwaaak-pwak-pwak ... [*He does a chicken impersonation to brilliant effect*].

As COXIE *makes for* SPIDER *he slams the car door, slides along the front seat and pops his head up over the roof on the other side.*

COXIE: Jeez, you asking for it ... !

SPIDER: Truth hurts, hey?

COXIE: It's my bladdy folks who want to emigrate, not me.

SPIDER [*in an Australian accent*]: Don't worry, Coxie, me ol' sport – they say the birds are a bit shit, but the beer's okay.

SPIDER squawks, circling the car.

COXIE: What is it with you? You jealous?

SPIDER: I've just worked out why they call you head boy. It's because you spend so much of your time with your head up the teachers' arseholes.

COXIE [*chasing* SPIDER *around the car, slamming the bonnet closed*]: Stuff you man!

COXIE exits, making for the road. SPIDER *is riding high now and begins singing to the tune of 'Tie me kangaroo down, sport' – a popular Australian song.*

SPIDER [*singing*]: 'Tie me kangaroo down, sport – tie me kangaroo down – bonk a wallaby! Intercourse with a horse, Nourse, intercourse with a horse – bonk a wallaby!' [*Shouting after* COXIE.] See you when the Abbos get too hot to handle! [*He stares after the disappearing* COXIE. *A sudden change of mood. He turns to the car and fetches his bottle. His tone is sullen.*] Don't feel you have to stay because a' me, hey. I don't sug. 'Strue's bob.

ALLIE: No, it's okay. [*Pause.*] I been thinking for a long time already of ways of getting out of the Army. Maybe this is it.

SPIDER: I wouldn't try Swaziland.

ALLIE: No?

SPIDER: Not a good idea.

ALLIE: I don't suppose you can ever get out of going to the Army, hey? Unless you were sort of – radically disabled. Permanently sort of – indisposed. [*Looks down at his bottle ... light bulb!*] Alcohol poisoning!

SPIDER: Huh?

ALLJE: How about if I drank this whole bottle?

SPIDER: Don't make me laugh. My old man's been on the bottle forty years – he's still alive.

ALLIE: Ja, but he's not drinking non-stop.

SPIDER: You don't know my Old Top. Only time the oke's not got a glass in his hand's when he's at work. And even then he's got the ol' flask in the back pocket.

ALLIE: He's obviously immune.

SPIDER: Immune? The oke's 100 percent proof, man. Clean burning Sasol! One day he's gonna strike a match – blow himself – the whole bladdy house up.

Pause.

ALLJE: Forty years.

SPIDER: Don't need any fly spray with him around, ou. He just sommer breathes them dead. We went to the Game Reserve, they wanted to keep him there. No mosquitoes for a ten kay radius.

Pause.

ALLIE: I suppose that must make him almost alcoholic?

SPIDER [*in a world of his own*]: I got two chances when I'm at home. I'm in my room at nine o'clock – or else I'm hanging around outside until the sun comes up. Anything in between – he nabs me. Musical appreciation. Among other things. [*Slight pause.*] He sits there. Little side light. His booze. His music. One ear on the door. He's waiting for me, you see. I try tip-toeing down the passage to get to my room – ZAP! Into the lounge. And it's King of Swing. Glen Miller. Perry Como. And all the time there's this dof smile on his face like it's supposed to be something fantastic.

ALLIE: Who's Perry Como?

SPIDER: You ever heard a' Bing Crosby?

ALLIE: Cosby?

SPIDER: Crosby, Bing.

ALLIE: Oh, Bing. Oh, ja. I know him. He's the bloke with the turned up nose.

SPIDER: That's Bob Hope.

ALLIE: Ja-well ...

SPIDER: Same thing. [*Takes comfort from his bottle, pausing before continuing.*] And it goes on and on. And all the time he's saying this is music. People don't know how to make music any more. And I'm nodding – ja, ja. And all I'm hearing coming outa' the speakers is this pure kak. This total unadulterated shit. Every time I try make a quick duck to go to bed, he says no, wait. And he plays me something else. It gets to the point where I'm virtually catatonic. I'm sleeping wide awake. Now he thinks he's got me, you see. The rigor mortis has sorta fooled him. So he starts expounding. He's lekker loose now. The 'philosopher' coming out. Waxing lyrical – you know – 'Man's higher purpose in life' – and all that shit. 'The fruits of your labour' – that's another one. He's big on that. 'Life's rich tapestry'. I mean you gotta picture it man – this thick tongue trying to get around 'life's rich tapestry'. [*Pause.*] My best was when he came out with how privileged we are to live in this beautiful country. And this on the same day a' the bladdy bomb. We'd just finished walking through the blood and the glass to get back to the car – he's talking about our beautiful country. His brain's gone, swear to God. It's like a piece a' blue cheese.

ALLIE: Hell, between bombs and car crashes, you having quite a year.

SPIDER: That smelly blue cheese that falls apart when you touch a' stuff.

Pause.

ALLIE: How does your ma take all a' this?

SPIDER: My ma? [*Smiling thinly.*] My ma comes along about six o'clock. She says, hey – how about getting some sleep? He gets up, he smacks her.

ALLIE: He smacks her!?

SPIDER: That's if he can catch her. She usually gets away. Ducks out the back. Goes and hides in the maid's room.

ALLIE: Hell, it sounds sort of ... [*Hesitates.*]

SPIDER: Say it. Insane. [*Smiling.*] You should come and visit some time. Bloody madhouse-de-luxe.

ALLIE: Do you ever try stop him?

SPIDER: What? Drinking?

He moves to the canopy and climbs up.

ALLIE: Your ma. Beating her up.

SPIDER [*scoffing*]: That's her worry. You make your bed, you must kip in it, boy. She's let him get away with too much crap down the years. [*Slight pause.*] I woulda kicked the bastard out long ago. Or buggered off myself.

Pause.

ALLIE: I've always wondered why you never liked going home.

SPIDER: Roll on the Army, boy. Next to my house – the Border's bladdy paradise.

He uses the Bedford frame as a jungle gym. Pause.

ALLIE: It's weird, isn't it? Here am I trying to avoid the Army – you can't wait to get in.

SPIDER [*smiles his old smile, more relaxed now*]: Army's a piece a' piss, man.

ALLIE: That's not what I've heard.

SPIDER: Get through the basics – the rest's a joke.

ALLIE: No, that's where you're wrong Spider. The joke comes when I try basics.

SPIDER [*guffaws*]: Come on – you know what it really is? A little clash, man. Test of wills. Them against you.

ALLIE: A test? Great. I can't even get through your traffic-light test.

SPIDER [*softens*]: There are ways of getting out of it, you know.

ALLIE: You can't get out of the Army.

SPIDER: You wanna bet?

ALLIE: It's impossible. I know guys who've tried.

SPIDER: They haven't tried hard enough. You got to go in there with a plot. Like ou Charlie de Wet.

ALLIE: Ja, hell-out complicated, I suppose?

SPIDER: Kak, man. Marshmallows.

ALLIE: Marshmallows?

SPIDER: The whole time he was there – only one thing on his mind – marshmallows. On top of his locker, under his pillow, inside his boots – where my marshmallows?

ALLIE: But that's plain stupid. Who's going to fall for that?

SPIDER: Exactly. That's why it worked so well. Took him three months to crack it. Always complaining about the other okes taking his marshmallows. Out on the parade ground. Where's De Wet? He's looking for his marshmallows.

ALLIE [*quietly, shaking his head*]: Huh.

SPIDER: So finally he reckons he's winning, hey. He writes to his family, his mates. Gets them to send him parcels of the stuff. Fifty-sixty packets – massive pile. Hides them, you see. No one knows he's got them. Four o'clock one morning he reckons this is it. Off he goes to the Commandant's bungalow – bang – bang – bang. [*Shouting.*] Hey, Commandant! It's okay! I got my marshmallows! The Commandant opens up – he just sommer checks this mountain a' marshmallows – this tiny head sticking out. He thinks – to hell with this! He sommer kicks the bastard out. Right there and then.

ALLIE: He kicks him out the Army?

SPIDER: First train. Gone. Finish. A for away. He got his discharge papers in fucken quadruplicate!

Pause.

ALLIE: I could never do that.

SPIDER: Not easy. Takes guts.

ALLIE: You'd have to be a bit crazy to begin with.

SPIDER: Not crazy. Just clever.

ALLIE: Eccentric.

Pause.

SPIDER: You could always fail the physical.

ALLIE: There's nothing wrong with me.

SPIDER: Not now there isn't.

ALLIE: What d'you mean?

SPIDER approaches him, threatening impending agony.

SPIDER [*a beat*]: I knew a bloke who put a garden fork through his foot.

ALLIE: No thanks.

SPIDER: Like you said – they can't take a cripple, hey?

ALLIE: I'd rather try the marshmallows.

SPIDER: Well, you better think a' something. Otherwise it's vasbyt, min hare and baie dae ...

ALLIE shakes his head, perturbed. There is a commotion off-stage. JESSICA and MYRTLE are charging down from the road, frightened but at the same time giggling as only schoolgirls can. They both head for the same downstage rear car door, but MYRTLE makes it first and jumps in.

SPIDER: What the hell?

JESSICA runs around the back of the car, taking the keys from the boot as she does so. She hops into the rear upstage door. They slam all doors and wind up the windows, locking themselves in. COXIE follows at a distance, obviously irritated with the whole affair.

COXIE [*to the girls, who ignore him*]: I suppose you expect me to fix it for you all of a sudden?

SPIDER: I thought you okes would be half-way home by now?

COXIE: Ag, man – they see some blacks go past in a bakkie, they decide they don't wanna hitch anymore.

SPIDER: Typical! Hey girls – you'd better get used to taking rides from the Affs, hey. They'll be running the country soon. [*Moves to the car, banging on the windows.*] Hey, check these chicks here – stealing my sleeping pozzie ... [*Bounces the vehicle, they shriek.*] Hey! Come outa' there ... Hey!

119

SPIDER bangs and shakes the car. The girls shout at him. COXIE is thoroughly disgruntled with the new turn of events.

COXIE: Hey, los it, Spider.

SPIDER: What d'you mean, los it? Since you guys decided to bugger off – this is what I would call trespassing, not so Allie?

ALLIE is lost in his own thoughts. SPIDER resumes his attack on COXIE, getting into top gear again.

SPIDER: Now, if you okes wanna park the night – I suggest you approach the management and do it along the proper channels.

COXIE: Piss off, man.

SPIDER: That's you out, for a start. We don't accommodate guests who use foul language. [*Turning to ALLIE.*] Allie? How's that for a plot? [*Indicating the car.*] The Royal Spider Spa. The Allister Lacey Holiday Inn?

ALLIE [*out of nowhere*]: The trigger finger!

SPIDER: No, kak name ...

ALLIE: No, no listen, man. What's a soldier without a trigger finger? What's a rifleman without a finger to pull his trigger?

SPIDER: A fuck-up.

ALLIE: Exactly.

SPIDER: So? What you saying?

ALLIE: What I'm saying is – forget about the fork through the foot or the stupid marshmallow junk. All I got to do is put paid to my index finger, and it's goodbye to Magnus Malan.

SPIDER: Good boy, Allie – you learn fast. Now. What you say? Forty bucks each – bed and breakfast?

ALLIE: I'm serious, man.

SPIDER: So am I. [*to the girls, through the closed windows.*] Forty-five rand a head. Stay now – pay later.

ALLIE [*exploding*]: Ag, hell – forget it.

Pause.

SPIDER: Whatsa' matter?

ALLIE: You just wanna joke all the time.

SPIDER: Look, I think it's a good idea, okay?

ALLIE: You do?

SPIDER: For sure. But it's no use just breaking it, hey.

ALLIE: Why not?

SPIDER: It heals. Broken finger heals like anything else. Put it in a splint – six weeks later, it's A for away.

ALLIE: Dammit.

SPIDER: Gotta think of something more drastic.

He takes out his flick-knife and pretends he is going to cut ALLIE's finger off. ALLIE shouts, pulling away.

ALLIE [*moving to COXIE*]: What do you suggest, Coxie?

COXIE: Hey?

ALLIE: My finger.

COXIE: Your finger?

ALLIE: What should I do?

COXIE: There's something wrong with it?

SPIDER: He's trying to get out of the Army.

COXIE: With his finger!?

ALLIE: No. Spider reckons if I can manufacture some physical disability, they'll release me from my call up.

SPIDER: We working on his trigger finger.

He jokingly goes for his finger again. ALLIE pulls away.

COXIE: Which one?

ALLIE: What do you mean, which one?

COXIE: You got one on your right hand and one on your left. Something happens to the one – they teach you to shoot with the other.

ALLIE [*beaming*]: Oh no, they can't.

SPIDER: Oh yes, they can.

ALLIE: Not with me they can't.

COXIE: You wanna bet?

ALLIE: My eye. I've got a corneal disfiguration in my left eye. That's one of the reasons I wear glasses. [*Immensely pleased with himself.*] There is no way I could shoot left-handed.

The car hooter parps loudly, catching the boys by surprise. JESSICA and MYRTLE begin chanting inside the car.

JESSICA & MYRTLE: We wanna go home, we wanna go home.

SPIDER: Check these chicks.

COXIE [*still peeved, through windscreen*]: Ja, don't talk to me. You had your chance.

JESSICA holds up one of SPIDER's bottles of Southern Comfort.

SPIDER: Shit. My booze! They drinking my booze! [*He tries the doors, windows and so on.*] Listen Jessie – leave those things. Don't break the seal, man. [*She sticks a tongue out, wiggles the bottle.*] I'm sorry what I said about your bum I didn't mean it, swear to God.

JESSICA [*methodically breaking the seal and opening a bottle, yells from behind the glass*]: Waa-la ...

SPIDER [*almost on his knees*]: You got a nice arse. You got a lovely arse. 'Strue's bob. A tit arse ...

ALLIE: Arthritis ... !!

SPIDER: Please, man ...

ALLIE: That's it – arthritis!

SPIDER: Jessie ...

ALLIE: Spider. How's about if I told them I had arthritis?

SPIDER [*at the window*]: Shit.

ALLIE: How's about if I told them it's congenital? It's been in the family for years ... ?

SPIDER [*to COXIE*]: Tell your chick to lay off my booze, man.

COXIE: Your booze ... !?

SPIDER: How am I gonna flog the stuff ... ?

ALLIE: Spider ... !

SPIDER [*angrily to ALLIE*]: What?

ALLIE [*holding up a finger*]: Rheumatoid Arthritis.

SPIDER: Ja.

COXIE: Don't tell me you wanna flog all that booze?

SPIDER: School got them for nothing, man. [*Indicating the car.*] What d'you expect me to do – leave the stuff?

COXIE: How can you sell something that doesn't belong to you?

SPIDER: Free enterprise, my friend. The Lord provides and Man divides.

ALLIE [*still pursuing his point*]: Maybe I could catch it ...

COXIE: Hell, you're a snake in the grass.

SPIDER: What? You think it's not ethical?

ALLIE: I wonder if you could ever catch it?

SPIDER: As head boy – you wouldn't do it, of course ...

ALLIE: Spider ...

SPIDER: As head boy, you wouldn't stoop so low.

ALLIE: Spider, what if I caught the damn thing?

SPIDER: Allie – shut up, man ...

ALLIE: No, I'm just trying to work out if there was any way you could actually catch arthritis.

SPIDER: You can't – now shut up.

ALLIE: No, that's what I'm saying. It's not like catching flu or catching chicken pox or any a' those things ...

SPIDER: The only thing you gonna catch just now's a stiff klap – now, can it, now!

COXIE: Who the hell would want to catch arthritis, anyway?

ALLIE: Have you seen what it does to your hands ... ?

SPIDER: Allie ... !

ALLIE: I'm serious. Have you seen what chronic arthritis does to your fingers? You couldn't push a doorbell – never mind pull a trigger.

The car hooter parps again. The girls giggle inside. This time JESSICA holds up a carton of cigarettes. She has two unlit smokes in her mouth – MYRTLE is assisting her.

SPIDER: What the hell ... ?!

MYRTLE: Hey, Spider! After action – satisfaction!

SPIDER [*trying doors again*]: These chicks are pushing their luck.

COXIE: Hey Jessie, that stuff's stolen goods, man.

SPIDER bangs on the roof. The girls laugh and pull faces. SPIDER looks about.

SPIDER: What we need's a bladdy can opener.

He moves off around the car, searching.

COXIE [*to the girls*]: Stop messing around. Come outa' there now. Let's work out what we gonna do now, man.

JESSICA: I can't hear you.

MYRTLE: You'll have to speak louder.

COXIE: Open the door, man.

SPIDER arrives, wielding a one and a half metre iron bar picked up near the Bedford canopy.

SPIDER: Okay, ladies.

SPIDER hammers the roof of the car with a particularly hefty blow. The girls scream. COXIE hares around to SPIDER.

COXIE: You outa' your mind!?

SPIDER hits the roof again. COXIE has to struggle to prevent him doing it once more.

SPIDER: Stick around ...

COXIE: What the hell you doing, man? You'll destroy the bladdy car.

SPIDER: Stuff the car. Think a' the bladdy insurance.

COXIE: What d'you mean – insurance?

SPIDER: Insurance, man. The more we mess it up – the more they pay out.

COXIE: You crazy, man.

SPIDER: Allie's folks'll thank us. Not so, Allie? Allie ... !

ALLIE has wandered off into the veld, bottle in hand. COXIE has succeeded in wrenching the iron bar from SPIDER's grasp and drops it near the car.

COXIE: Maniac.

SPIDER [*to* COXIE]: For a oke who's supposed to be good at maths – your grasp of economics astounds me.

MYRTLE [*opens the rear upstage door and props her head over the roof*]: Are you guys getting this car going now, or what?

JESSICA [*opening the front downstage door*]: Look sharp, man.

MYRTLE: Some of us have to get home, you know.

COXIE: Don't moan at me, Myrtle. You're the one who didn't wanna hitch.

SPIDER [*to* COXIE, *sarcastic*]: Hitching's supposed to be dangerous, didn't you know that?

COXIE [*who has resumed his position at the engine*]: What happened to your partner, Myrtle?

SPIDER: Good question.

COXIE: Why didn't you get a lift home with him?

SPIDER: Because he buggered off with Cornelia Snyman, that's why.

MYRTLE: No, he didn't.

SPIDER: So where is he?

MYRTLE: You didn't even have a partner – so weh!

SPIDER: I must waste my time trying to chat up a chick?

JESSICA: You were just too scared you'd get no-one to go with you.

SPIDER [*glaring at her, stung by this remark*]: You owe me for that booze, hey.

> JESSICA *clutches the bottle, sticking her tongue out at him. He moves slowly off, in the direction taken by* ALLIE. JESSICA *climbs up onto the roof, sitting with one foot resting on the fender, the other tapping the open car door.*

COXIE: Now where's he going now?

JESSICA [*watching* SPIDER *exit*]: That'll teach him. Swine.

COXIE [*shouting*]: Spider. Go flag down a car! Tell 'em to get hold of the AA!

JESSICA [*heavily sarcastic*]: What is that? Alcoholics Anonymous?

MYRTLE: God, I'm gonna get into such trouble. I've never been up this late in my whole life before.

JESSICA: Relax, Myrtle You haven't turned into a pumpkin yet.

> COXIE, *back at the engine, grins at this.*

MYRTLE: Ja, but isn't your dad going to have an absolute fit?

JESSICA: I'm not staying at my dad's thank God! And even if I was, he couldn't give two hoots.

COXIE [*indicating the bottle*]: Go easy with that stuff, hey.

JESSICA: Him and his bladdy women. [*Smiles, changing mood.*] Did I tell you he's divorcing his new wife?

COXIE: Which?

JESSICA: What d'you mean – which? He's only had two.

COXIE: The blonde?

JESSICA: The bottle blonde. Dalene.

COXIE: The one who thinks she's a beauty queen.

MYRTLE: I thought she *was* a beauty queen.

JESSICA [*sipping at her bottle, unable and unwilling to hide her cynicism*]: He certainly knows how to pick them I tell you. When they got married, she put it in the contract that he had to provide a special fund for her facelifts.

COXIE: Bull.

JESSICA: 'Strue's bob. One at thirty-eight – one at forty-two – and one if she ever needed it again.

MYRTLE: How many facelifts can a person have?

JESSICA: I suppose if you have enough of them – your bellybutton could end up somewhere near your chin.

MYRTLE: Sis, man.

JESSICA: Imagine being that afraid of getting old?

MYRTLE: Would you ever?

JESSICA: Be afraid?

MYRTLE: Have a facelift?

JESSICA [*a beat*]: I don't know. Would you?

MYRTLE: I don't know.

Slight pause.

JESSICA: He's just like a little boy sometimes. It's kinda' sad. The other day he went out and bought one of those new Range Rovers. Four-wheel drive. Brought it round to the house to show my ma. I think he thought he was going to impress his ex or something. He came roaring into the drive – hooting away. Then, all of a sudden – CRASH! Right through the carport. He nearly took the whole side a' the house away.

COXIE: So daddy number one's in the dog box.

MYRTLE: Shame, man.

JESSICA [*washed out*]: Hell, I tell you, man – the sooner I get out of that lot the better. My own little flat. My own furniture. So what if it's tomato boxes – as long as it's mine.

MYRTLE: Same here. [*A beat.*] Not that I'd leave home. Not now, anyway.

COXIE: Why not?

MYRTLE: My folks wouldn't let me. Anyway, where would I go?

JESSICA: To a place where they got no lawnmowers.

COXIE: No lawnmowers.

JESSICA: Isn't that your worst? Sunday afternoons. You lying on your bed. All you hear are lawnmowers. Hundreds of them. It's like a disease. Every weekend the whole neighbourhood gets lawnmoweritis. One house catches it and they all follow. Whining. Buzzing . Poeping along ...

MYRTLE: Oh, ja. Like the one Mr Fencham's got.

COXIE: Like a go-cart.

JESSICA: I stick on my headphones and try to blast my brains with Dire Straits – but even that doesn't help. [*Pause.*] Huh. That's probably where I first got the crazy idea to become a bio-chemist – subconscious desire to invent some poison to kill off all the lawns.

MYRTLE: Something I can't stand are Kreepy Kraulies.

JESSICA [*a beat*]: Those ones in the swimming pool?

MYRTLE: I dream about them.

COXIE: Hell. Kinky.

JESSICA: No. Krauly.

MYRTLE: It's not funny. They come out of the pool and into my room. I always dream they're coming to suffocate me.

COXIE [*quietly*]: Shit.

MYRTLE: My ma was talking to someone. They just said it's anxiety.

JESSICA: Is that all?

MYRTLE: Anyway, it should be okay now. My dad went out and bought an Aquanaut.

They smile at her.

JESSICA: Ja, we've got a Barracuda.

There is a shout off. ALLIE *approaches, perceptibly staggering now. His bottle has less liquor in it and his right index finger has a long length of electrical wire tied to it.*

ALLIE: Hey chaps – do me a favour. Give us a hand here!

COXIE: Where the hell you been, man?

ALLIE: Me? Nowhere. Here. [*He holds out the end of the flex.*]

COXIE: What?

ALLIE: Grab.

COXIE: Bugger off, man.

ALLIE: Jessie.

Almost in one motion, he moves to the upstage side of the car, holding the end of the flex before him.

COXIE: What's happened to the other idiot?

ALLIE: I dunno.

COXIE: What you mean – you don't know?

ALLIE: Jessie?

He places the end of the wire in JESSICA's *hand.*

JESSICA: What's this?

ALLIE: Hold it.

JESSICA: Why?

ALLIE [*looking about*]: You'll see. Get down.

JESSICA: Hey, you're not going to fart or something stupid, are you?

ALLIE: Don't be mad ...

JESSICA: Because Allie, I'm warning you, if you poep ... !

COXIE has done a bit of a walk around the car, looking off. He shouts into the night. JESSICA *climbs down ...*

COXIE: Spider ... ! Spider ... !

MYRTLE: Maybe he's gone to get help.

COXIE [*tongue-in-cheek*]: You don't wanna go look for him, do you, Myrt?

MYRTLE [*unamused*]: Are you mad.?

ALLIE has been leading a bemused JESSICA *this way and that. Finally, he leads her away from the car, posting the wire through the car door window and sitting in the front seat. The entire operation takes place over the following dialogue:*

JESSICA: What're you doing now, man?

ALLIE: Wait a minute. Stand there.

COXIE: Look, I think it's time we worked out a proper plan of action now.
This is getting ridiculous. Jessie. What the hell you doing?

ALLIE has by this time positioned himself inside the closed car, feet braced against the door with the flex leading out through the window to JESSICA.

ALLIE: Okay. Now, yank it.

JESSICA: What?

ALLIE: Just pull it.

JESSICA: Are you crazy? You could damage your finger!

ALLIE: That's the whole idea. Now pull it.

JESSICA: Allister Lacey – you've been drinking.

ALLIE [*his eyes shut tight*]: Please!

JESSICA [*dropping the wire*]: No.

COXIE: What's your case?

MYRTLE: What you trying to do?

JESSICA: He's out of his mind ...

COXIE: Get outa' the car, man ...

JESSICA: Stop being stupid now.

ALLIE can take it no longer. He pours out his feelings in one long intoxicated babble.

ALLIE: I'm not going to the Army, okay!? I'm not fighting any mad military war for any fascist minority one party mish-mash. Not for Magnus!! Not for my dad. Not for anyone.

JESSICA [*a beat*]: God. You really *are* drunk.

ALLIE: Okay, I'll do it myself. [*Hurting his finger in his haste to get out.*] Ow!!

JESSICA [*kicking at the flex*]: Stupid.

ALLIE [*getting out of the car, untangling himself as he does so. He moves away, still intent on doing damage to his finger*]: Tree. I need a tree.

There is another off-stage commotion. Spider appears, banging a hubcap and a metal hub rim together and singing a rather wild and raunchy Rolling Stones classic.

SPIDER [*singing*]: 'Jumpin' Jack flash is a gas-gas-gasss'!

JESSICA: And now?

SPIDER [*holding out a hubcap, pleased with himself*]: How's this? Genuine VW. Collector's item. What am I bid?

COXIE: Where's Allie going? Allie ... !

SPIDER: Thirty bucks. Cheap at the price.

COXIE [*turning to him*]: Listen – what the hell are we doing now, man?

SPIDER: Right now we looking at some vintage archaeology here.

COXIE [*under his breath*]: Jissus!

SPIDER: Jess. For you. Twenty-two rand seventy-five cents.

JESSICA: Give it a break, Spider.

SPIDER: You know what this is? Talk about history!? Hey? Genuine Volksie Beetle – AD 1970. Eighteen bucks.

MYRTLE: Michael ...

SPIDER: I don't believe you okes. I know people who'd crack heads for this.

JESSICA: Any chance of meeting any of them?

COXIE [*exploding*]: Look, for heaven's-sake, man – are we going? Are we staying? Are we fixing this car now, or what?!

SPIDER: Oo ... temper ... temper.

COXIE: I wanna know what the hell the plan is now, man.

SPIDER [*staring at COXIE – aware that COXIE is rattled. His response is calculated, cool.*] You tell us. You're the 'head boy'.

COXIE [*knowing that he cannot give ground, he appeals to reason – hoping that SPIDER will bend*]: Why don't you just help me, man – instead a' buggering around? You know as much about bladdy cars as I do.

SPIDER: Ja, but then I'm in no hurry to get home.

MYRTLE: I'll help you, Michael.

COXIE [*his turn to stare SPIDER out*]: You think this is a game, don't you? You think this is one big jol.

SPIDER: For sure. And it might be the last jol we ever have – so I'd bladdy-well enjoy it.

MYRTLE: How can you talk about having fun at a time like this?

SPIDER: I wasn't including you, Myrtle.

JESSICA [*on the other side of the car*]: Allie ...

SPIDER: Everybody knows your idea of a good time is playing with your Barbie Dolls ...

COXIE [*to* MYRTLE]: Just do us a favour. Get behind the wheel.

SPIDER: Ring-a-ring-a-rosies. Oranges-and-lemons.

JESSICA [*still looking off*]: What's he up to?

> MYRTLE *has got into the car and positioned herself behind the wheel.* COXIE *is over the engine.* SPIDER *cannot resist taunting* MYRTLE.

SPIDER: If we had a skipping rope here – you'd be A for away.

COXIE [*to* MYRTLE]: Now I'm gonna want you to turn the ignition, okay.

SPIDER: I tell you what. Just for Myrtle. I-spy-with-my-little-eye ... [*Climbing onto the drum*].

COXIE: Okay. Turn it.

MYRTLE: The key?

COXIE: Ja. Turn it on.

SPIDER: Come on. Who's to start?

COXIE: Again.

MYRTLE: Again?

> *She turns the ignition once more.*

SPIDER [*bumbles on*]: Fixed up. You guys look sharp, hey? [*He looks about.*] I spy with my little eye – something beginning with ...

COXIE: Is it turned?

MYRTLE: Ja.

COXIE: Push the pedal.

SPIDER: Something beginning with ...

JESSICA: I'm beginning to get worried about Allie, man.

COXIE: It's the accelerator, hey?

MYRTLE: Ja.

COXIE: Pedal on the right.

SPIDER: I spy – something beginning with ...

JESSICA: He's in no fit state to be wandering around in the veld.

COXIE: You pushing?

MYRTLE: I'm pushing.

JESSICA: Michael ...

SPIDER: I spy with my little eye, something beginning with ...

COXIE: Shit!

SPIDER: That's 's' – against the rules. Anyway, it's my turn.

COXIE: Piss off, man!

SPIDER: Disqualified. Jessie – you next.

JESSICA: I think someone should go look for Allie.

COXIE: Did you have the key turned the whole time?

MYRTLE: All the time I was pushing.

SPIDER: Okay – K–I–N–G – spells king – how's that?

JESSICA: Michael ,,,

SPIDER: Pin-the-tail-on-the-donkey – who's bok?

He jabs a finger in COXIE's backside.

COXIE: Look, will you bladdy can it now, man!

SPIDER: Shit, you guys don't wanna play games. You don't wanna sing songs. You don't wanna boogie.

MYRTLE: You want me to push again, Coxie?

SPIDER: How's about three cheers for the teachers?

JESSICA: How's about someone trying to find Allie?!

SPIDER: Hell – Frank Zappa was right. The art of discourse is dead. It's no wonder the school debating society got wiped out this year. Bunch a' bladdy dum-dums.

Now SPIDER is sitting on the roof.

MYRTLE: I'll have you know, we did not get wiped out, Mr Smarty Pants.

SPIDER: We?

MYRTLE: In fact we did quite well.

SPIDER Oh, ja – I'd forgotten – you're one a' them, aren't you?

JESSICA wanders off into the veld.

MYRTLE: We only happened to beat one of the best schools in Bloemfontein – and that was even without Shirley Rabinowitz.

SPIDER: I'm impressed. What did you discuss? Conservation versus growth?

COXIE [*noticing JESSICA moving off*]: Where's *she* going now?

SPIDER: Sport versus culture for healthy recreation?

COXIE [*shouting into the night*]: Jessie ... !

MYRTLE: I'm not wasting my breath on you.

SPIDER [*hitting top gear again*]: No, please – enlighten me. I wanna know what earth-shattering topics you okes discuss. Enid Blyton versus Winnie the Pooh? Hey? Or do you debate totally irrelevant issues – such as crime versus political agitation in the townships?

MYRTLE: Drop dead, man.

SPIDER: They do that, don't worry.

COXIE: Hey, cool it ...

SPIDER: Poverty and unemployment in Umlazi. Oh, no – of course – you don't know where Umlazi is, do you? Whole life living in Durbs – you never heard of Umlazi ...

MYRTLE [*who knows it is true as do they all, quietly*]: Ag, man ...

SPIDER: Mamelodi? Langa ... ? How about Tembisa? Twice the size a' Maritzburg. [*Slight pause.*] You know when Napoleon sent a piss-willy little telegram to Bismarck, but I bet you know stuff-all about what happened in Soweto on the 16th a' June, 1976 ... !

COXIE [*topping him*]: Give it a break now, okay!?

MYRTLE: We're not allowed to discuss politics – you know that ...

SPIDER: Who said anything about politics? We discussing everyday issues here. Why Spear a' the Nation are planting bombs instead a' talking ...

COXIE: You're talking a load a' crap – that's what you're talking!

SPIDER [*hitting COXIE where it hurts*]: Then crap's the reason you're crawling off to Australia!

COXIE: Oh, jeez ...

SPIDER: Or wait – don't tell me – it's a forced removal? You going to Sydney at gun point?

MYRTLE: Stop it ...

SPIDER: They bulldozed your house – now you packing for Perth!

MYRTLE: Stop it, man – leave him!

SPIDER [*turning on her*]: You stay outa' this ...

MYRTLE: His dad's got a transfer, orraight?

COXIE: Los it, Myrt ...

SPIDER: A what ... ?

COXIE: Forget it, now.

SPIDER: No-one gets 'transferred' to Australia, dof-brain! South Africans don't get 'transferred' anywhere. We dirt. We scum-bags. We the polecats a' the fucken world – where's your head?

COXIE: Jissus ...

SPIDER [*eyes blazing*]: We racist pigs. We practise chocolate fucken genocide, didn't you know that? We slaughter schoolkids, just for fun. We shoot them in the streets ... !

He mimes a machine-gun, mowing people down.

COXIE [*tries to intervene, but is thrust aside*]: Spider!

SPIDER: I'll tell you why he's going. He's kaking off for the day they come get us ... [*Turning to COXIE.*] Isn't that right? He doesn't wanna be here. But you gonna be here, aren't you, Myrt?

He pins her against the car, metal hub rim in his hand.

MYRTLE: Ow!

SPIDER: But you're so bladdy thick, you won't even see it coming. You won't know what's hit you 'til it's too bloody late!

SPIDER thrusts the rim brutally over her neck. She tries to struggle free. SPIDER spins her around, keeping COXIE away.

COXIE: Jesus, you sick, man!

MYRTLE *is trying softly. SPIDER's face is close, hateful.*

SPIDER: You scared? I'm scared too. But you know what scares me, Myrtle? You do! You dangerous, you know that? You live behind your high walls – your bladdy burglar bars, and there's bugger all you know. And what's worse is, you don't even *wanna* know!

SPIDER shoves MYRTLE and walks away, making for his booze bottle. She whimpers. COXIE moves to her, staring at SPIDER.

COXIE: You got a problem, pal. You better see a doctor. [*Comforting MYRTLE.*] You okay?

MYRTLE [*softly*]: Ja.

SPIDER is drinking deep from the bottle.

COXIE: You're right outa' your tree, man.

MYRTLE: Leave it ...

COXIE [*anger building*]: Do yourself a favour. Next time you in Pick 'n Pay and there's a bomb about – stick around and wait for it.

SPIDER: I'll do that. [*A wicked glint in his eye.*] In fact, I might just plant it myself. Cheers. [*He raises the bottle and drinks.*]

COXIE: What is it with you?

MYRTLE: Michael ...

COXIE: You been sniffing tonight? You been rooking ...

MYRTLE: It's enough now.

COXIE: Shit, talk about bladdy hang-ups.

SPIDER: Oh, I got a hang-up now, have I?

COXIE: Bladdy sure.

SPIDER: You the one with the hang-ups, my friend. You think because you captain a' the first fucken rugby team, you well-balanced? I got news for you ...

COXIE: Shit – you wanna wraught? Come ... [*He gets into a fighting stance, ready for action.*]

MYRTLE: No!

COXIE: Come on. Come dip. Come ...

MYRTLE: Stop it!

COXIE: Take a dip.

SPIDER: Fuck off.

COXIE: So what's your case?

SPIDER: Can't talk to you anymore, man ...

COXIE: You been gunning for me for I dunno how long ...

SPIDER: That's right.

COXIE: You been pushing and stirring ...

SPIDER: Ever since Standard Eight, and you know why?

COXIE: You been a pain in the arse ... !

SPIDER: And you know why ... ?

JESSICA [*appears, highly agitated*]: We've lost Allie!

SPIDER [*bashing* on]: The day you became a prefect – you blew it.

JESSICA: Allie's gone.

COXIE: A prefect?

SPIDER: Blew your chances – one shot.

JESSICA: Allie's disappeared, man!

COXIE: Just hang on ...

MYRTLE: Huh?

SPIDER: You went from being quite an alright sorta oke – to a total supercilious
    bastard.

JESSICA: Are you listening to me?

COXIE: Me?

SPIDER: And then when you became head boy, I mean that was it. You wrote
    yourself off.

COXIE: Me!?

JESSICA: Michael!

SPIDER: You.

JESSICA: Michael!!

COXIE: That's your opinion. [*to* JESSICA.] I'm coming.

SPIDER: Total sell-out.

COXIE [*starts following* JESSICA *around the car*] [*to* SPIDER]: In your opinion.
    [*Shouting.*] Allie!

SPIDER: Power corrupts, my friend. They offered you the red fucken apple and you
    took the bite. Couldn't resist.

Both JESSICA *and* COXIE *are upstage of the car now, looking out across the veld.*

JESSICA: I've looked all over the place. I can't find him anywhere.

COXIE [*shouting*]: Allie!!

MYRTLE: I could see he was drinking too much.

COXIE: He can't be lost, man. [*Shouting.*] Allie!

SPIDER perches once more on the roof with his bottle. The other three look anxiously off. COXIE *climbs the metal frame, getting as high a vantage spot as possible. He scours the moonlit veld.*

JESSICA: Maybe he's fallen down a donga or something ...

COXIE: Allie!!

MYRTLE: He could be trying to find a house.

SPIDER. He could also be deceased.

MYRTLE [*nervous*]: Stop it, man, Spider.

SPIDER: One down – four to go.

MYRTLE *begins moving tentatively towards the car.* COXIE *and* JESSICA *are up on the canopy, calling off into the night.*

COXIE: Allie!

JESSICA: Allie!

SPIDER [*as* MYRTLE *reaches the back door*]: I wouldn't get in the car, Myrtle.

MYRTLE: Why not?

SPIDER: They burn the car – you'll roast alive.

She retreats, going back to the others.

JESSICA: God, this is spooky, man.

COXIE [*spotting* ALLIE]: Ah, wait a minute – shit, man. There he is ...

JESSICA: Where?

COXIE [*pointing*]: There [*Shouting.*] Allie!

MYRTLE: Is he okay?

JESSICA: Someone's with him.

COXIE: Bull.

JESSICA: Someone's standing next to him – holding him down.

MYRTLE: Who is it?

COXIE: Rubbish, man. It's a tree trunk.

MYRTLE: What's he doing?

SPIDER: Looking for someone else to pull his wire.

MYRTLE: Shouldn't someone go and fetch him?

JESSICA: That's not a tree-trunk, it's an anthill!

MYRTLE: An anthill?

SPIDER [*smiling*]: The guy's nuts, man.

JESSICA: What's he doing with it?

SPIDER: Probably got his finger in it.

COXIE [*his head in the engine again*]: Myrtle, I'm gonna need you again just now.

MYRTLE: Why would he want to put his finger in an anthill?

JESSICA [*waving*]: Allie!

SPIDER [*watching* COXIE *tinkering with the engine*]: Don't waste your time with it, man. Your best bet is to dismantle it. Sell bits off as spare parts.

JESSICA has been trying to attract ALLIE's *attention all this while.* MYRTLE *has not moved from the base of the frame.*

JESSICA: He doesn't want to know – just look at him.

MYRTLE: Let's see ...

MYRTLE also climbs up the steel frame. SPIDER, *by this time, has made himself comfortable on the roof by lying face down. He still peers into the engine, much to the discomfort of* COXIE.

SPIDER: You check the plugs?

COXIE: Of course I checked the plugs, man.

SPIDER: Points?

COXIE: Piss off, man.

MYRTLE and JESSICA have been waving at ALLIE.

MYRTLE: Why doesn't he want to come?

JESSICA: It's Allie being otherwise ...

SPIDER [*with a self-satisfied chortle*]: Hey, tell me something. How many cars you fix?

COXIE: What's it to you?

SPIDER: I may know stuff-all about cars, but one thing I do know you need a bladdy rotor to start the thing.

COXIE [*stares at the engine, aghast*]: Oh, my ...

MYRTLE [*waving*]: Allie ... !

SPIDER: Expert, hey? Bladdy mechanic?

COXIE: I never said I was a mechanic.

SPIDER: Who's the monkey now, hey?

COXIE [*looking under the car with the torch*]: Jessie! You see the rotor? Little black thing. [*He searches the ground.*] Shit, why didn't I see it, man?

SPIDER: 'Cos you're not a mechanic's poephol!

COXIE: Hey, Myrtle – come help me look. We find the rotor, we can start the car.

MYRTLE: We can what?

COXIE: We can get going. Hey, come on – give us a hand. Jessie, call Allie.

JESSICA: Coming.

SPIDER: Hey, you pay me fifteen bucks for this hubcap – I'll help look.

COXIE: Bugger you.

COXIE searches the area immediately around the car, shining the torch this way and that.

MYRTLE: What is it we're looking for?

COXIE: Little black thing, man. Goes in the engine. Come on, you guys.

MYRTLE [*searching*]: You mean you put it in the car, it'll start?

COXIE: We gotta follow the path we came down in the car. Musta' come out when we rolled. Jeepers, what an arsehole ...

COXIE begins moving off along the path the car took in its journey from the road. MYRTLE follows him, her eyes on the ground. JESSICA has not moved from her perch – staring up at the stars.

JESSICA: Amazing how bright the moon is when you're in the veld.

COXIE [*off*]: Jessie ... !

JESSICA: In town you never see it as bright as this.

SPIDER: Your boyfriend needs a hand.

JESSICA: I like it best when it reflects off the water. Sorta shimmers.

SPIDER: They find that rotor, the party's over, you know that? The party's finish and we all go home. When you get right down to it, Jess, we're all a buncha' party poopers. The whole bang-shoot of us. Sad, isn't it? Don't you think?

Pause.

JESSICA: I wonder if you could ever catch a tan from the moon?

SPIDER looks up at the full moon as JESSICA moves from the canopy to him.

SPIDER: You mean like a – tan-tan.

JESSICA: Ja. A moon tan.

SPIDER [*slight pause*]: Come out all blue.

JESSICA: Translucent

She starts to flirt with him.

SPIDER: Transparent. [*Slight pause.*] Sorta' see-through.

JESSICA: When my grandmother used to come out from England, she was so pale your eyes used to hurt just looking at her.

SPIDER: The glare?

JESSICA: Ja, sun off her skin.

SPIDER: Ei-na!

JESSICA: It was vanilla one day – strawberry the next.

SPIDER: Day after that – full-on bladdy lobster.

JESSICA: Don't tell me. Crayfish thermidore.

She unties his shoelace. Strokes his leg.

SPIDER [*not responding to her come-on*]: Come on, Jess – make me an offer here. [*Holding up the hub-cap.*] Ten bucks.

JESSICA: She had this little stone cottage in Tunbridge Wells.

SPIDER: Nine Rand fifty ...

JESSICA: Bognor Regis.

SPIDER: Bogyor-what?

JESSICA: It's down at the seaside. We went there once for crumpets and tea.

SPIDER: Hell, that must be tit, hey?

JESSICA: Bladdy fattening, is all I can say.

SPIDER: No, I meant overseas. England.

JESSICA [*a beat*]: Ag, it wasn't so great. Rained the whole time we were there. [*Slight pause as she checks his chest, undoing a shirt button.*] It's no wonder they can never catch a proper tan.

SPIDER: Okay. My final offer. Eight Rand fifty.

JESSICA [*shaking her head*]: Spider.

SPIDER: Keep it for the kids, man. In 1999 you show it to your kids – you say that's how they drove around in the olden days.

JESSICA: No thanks. [*She is not giving up on him.*]

SPIDER: Two bucks.

JESSICA: Uh-uh.

SPIDER: One buck.

JESSICA: You don't give up, do you?

They kiss – a long one. He pushes her away from him. There is an awkward silence.

SPIDER [*taking the hubcap*]: Okay, stuff it. Free a' charge. Present. [*He holds it out, trying to give it to her.*] Take it. It's a gift. Me to you.

JESSICA: It's okay.

SPIDER: Keep it for the kids, man ...

JESSICA: I'm not having any kids.

SPIDER: You can tell them who gave it to you ...

JESSICA: I'm not getting married.

SPIDER: You can say you once knew a oke at school called Spider the Rock and he gave it to you on the night of the Matric Farewell. [*Slight pause.*] What d'you mean you're not getting married?

JESSICA: Kids, maybe – marriage, no ways.

SPIDER: Haa-ha. That's what they all say.

JESSICA: You just watch me.

SPIDER: Whatsa matter? You got something against men?

JESSICA: Hah!

SPIDER: No, come on. Because that's something I've sussed ...

JESSICA: Oh, ja?

SPIDER: Ja. You. You want them, but you're scared.

JESSICA: Ag, it's men in this country ... They're either overgrown teenyboppers – or just a bunch a' animals.

SPIDER [*slight pause*]: Thank God for okes like me, hey?

JESSICA: Huh, don't flatter yourself.

SPIDER [*slight pause*]: Ja. Figures. Makes sense.

JESSICA: What?

SPIDER: That's your buzz, man. You and ol' Coxie. He's safe. He's dependable. The solid bladdy citizen. [*Looks up to the road, where* COXIE *and* MYRTLE *continue their search.*] The arsehole. Still looking for the bladdy rotor. [*Chuckles wickedly.*] What you say we go tell him I got it ... ? [*She looks at him.*] Just for fun.

JESSICA: You haven't really got it, have you?

SPIDER: Which hand?

JESSICA tries to open his hands. He grabs at her, playfully.

JESSICA: Why you such a bastard tonight man, Spider?

SPIDER: Who?

JESSICA: You.

SPIDER [*knows he cannot deny it*]: I'm surrounded by a bunch a' faders, man. Tonight's the night, and it means nothing to you okes.

JESSICA: Of course it does.

SPIDER: So why you wanna split? A Farewell's supposed to be something special, isn't it ... ? Isn't it? I mean that's what they all tell us ...

JESSICA: What is it you want Spider?

SPIDER: I just want to remember it, that's all ... I wanna ... I just wanna know the bladdy thing happened.

JESSICA [*seeing a vulnerability in him she never knew existed*]: You're scared, aren't you?

SPIDER: Bullshit!

JESSICA: You're frightened for next year.

SPIDER: Aren't you?

JESSICA [*a beat*]: I don't know. A bit. [*Slight pause.*] I don't even know what I'll be doing yet.

SPIDER: I thought you were going to varsity?

JESSICA: I am. But I still don't know what course to take.

SPIDER: What's the diff, man? They're all the same.

JESSICA: I suppose so. [*Pause.*] You guy's have got no choice, hey?

SPIDER: What a kwes! Go face the Total Onslaught. [*Miming his machine gun.*] Both inside and out. [*Looks up toward the road.*] That's one thing Coxie's sure of. He's not gonna die for any lost bladdy cause.

JESSICA: And after that?

SPIDER: Hell – one step at a time, ou. [*Shrugs.*] Ag, I dunno. I s'pose me and ol' Freddy will eventually form the band.

JESSICA: What band?

SPIDER: Band, man – TA-RRAAAANG! [*Miming a guitar.*] Sex, drugs and Rock 'n Roll.

JESSICA: You're not serious? What you gonna play?

SPIDER: Heavy Metal, Acid Punk ... [*Sings.*] 'Baby, baby, baby ...'

JESSICA: But you can't sing a note.

SPIDER: So what? It's not what you sound like – it's how you do it. It's style. It's presentation – TARRAANG! It's what you got up front.

JESSICA: Up front?

SPIDER: Good front man – that's what it's all about. Anyone could do it – good enough gimmick. Even you. [*Slight pause.*] Actually, come to think of it, you wouldn't look too bad as a front man. Sorry – woman. Kate Bush.

JESSICA: Hah!

SPIDER: No, it's true. You look a bit like her. Anyone ever tell you that? A mixture between Kate Bush and whats-her-name ... ?

JESSICA: Talk junk now, man.

SPIDER: I'm serious. A cross between her and that chick who won that Oscar for what was that movie ... ?

JESSICA: *Jaws.*

SPIDER: No, man. Tall chick. Sexy chick. She gets raped in this concentration camp and she comes out all stuffed in the head and then she meets this oke who fixes her up and after that she's all okay again.

JESSICA [*a beat*]: I didn't see it.

SPIDER: You didn't see it? Great movie. [*Pause.*] Her.

JESSICA: Thanks.

SPIDER: And Kate Bush. Sorta' fifty-fifty. More or less. Bit more than less ...

JESSICA: What do you want, Spider?

SPIDER: Hey?

JESSICA: What is it you really want?

SPIDER: Nothing. I'm just – you know. I'm just trying to work out how a smart chick like you can hang around with an arsehole like ...

JESSICA: Look, I'm nobody's 'chick' okay?

SPIDER: You don't dig him?

JESSICA: God, you guys are pathetic. You really believe a woman lies around on a bean bag all day, just waiting for some bloke to phone her up.

SPIDER: Depends who she is.

JESSICA: Ag, hell – drop dead, man.

With a toss of her head, she plunges into the back seat of the car. SPIDER is genuinely thrown by this.

SPIDER: What's up now?

JESSICA: Go play with yourself!

She tries to shut herself in, but SPIDER holds the door.

SPIDER: Listen, man – stop being so ... hey ... !

JESSICA [*struggling*]: Get out of here!

SPIDER: Why you so bladdy 'touchy', man – you like a ... you like a bladdy ...

He has managed to get into the back. His mood is still 'playful', whereas she is for real. She hits him, half holding back. They speak while they struggle.

JESSICA: Because you don't think. Try thinking! Try bladdy – ag, push off, man!

SPIDER: Don't tell me to ...

They clinch and kiss passionately. The 'fight' has been the emotional smokescreen for what they have been wanting to do all along. As they grip and grope, moving towards what looks like being the inevitable backseat screw, ALLIE staggers on, without the wire now, and totally plastered. His right index finger is lodged firmly in the empty bottle neck. He holds the bottle up, seeking assistance.

ALLIE [*approaching the rocking car*]: Spider?

At first the two inside are totally unaware of his presence, so involved are they with each other. ALLIE would not know what they were doing even if he were not stone drunk. He circles the car, calling out for help.

ALLIE: Spider ... hello ... ? Spider, help me.

JESSICA is the first to notice ALLIE. Her initial instinct is to freak, but she is so determined not to let this 'chance' slip away, she shouts at him.

JESSICA: Allie, go away! Get away, man!

ALLIE: Huh? I want you to – er ...

JESSICA: Voetsek, man!!

SPIDER [*more embarrassed than angry*]: Bugger it ...

ALLIE: Sorry, chaps – I was only ...

JESSICA: Look, just get *lost*, man, Allie, man!!

SPIDER: Shit ...

ALLIE: Ja, okay – well, I'm sorry ... I'm ... Oh, hell, man ... I'm ...

He wanders off, still holding his stuck finger aloft. SPIDER's ardour has been totally cooled by ALLIE's intrusion. He steps out of the car, zipping up his fly, straightening up his clothes. JESSICA, on the other hand, is not about to be denied.

JESSICA: What're you doing?

SPIDER: Ah, crumbs, man! We can't just ... how can we ... ? [*Points off in the direction in which ALLIE has gone.*]

JESSICA: He's gone now. Come on ... !

SPIDER: Jess ...

JESSICA: Please!

She reaches out to grab him, but he shrugs her off. Suddenly she is dead still. Their eyes lock. They are both breathing heavily.

SPIDER: Look, I'm sorry.

She realises she is making a fool of herself. She slowly makes for the road.

JESSICA: Okay.

SPIDER: Jess ... come back here ...

JESSICA: Forget it ...

SPIDER: Jessie, I'm ... Jess ... !! [*She is off now, striding purposefully to where COXIE and MYRTLE are, up on the road.*] I don't mean it like that. It's not that I don't wanna ... ah, shit ... !! Jessie!! Ag, voetsek– you got a big bum anyway!!!

SPIDER spins and kicks the drum viciously, knowing he has blown his one and only chance. He goes to the car and hits that too. He jabs the tape back into the cassette deck. Corey Hart 'Komrade Kiev' obliges at full volume. SPIDER picks up the steel pipe lying near the car and launches into a guitar 'solo'. He vaults back onto the car roof, there to give his version of a rock star in full flight.

ALLIE enters. He holds the bottle up to SPIDER who ignores him, lost in the music. ALLIE staggers around the car, considering whether he should risk smashing the bottle. It is during all this that a fuming COXIE enters, followed closely by the girls.

COXIE [*to SPIDER, shouting over the noise*]: So where is it ... !?

ALLIE approaches COXIE, holding up the bottle. SPIDER goes on raving it up on the roof, using the pipe as a microphone now. COXIE pushes past ALLIE and snaps the tape deck off. He stares up at SPIDER, seething.

COXIE: Jessie says you've got the rotor! Let's have it!

SPIDER [*ignoring him*]: Who's this, guys? Who's this? [*He goes into a Jaggerstrut and begins a passable impersonation of the man himself. Singing.*] 'Jumping Jack flash is a gas-gas-ga-asss ...'

141

COXIE, unamused, tries to get up onto the roof. SPIDER prods him with the pipe, keeping him at bay.

COXIE: For Pete's sake, man!

SPIDER: Ah, come on – it's not that hard ...

COXIE: I'm tired of this crap, now!

SPIDER [*singing*]: One hit to the body – One kick to your aaaa-ss ...

ALLIE: Hey, it's Perry Como ...

JESSICA: It's not funny anymore, Spider.

MYRTLE: Give it to him, man

COXIE: We wanna get going now, okay!?

SPIDER: Shame, he wants to go home ...

MYRTLE: We all do.

SPIDER: Who else? Allie?

ALLIE: I want somebody to get this thing off my finger.

SPIDER: Jessie? You don't really wanna go?

JESSICA: It's over now, Spider.

SPIDER [*staring down at them. Stalemate*]: Shit. Outvoted.

Pause.

JESSICA: Get down now.

COXIE: Come on.

COXIE holds out a hand, expecting SPIDER to give him the rotor. In order to save face, SPIDER employs delaying tactics.

SPIDER: Okay. okay. Home time. Before we go – I wanna make a proposal.
A toast.

COXIE: Jissus!

They all freak.

SPIDER: No, no – this won't take long. I'd like to propose three boos to Bloubal,
Death Breath and all the other bastards who gave us uphill while we were still at
school.

ALLIE: Yaaay!

COXIE: To hell with you, man.

SPIDER: Who's bok?

ALLIE: Three boos?

SPIDER: Three massive boos especially for Weasel, Zombie and the Dragon.

JESSICA: Spider ...

SPIDER: Spider too, if you want ...

MYRTLE: I'm not going to do that.

SPIDER: You don't wanna go home?

MYRTLE: I'm not going to boo Miss Wheatley.

ALLIE: Why not?

MYRTLE: Because.

SPIDER: Because why?

MYRTLE: Because she's nice.

ALLIE: Nice? You think Weasel's nice?

SPIDER: She thinks everyone's nice. That's her biggest fucken problem in life.

MYRTLE: I don't think you're very nice.

SPIDER: Thank God for that. If you thought I was nice – I'd go drown myself off the Bluff.

ALLIE: Come on – who's starting? [*Shouting.*] Boo ... ! Boo ... ! Boo to Death Breath!

SPIDER: Boo to Death Breath ... !

ALLIE: Boo to Zombie ... !!

SPIDER: Zombie ... ! Booo ... !!

ALLIE: Boo to the Army!!

SPIDER: Boo to the Army!!

ALLIE: Booo ... !! Boooo ... !!

SPIDER: Booooo ... !!

> ALLIE *dances around the car while* SPIDER *struts on the roof. Their cries top and tail, growing louder all the time.* COXIE *has moved to the canopy.* JESSICA *sits on the oil drum,* MYRTLE *beside her.*

ALLIE: Boo to Perry Como!

SPIDER: Boo to Frank Sinatra ... !! Booo ... !!

ALLIE: Bing Crosby ... !! Booo ... !!! Boooo ... !!!

SPIDER: Boo to bladdy orchestras and jazz, clarinets ... !!

ALLIE: Boo my ma ... ! Boo the car ... !!

SPIDER: Boo to three-piece suits, formal dinners and official fucken functions!!

ALLIE: Boooo ... !!! Booooo ... !!!

> SPIDER *peters out, noticing the lack of response from the others.* ALLIE *continues at full volume – opening up – pouring out. He swears, perhaps for the first time in his life.*

SPIDER: Okay, Allie ...

ALLIE: Stuff my father!! Fuck all his shit ... !! [*Clamps a hand over his own mouth – shocked at his 'bravery'.*]

SPIDER: Cool it, Allie!

ALLIE: Fuck 'em all! Booo ... !!

SPIDER: Allie!!

143

ALLIE [*quietly*]: Boo ...

Pause.

SPIDER: Forget it, man. It's a dead loss. Between the Bees Knees and the two ol'
Goody Two shoes here – we'd get more joy shouting boo to the bladdy moon.

ALLIE [*his cue to start up again*]: Boo ... ! [*Cupping his hands.*] Boo to the moon ... !

COXIE [*to ALLIE who is beside him*]: Just get a hold a' yourself, okay?

ALLIE: Hey?

COXIE: You pissed, man!

ALLIE: Mooooo!

COXIE [*pointing to the bottle*]: Did you drink that whole bottle?

ALLIE: Just help me pull it off [*He offers his bottle-finger to COXIE, who ignores him.*]

SPIDER [*surveying the others*]: We got the wrong mob here, Allie. They not even into
raa-raa-raaa ...

ALLIE [*chanting*]: Raa-raa-raaa! Chakka-chakka-chaaaa ... !!

COXIE: Shut up!

SPIDER: No school spirit.

ALLIE [*chanting*]: Who are – who are – who are we ...

SPIDER: Come on, Jess. Let's see some school spirit.

ALLIE [*singing*]: Excelsior, Excelsior – to you we will be true ...

SPIDER: Come on, Jess – no school pride?

ALLIE: For the school, Jess ...

SPIDER: Old times' sake ...

ALLIE [*with drunken abandon*]: Excelsior, Excelsior ... !

MYRTLE: I'll sing.

JESSICA: No, you won't.

SPIDER: I don't believe it. They don't want a party.

ALLIE: Let's have a party!

SPIDER: Last night as classmates, and they don't want a party.

COXIE [*leaps to his feet, exploding*]: For fuck's-sake, can't you get it into your fucken
head – we've had the bladdy party, man!!

SPIDER: When? Where? What party? You think a few coloured lights and a fucken
disco makes a party!?

JESSICA: Spider, it's enough now ...

SPIDER: You been conned, my friend. The lota' you ... It's their party. It's always been
their party. Don't you see that!?

MYRTLE: I want to go home.

SPIDER [*on a roll now and cannot stop*]: The teachers. Your parents. You dance to
their tune every day of your lives ...

COXIE [*quietly, his anger building*]: Jislaaik!

SPIDER: If they told you the fucken world was flat, you'd believe them.

JESSICA: Spider!

SPIDER [*turning on her*]: Tell me you weren't clapping for Bloubal tonight! Come on! His farewell speech!

JESSICA: Michael.

SPIDER: You were applauding the bastard. There he was, practically telling us that they'd succeeded in turning us all into sheep – and you were thanking him for it!

COXIE: Talk crap now, man ... !!

SPIDER: Of course I'm talking crap. To you I'm talking crap because you'd been bought! You're head boy. You're part a' their whole bladdy picture, man. Braaivleis, sunny skies and fucken Chevrolet!

JESSICA: No, man – I can't take this ...

SPIDER: Where's the bladdy song that goes - burning tyres and petrol bombs!?

MYRTLE: Stop it, Spider ... !

JESSICA [*moving to* COXIE]: I don't wanna hear this ...

ALLIE [*singing*]: 'Popcorn, chewing gum, peanuts and bubble gum. Ice cream, candy floss and Eskimo Pie ...'!

SPIDER [*holding the metal pipe like a microphone, assuming the headmaster's clipped tone*]: Boys and girls, it saddens me to say goodbye after so many years ...

COXIE [*who has been staring at* SPIDER, *aware of his game*]: You haven't got it, have you?

SPIDER: But I'm happy to say – thanks to the staff and myself – you have been fully equipped for life's journey ...

COXIE: You haven't got the rotor ...

SPIDER: You can go out into the world with confidence, with fortitude – future leaders of our society.

COXIE: There was no dassie either, was there?

JESSICA [*nervously*]: Michael ...

SPIDER [*to* COXIE]: I'll tell you something, boy – our Christian National Education works like a dream. Our classrooms are sheep dips. Free fucken brain wash – five days a week!!

COXIE [*on his way up to the road*]: I don't have to listen to this!

SPIDER misreads his actions as fear of the truth. He rams home the final barbs, taunting COXIE *for all he is worth.*

SPIDER: That's it. Run away. Australia's ready and waiting! [*Shouting after him.*] The best sheep country in the world, so they say! Just think – you work hard enough at it, you could become Head Sheep! [*Begins a sheep impersonation – not as good his chicken imitation.*] Baah-baahh!!

ALLIE [*singing, his drunken euphoria showing no sign of abating*]: 'Ag, daddy – how we miss – nigger balls and liquorice, Pepsi-Cola, ginger beer and Canada Dry ...'

COXIE has charged off only to pick up a metal bar he remembers having seen earlier somewhere near the road. JESSICA sees him storming back brandishing it and senses his mood.

JESSICA: Michael ... !

He shoves her aside and moves purposefully to the car. ALLIE is still singing, SPIDER's 'baahs!' have turned to clucks – the fight he has been looking for is tantalisingly close now.

SPIDER [*squawking*]: Pwaaak-pwak-pwak ...

COXIE lashes out at SPIDER, who parries the blow, squawking in mock-terror. COXIE's second swing strikes the roof of the car, forcing SPIDER to leap back off it. COXIE moves around the car, stalking him – lashing out at the upstage doors as he does so. JESSICA and MYRTLE are terrified. JESSICA calls to ALLIE to do something. He holds out his bottle-finger and tries to dislodge it, switching on the tape deck in an attempt to distract them. In the meantime, SPIDER has backed against the upstage canopy frame. COXIE swings a blow to the head and SPIDER ducks – the sound of metal against metal is brutal, frightening. They strike out at each other broadsword style. SPIDER knows he is in a fight. They are around the front of the car now. COXIE lashes out, hitting door, roof and so on as SPIDER ducks and dives, trying to get in his own odd shot, all the time moving around the car in an anti-clockwise direction. The music blares on, adding to the chaos.

MYRTLE [*terrified*]: Michael, stop it! Spider ... !

By this time, JESSICA has succeeded in pulling the bottle from ALLIE's finger. He lurches about, unsure of what to do. SPIDER and COXIE are again behind the car. SPIDER trips on a storm drain pipe and COXIE has him where he wants him. Since they are quite well hidden from view, COXIE is able to lash at the doors with his weapon – making it sound much worse than it really is.

JESSICA: For God-sake, give it up!
MYRTLE: Michael!!!
ALLIE [*still at a distance*]: You guys ... !!

SPIDER has succeeded in yanking the bar away, and a fist-fight ensues. The audience sees only flashes of fists, arms and so on, as the antagonists are still hidden by the car. COXIE begins to get the upper hand and proceeds to ram SPIDER's head against the front door. He batters once, twice, three times – again, it must sound far worse than it actually is – brutal as only a full-blown schoolboy fight can be.

COXIE [*ramming SPIDER's head*]: Bastard!!

ALLIE has now placed himself as close as he dares to the action. He stands protesting, against the downstage front wheel – his hands on the mudguard near the open bonnet. In his fury, COXIE steps back and hurls the bonnet closed – trapping ALLIE's right index finger (the final irony!). ALLIE screams hideously.

COXIE [*screaming at SPIDER*]: You're sick. You know that? You're fucken sick!

He heads off. A panic-stricken MYRTLE snaps off the tape.

MYRTLE: Allie ... ?
JESSICA: Oh, no – man ...
ALLIE's *finger is pumping blood.*
COXIE [*grabbing ALLIE*]: Come on ...
ALLIE [*in great pain*]: Ei-naaa!
MYRTLE [*with ALLIE*]: He's bleeding!

ALLIE, very pale, has sobered up completely. COXIE takes out a hanky and tosses it at him. He is cold, unbending.

COXIE: Come on. Let's go.

He begins to move off.

MYRTLE: Michael ...
ALLIE: Eina-eina-eina!
JESSICA [*concerned*]: Spider ... ?

COXIE is well on his way already. MYRTLE and ALLIE, the hanky around his finger now, sit on the drum. JESSICA stands, unsure of what to do.

JESSICA: Michael, we can't ... Spider ... ?
COXIE [*shouting off*]: Come on!!

SPIDER has been hidden from view ever since the fight. JESSICA moves around the back of the car.

JESSICA: We can't just leave him ... ! [*Looking behind the car.*] Spider ... ?

Slowly, painfully, SPIDER emerges from behind the car. He dabs at his bleeding nose and mouth and goes to the front seat. He takes out a bottle of booze and splashes it over his face. The violent sting forces him to shake his head in agony. He feels his nose – looks at the blood on his hands in a clinical, almost detached way. It is sublime release, sublime relief. COXIE returns slowly, a lot more in control now.

JESSICA: Spider ... God, just look at you.
SPIDER [*dabbing at his face*]: Huh! Sorta' different when it's your own.
JESSICA: We'd better get you guys home.

SPIDER [*inspecting the blood*]: There's always so much of it. You kinda' wonder where it all comes from.

COXIE moves towards him, keen to apologise – but somehow unable to voice it.

COXIE: Look, I'm – I'm ... ah, dammit ...

SPIDER: We were halfway across the car park when it went off. I don't know why, but I ran back inside. There was this mess – you can't believe. People ... trolleys ... and blood, man – glass – everywhere.

JESSICA: Spider ...

SPIDER: And then there was this noise. [*He does an eerie slow-motion demonstration.*] All those who were still on their feet were kinda sleepwalking ... Like they knew it had happened, but they didn't really wanna believe it ... [*No-one stirs, they are totally captivated by his description.*] I turned around and looked at the tills. And then it hit me. Number seven wasn't there anymore. I knew we'd used number seven, because all the others were full. I'd run to the cashier and said fantastic, seven's my lucky number.

MYRTLE: Spider, you don't ...

JESSICA: Shhh ...

SPIDER: She wasn't there anymore. She was gone.

COXIE: It's okay ...

SPIDER: Number seven was gone ... !

COXIE: It's okay now ...

SPIDER: She'd been blown away ... just ... just blown away ... !

JESSICA [*putting her arms around him, cradling his head*]: Shh – it's all right now. It's over. It's all okay now. Shh.

SPIDER has his head buried in JESSICA's shoulder. COXIE reaches out tentatively to touch him. MYRTLE moves to join the trio, but COXIE gently leads her back to ALLIE. He studies the bloody hanky around ALLIE's finger.

COXIE: You reckon it's broken?

ALLIE: I dunno. I can't feel anything.

MYRTLE: We got to get him to a doctor.

COXIE [*aware of being responsible, looks to SPIDER then back to ALLIE*]: God, what're we *doing* to each other?

JESSICA: Come on, let's get up on the road. We can start walking. As long as we all stick together ...

COXIE [*moving to SPIDER*]: Hey, I'm ... I'm sorry, Spider.

SPIDER: Forget it.

COXIE: I shouldn't of ... I lost my cool ...

SPIDER: It's okay. Forget it. I was asking for it. [*Squeezing COXIE's shoulder.*] Dinkum.

The two share a look. SPIDER's *eyes say 'quits'.*

COXIE: Shit, what the hell's happened to us?

JESSICA: It's over now.

COXIE: No, I'm talking about the lot of us. I feel like I don't know you guys anymore. Any of you.

ALLIE [*cradling his finger*]: So what's new? I don't even know myself.

MYRTLE: Join the club.

JESSICA [*searching for her handbag*]: It's getting late. Come on.

COXIE: No, but ... but five years ... ! It's been five years, you guys. Five long years since Standard six ...

SPIDER: Seven for some.

MYRTLE: What d'you mean? It's *twelve* since nursery school!

JESSICA: Twelve ... !? Yeeugh ... ! What a waste!

SPIDER [*singing*]: 'We don't need no education ... '

> JESSICA *does a mock strangulation of her own throat and she and* MYRTLE *pack up laughing.* ALLIE, *in spite of his mood, picks up the vibe.*

ALLIE: I can't imagine not sitting in the lab next year – waiting for Death Breath.

JESSICA: Thank God for that.

MYRTLE: History with Dopey!

SPIDER: PT with Bloubal ...

> *They all laugh.*

COXIE: Hey, listen – I'm serious, man.

JESSICA: Don't get serious, Micka-lix. Not now.

COXIE: No, what I'm saying is ... [*He peters out.*] Ag, dammit – I dunno what I'm saying, man.

JESSICA: What you're saying is – we won't be *seeing* each other anymore ...

COXIE: Ja ... I mean, no – I mean ... ugh!

JESSICA: What are you trying to say, Michael?

COXIE [*blurts it out*]: Look, I don't want to go to Australia, okay? [*There is a pause while they all stare at him.*] I've never wanted to go! It's not just not being with you guys anymore, it's ... it's ... [*Petering out again.*] Ah, dammit, man – life without Durbs is like ... is like ... life without Durbs.

SPIDER [*slight pause*]: And what's life without Durbs?

COXIE: Exactly.

ALLIE: So, don't go.

COXIE [*wry smile*]: Huh.

MYRTLE: Ag, you could always come back, man.

ALLIE: It's easy to come back.

COXIE [*unconvinced*]: Ja.

JESSICA: People always come back.

ALLIE: Always.

MYRTLE: All the time ...

COXIE: Ja.

There is another long pause as they watch him, knowing that he will not be back.
SPIDER, at a distance, watches silently. MYRTLE is ever hopeful.

MYRTLE: You must come back and visit. You must promise. You must come back and stay.

COXIE: For sure. [*A pause.*] For sure.

They look at each other, COXIE and MYRTLE, for a little longer than is comfortable.

JESSICA [*breaking the mood*]: Listen, has anyone seen my handbag?

She begins searching for it again. COXIE moves off slowly – up towards the road.
MYRTLE turns her attention to helping JESSICA find her handbag. As she passes
near SPIDER, he reaches out to her.

MYRTLE: Where did you drop it? Did you look by the ... ?

SPIDER: Myrtle – um ... Listen, Myrtle – er ... Wait a minute ... [*He unpins a shiny*
badge from his lapel.] Here. Stick around.

MYRTLE: What?

SPIDER: Take it. [*Offering her the badge.*]

MYRTLE: What's this?

SPIDER: Nothing, it's ...

MYRTLE: For me!?

SPIDER: Look, I'm ...

MYRTLE: Gee, thanks, Spider – who is it? [*Examining the badge.*] He's nice.

SPIDER [*a beat*]: Them.

MYRTLE: Hey?

SPIDER: Them. It's a group. Pink Floyd.

MYRTLE [*admiring it*]: Pink who?

SPIDER: Floyd. Pink – Look, if they too radical, I can give you a ...

He begins searching his lapel for another badge.

MYRTLE: No, no – it's lovely, they fantastic ... ah, gee ... [*Gives him the swiftest peck*
on the cheek in the history of kissing].

SPIDER: Ja, look – I wanna sorta apologise.

MYRTLE: It's okay.

SPIDER: No, it's not okay – I been a real prick – sorry, I mean a real cu ... I mean a ...
a ... Ah, fuck.

MYRTLE: It's okay, Spider, I made up my mind – I'm gonna talk to our maid.

SPIDER: Huh?

MYRTLE: I'm gonna open my eyes. I'm not gonna be stupid anymore.

SPIDER: Myrtle, you're not stupid ...

MYRTLE: No, I know. I'm gonna learn Zulu and Xhosa and Sotho and I'm gonna talk to our garden boy and the delivery boy and the postman and anyone who wants to talk to me. I'm gonna talk to them even if they don't wanna talk to me ...

SPIDER: That's great, Myrtle – great ...

MYRTLE: Because we all got to talk to each other.

SPIDER: For sure. Listen ...

COXIE [*charging down from the road in a state of high excitement*]: Hey, come on, you guys – quickly! We got a lift!

JESSICA: We got a what!?

COXIE [*urgently*]: Come on, he's waiting, man. It's a dude going to Maritzburg, but he says he'll drop us off.

MYRTLE: Yayyyy – we going home!!

JESSICA finds her bag. MYRTLE almost falls out of her high heels in her haste.

JESSICA: Hang on, hang on.

COXIE is on his way back to the road, the girls following. As they move off, expecting the others to follow, MYRTLE chats ten to the dozen.

MYRTLE: Is it a white man, Coxie?

COXIE: Move it, Myrt.

MYRTLE: It's not a bakkie or anything, is it – because if it's a bakkie maybe we should wait for a proper car or something like that or something we can be sure is going to be safe ... I mean, you never know ...

Her voice trails away. ALLIE looks up to the road. Although reluctant to budge, he looks down at his finger and thinks better of it. He slowly gets to his feet. He looks at SPIDER, then back to the road.

SPIDER: Go on, man.

ALLIE: You're not coming?

SPIDER: I'll see you around.

SPIDER moves to his spot in the front seat and hauls out his bottle. The others begin shouting from the road.

COXIE [*off*]: Hey, you guys, look sharp, man!

MYRTLE [*off*]: Al – lie!!

ALLIE [*hovering, then turning to SPIDER, holding up his finger swathed in the bloody hanky*]: It nearly worked, hey?

SPIDER: Close, pal. Close. [*Smiling.*] Better luck next time.

ALLIE [*studying his finger and shrugging philosophically*]: Ag, what-the-hell? If you gotta go, you gotta go. [*Turns to go.*]

SPIDER: Hey, Allie.

ALLIE: Ja?

SPIDER: Marshmallows.

ALLIE [*his face cracking into a broad grin*]: Marshmallows.

He leaves.

JESSICA comes running down past him from the road.

JESSICA: Hey, look – this guy hasn't got all night, hey.

SPIDER is playing with his lighter. He is flicking it on – blowing it out. Flicking it on – blowing it out.

SPIDER: Cheers, Jess.

JESSICA: For God-sake, what the hell you trying to prove ... !?

COXIE [*off*]: Je-essie!!

JESSICA: Come on, now! [*SPIDER stares at her. She is genuinely irritated.*] Ag, to hell with you, man.

She turns to leave.

SPIDER [*calling her back*]: Jess ... ! We had some good times, hey?

JESSICA: Ja. Come on. [*He does not budge.*] We're going home. Come on!

She turns to go.

SPIDER: Listen, do us a favour. New Year's Day – the Aquarium. I'll meet you there.

JESSICA: The Aquarium?

SPIDER: Twelve noon. The Shark Tank. We'll make a day of it?

JESSICA: I don't know.

SPIDER [*he shrugs*]: No big deal.

ALL [*off*]: JESSIEE!!

JESSICA: How about the Dolphinarium?

SPIDER: Done.

JESSICA [*looks at him, considering this*]: I'll see. I'll try.

She goes as SPIDER watches her. He swigs at his bottle, leans across and snaps on the radio. It is Radio Orion. Robin Alexander is in the process of delivering a chunk of particularly useless information which gives way to Waylon Jennings singing 'Hello John'. SPIDER lights up a smoke and settles back. He sips. Waylon croons.

The lights fade to blackout.

Smallholding

A TWO-ACT PLAY

Louis Sebeko as GIDEON, Nicky Rebelo as CHRISTIAAN and Kate Edwards as EVIE.
Photograph by Ruphin Coudyzer.

Cast

PA, a Boere-Rambo, shot to ribbons. He looks a lot older than his 48 years. Diseased, debauched and prone to *Dallas* and dronkverdriet.

EVIE, his daughter, mid-twenties. There is a brittle quality about her facade of independence. Out of place (as was her English rose of a mother) in a harsh, unforgiving landscape.

JJ, son of Rambo. Heir apparent to the smallholding. A regular 23-year-old stormtrooper – possessing neither the skills nor the intellectual capacity to take on much more than tasks requiring power-saws, power-drills, jackhammers and the like.

GIDEON, a black farmhand, mid-twenties. Very aware of the fact that his father and his father's father worked Sweetfontein long before it was a smallholding.

CHRISTIAAN, a young Afrikaner, late-twenties. High up in the Post Office. God-fearing, and of sober, compassionate habits.

The action takes place on the smallholding Sweetfontein on the outer reaches of the far East Rand. The time is 1989.

Smallholding was first performed at the Standard Bank Festival of the Arts in Grahamstown on 6 July 1989.

A national tour followed, culminating in a highly successful ten-week season at Johannesburg's Market Theatre.

At Grahamstown and on tour, Nicky Rebelo played Christiaan, Paul Slabolepszy, Pa, Sello Maake, Gideon, Martin le Maitre, JJ, and Kate Edwards, Evie. At the Market Theatre, the role of Gideon was played by Louis Sebeko. The production was directed by Bobby Heaney with set design by Nadya Cohen and lighting design by Mannie Manim.

TREKLIEDJIE
Met jou aan my sy
O liefste van my
Dan vrees ek g'n gevaar
Die wildernis in
Om die vryheid te win
Daar word ons drome waar

On 6 May 1987, the National Party (in power since 1948) again won a general election that was characterised by a swing to the right. On the day the results came through, I stumbled upon an untitled poem by Matsemela Manaka:

Let us create and talk about life
Let us not admire the beauty
But peruse the meaning
Let art be life
Let us not eye the form
But read the content
Let creativity be a portrait of one's life ...

I immediately set to work on *Smallholding*.
Paul Slabolepszy

Note on music:
The old Boer folk song 'Trekliedjie' was used by Glynn Storm as the basis of the sound track. Rearranging the melody and using guitar, strings, choral voices and so on, he created a wonderful musical backdrop to the play. This tape is available to future producers of *Smallholding*.

ACT ONE

Scene One

*The smallholding of the title comprises a much greater area than the corner depicted
on stage. In it is an old, small-to-medium sized caravan, propped up on bricks. The
name 'Costa Lotta' is splashed across it. The caravan stands on the diagonal, stage
left. There is a makeshift wooden step in front of the door. An outside patio area is
bordered by tatty fairy lights. On it is a braaiplace, a double car seat, potted plants
in petrol tins, and so on. To one side, there is a sawn-off forty-four-gallon drum with
the name 'Sasol' stencilled onto it. It has a lid. Next to it is a wooden box containing
cabbage leaves. Beside the caravan is a lounge chair displaying signs of flood damage.
The caravan itself is decorated with kudu horns, buffalo horns and other bric-a-brac.
A complex, elaborate television aerial is perched atop, complete with plastic orange
– an eccentricity that smacks of boere-kitsch. A working water tap is located at the
downstage corner of the caravan. The entire area should exude an atmosphere of gaudy
domesticity. It is all too much, and quite over the top.*

*The play begins with a jaunty rendition of 'Trekliedjie', sung with gusto. As the
stage pre-set fades to blackout, the song echoes away and cross-fades into a slower,
instrumental version of the same tune – the atmosphere is lyrical, romantic.*

*A pin-spot (follow-spot) picks up a young man, centre-stage. He is dressed in a suit and
has a loose tie around his neck. He wears glasses. His tone is personal, measured. his
Afrikaans accent easy on the ear.*

CHRISTIAAN: There are things that happen in your life every day. Everyday things.
They happen and then – that's it – they finish. [*He turns slowly to look at the
caravan. As he does so, a soft yellow glow emanates from the net-curtained
windows and the fairy lights that surround the patio fade up.*] But then there are
things that happen – strange things. So strange, you think – no, wait a minute
– did that *really* happen? Or did I just imagine it? Maybe it was just a dream. A
dream that seemed real, but a dream all the same. You say – okay – you leave it
at that. I mean, why place any importance on a dream?
[*He turns, as though to leave, but is arrested by the further illumination of the
area – the 'picture' coming to life, as it were.*] But then that dream stays with you.
Only it's more than a dream. It's more of a kind of a – nightmare ... [*Beyond the
fairy lights, distant and haunting, we hear the long mournful sound of a howl.
Whether we identify it as man or dog, makes no difference. It feeds* CHRISTIAAN'S

story and – almost as if he is creating it for us (and, perhaps, himself) – he pauses to register it fully before going on.] Not only because of what it is, but because it won't go away ... [*Cackling, drunken laughter off. Closer now.*] You try to push it out, but it stays with you. It's so real, so clear, it's as if you're somehow inside it. You can smell it. You can feel it. Like it's living. Breathing. Like it's happening – right now ...

There is a noise off stage, something is being clumsily kicked over. A drunken voice, singing – howling. CHRISTIAAN witnesses – along with the audience – the progress of a bearded, inebriated PA, as he staggers toward the caravan, half-empty brandy bottle in hand. We cannot make out his age, although he looks a lot older than someone who is in fact only forty-eight years old. Haggard, world-weary – as though the game of life has dealt him a considerably cruel hand.

PA [*as if talking to some invisible presence*]: How's this – how's this ... ? [*Throwing back his head and howling like a dog.*] Howwwww! Ho – wooowooo ... ! [*Singing drunkenly.*] 'I'm Dreaming of a White – Mercedes. Just like the one I saw before ...' Huh! Rotate your crops ... [*Looking about, his voice dripping with sarcasm.*] In order to rotate your crops, dear Mr Bank Manager, you got to have a crop to begin with. And – as you can see – the only crop I got, is Sweet Bugger All ... ! Bow – wowoooo .. .! [*CHRISTIAAN watches him lurch slowly to the caravan door.*] Knock-knock – anybody home ... ? Yes? No? Going once – going twice –gone to the man with the Klipdrift! Bugger it. [*He turns away and empties his pockets of keys onto the car seat.*]

While PA goes through his keys, bunch by bunch, CHRISTIAAN resumes his discourse – there, but not there – in front of the old man.

CHRISTIAAN: Pa. If Pa had a name, I never heard anyone use it. Oom? [*Smiling at some private joke.*] But then again, if someone is Pa, that's all one needs to know, isn't it? Father. Protector. The One Who Makes the Rules.

PA [*getting frustrated with his keys*]: Caravan, caravan, caravan ... !

CHRISTIAAN: And what a caravan ... [*Moving past PA to inspect it again.*] That's something else about the place that makes it so hard to forget. Or believe ...

PA moves to the door with a key, swaying all the while, humming 'White Christmas'. In the wrong key.

CHRISTIAAN: No, but – wait a minute! Hold on! How could it have been like this? How could anyone's home be like this? But it was. I'm sure it was ...

PA [*through a drunken haze*]: All these bladdy keys, man ... !

CHRISTIAAN: And what about him ... ? [*PA passes out like a giant blue gum, pitching face first onto the car seat.*] Is this what he was like? [*Staring at him.*] Maybe that's what it is? Maybe by trying to forget it or pretending it never happened, I'm imagining all sorts of things that were never there. I'm being frightened by a dream ... [*PA groans.*] Only it *wasn't* a dream. I was there. I was here ... [*He wanders stage left, looking off, trying to place something.*] I'm here now as sure as the day I ran out of petrol. Yes ... ! That broken sign by the gate. [*A beat.*] Let me tell you about it. [*He comes down to the audience again as 'Trekliedjie' folds in gently beneath his dialogue. There is a lighting cross-fade during which PA gets up and enters the caravan. It is early evening now. Standing beside the braai area, still and unmoving, is a young black man (GIDEON). He is plainly dressed. Neat, well-worn white shirt and dark trousers. He has a vicious (though old) rope-like scar in the region of his Adam's apple. The scar is partially hidden by a tattered red rag, tied like a scarf around his neck.*] Sweetfontein. At least, that's what the locals called it. Except there was nothing sweet about it. In fact, it might just as well have been called *Sweat*fontein – a lot of sweat and toil and nothing to show for it ... [*CHRISTIAAN walks about the set. Having created the new scene for us, he continues mapping out the territory.*] A smallholding. Not unlike many farm plots you find scattered around the edges of towns and cities all over the country. Part-time farmers. Sort of – sometime mechanics. Odd-job operators trying to keep going any way they can ...

The distant 'Trekliedjie' is replaced by the sound of Roy Orbison's 'Only the Lonely' emanating from inside the caravan. CHRISTIAAN pauses, smiling. PA's voice joins in the singing on the record. He croons lustily and, very soon, the sound becomes irritating. A young woman's voice is heard – sharp, insistent.

EVIE: Shaddap! [*PA drones on.*] Shaddap, man ... !

PA sings even louder now, butchering Roy Orbison's lyrical tones. The music is abruptly snapped off.

PA: What the bladdy hell you do that for?
EVIE: Because.
PA: Because!
EVIE: Because.
PA: Because why?
EVIE: Because. I'm trying to listen to the song.
PA: So, listen to your song!
EVIE: With *you* singing!?
PA: What's wrong with a person singing along with a bladdy song, man!?
EVIE: You kill the song.
PA: I kill the song!? The song's dead long time already! It's a kak song ... !
EVIE: So why you sing it?
PA: Why?

EVIE: Why?

PA [*a beat*]: Y's a crooked letter, you can't make it straight.

EVIE: Very funny.

There is a mumbling and a grumbling from PA. CHRISTIAAN *stands beside* GIDEON *– looking at him, but addressing the audience.*

CHRISTIAAN: The one they called Gideon was the first one I met. I knew nothing about him then, but there was something that told me he wasn't here part time ...

Inside the caravan, PA *has sat down to supper.*

PA: What's this?

EVIE: What's it look like?

PA: Is this *our* chicken or *town* chicken?

EVIE: Our chickens are all sick, you know that.

PA: So's this, by the looks of it.

EVIE: A chicken is a chicken is a chicken.

PA: Strangest chicken I've ever seen. Looks like aasvoel.

EVIE: You don't like it, don't eat it.

PA: I don't have much choice, do I?

EVIE: No. So, shaddap and eat!

CHRISTIAAN: And then – there was JJ.

PA: Where's JJ?

EVIE: How must I know?

PA: JJ! Where's that bladdy ... !? [*The door to the caravan is swung open and* PA *sticks his head out. He shouts at the top of his voice.*] JJ ... !! Come eat your supper! It's aasvoel! Aasvoel-a-la-king! Aasvoel-on-the-spit!

He slams the door, returning to his meal.

EVIE: Haa-bladdy-haa ...

They continue eating. CHRISTIAAN *thinks aloud, conjuring it up again – moving the story forward.*

CHRISTIAAN: Who was his favourite? Charles Somebody. Charles Jacoby. That's what he said. [*Considering this.*] Or Elvis. Maybe Elvis? [PA *begins humming – quietly at first. We recognise the tune* ('Are you Lonesome Tonight?'). CHRISTIAAN *smiles – he has guessed correctly.*] Elvis Presley ...

PA *hums louder now. It is inevitable that* EVIE *will respond.*

EVIE: Ag, man ... !

PA [*singing*]: 'Are you lonesome tonight ... ?'

EVIE: Shaddap!

PA: Hey-hey-hey – who you talking to!?

EVIE: You won't let me listen to *my* stuff, I don't wanna listen to yours ...

PA: You'll catch a klap, my girl ...

EVIE: I don't care ...

PA: Just now I'll send you outside ... !

EVIE: I'll *go* outside ... !

PA: No, you won't – *I'll* go outside ... !

EVIE: Then go ... !

They speak over each other now, a full scale fight, pots and pans clattering to the floor, amid shouts and general abuse.

PA: Bladdy hell ... ! I don't see why I should put up with a lot of nonsense from a silly bitch who can't even cook a decent bladdy meal, let alone let a oke sing at his own bladdy dinner table ... !!

EVIE: Nothing would make me happier ... ! Moaning about the way I cook all the time! If you hate the way I cook, why the hell don't you try it yourself sometime!? Go ... ! Get out ... ! Go ... !!

PA stumbles out of the caravan with his plate of food, the door slams and is locked behind him. For one blissful moment, there is absolute silence. He shakes his head and seems to address CHRISTIAAN. This provides the younger man with an opportunity to study him afresh.

PA: No respect for her father, that one. A father is king in his own castle, that's what they tell you. But it's a klomp twak. Nothing but a moersa klomp twak.

CHRISTIAAN [*studying him close up*]: Yes. Yes, that's the face. The face is right ... [*PA turns and heads for the car seat. CHRISTIAAN studies his gait.*] And the walk. The walk of a man who's had too much to carry.

PA plonks himself onto the car seat, addressing the black man angrily.

PA: What you doing here, Gideon? You not here anymore. Bugger off, man.

GIDEON does not budge. PA chomps at the chicken.

CHRISTIAAN: Yes, that's him. That's him orraight. An old man. A young man. A man old – before his time.

PA holds up a drumstick, his tone is pure vitriol.

PA: Chicken, she calls it. Poultry ... ! I wouldn't even give it the dignity of calling it fowl. [*What follows is for EVIE's benefit.*][*Shouting.*] You'll be rid of me one day, don't worry! One day, I'm putting the wheels on this caravan and I'm trekking off. I'm pulling out. Leave all you bastards to yourselves! [*to GIDEON.*] You included. Bugger off, Gideon, you spoiling my supper now!

CHRISTIAAN: Supper was one thing. But to spoil his TV!

PA [*checking his watch and exploding off the car seat*]: Shit! Evie ... ! [*Haring to the caravan door and hammering at it.*] Evie, open up, man! Evie ... !

EVIE: Go to hell!

PA: Please, man – it's Murder, man! Bladdy Murder She bladdy Wrote, man!

EVIE: Shoulda' thought of that before.

PA: No, no – I apologise. From the deeps of my heart. As it says in the Bible, I'm repentant – like Joshua. [*Half to himself.*] Or was it Abraham?

CHRISTIAAN: Isaac ... ?

PA: One a' those okes. Evie? Evie-weevie ... ?

EVIE: Don't waste your breath.

PA: Okay. Okay. Be like that. See if I care. [*Turning and going back to the car seat.*] I got a little black book, up here in my head. Your name's written down in big neon letters.

EVIE: My heart pumps custard.

PA [*resuming his meal*]: Fine. Okay. Fixed up.

> CHRISTIAAN *is at the Sasol drum. He removes the lid and checks inside it. He gives a surprised chuckle.*

CHRISTIAAN: Huh. I'd almost forgotten about this.

> *A big blond youth in his early twenties enters. He wears overalls and is covered in grease. He carries a tool box and curses under his breath, heading for the tap beside the caravan.*

PA: Yes-yes-yes. What took you so long?

JJ: That's the last time I do bogger-all for nobody!

PA: Good.

> JJ *slams the box down, washes his hands. He is livid.*

JJ: This bastard asks me to fix a' brake pads, okay? His clutch is shot to ribbons, so I replace a' clutch for him. Big favour. He says, no, it's the brake pads. I say, ja, ja – I know it's the brake pads. I'm still gonna do the brake pads. I'll do the brake pads tomorrow – meantime, I'd like a' money for the clutch, please ...

PA [*knowing what is coming*]: Haa-ha ...

JJ: He tells me to go get stuffed!

PA: Shoulda' done the brake pads.

JJ: And then what? He sits with a clapped-out clutch ... !?

PA: Customer is always right.

JJ: Customer's a fucken doos!

PA: Language! Language!

JJ: 'Strue's bob, I'm gonna get that car – stick back his old clutch and strip his brakes, sat. Front, back – the works!

PA: What's that gonna achieve?

JJ: Hopefully, one dead doos – smack against a brick wall!

PA: My son, the Good Samaritan.

JJ: Ungrateful bastard.

PA pokes at his chicken. JJ washes his hands at the tap.

CHRISTIAAN: I never knew what it stood for – JJ. I never had time to ask.

PA: Pull finger. Your supper's getting cold. Huh! Probably better that way.

JJ: What you saying to me?

PA: What pisses me off most is that, these days, they feed them so much fish meal you don't know if you getting chicken or Kentucky Fried Fucken Kingklip.

JJ: Shit ...

PA: They give you all that Festive-Rainbow-Farmer Brown-balanced bullshit, meantime baby chicks are growing fish fingers. Scales instead a' feathers! Soon you gonna have to start catching your bladdy chicken with a fishing rod – [*Demonstrating casting.*] hook – bait – and off you go ... ! Vizzzzz ... ! Kiep-kiep-kiep-kiep! [*JJ is shaking empty turps bottles, becoming frustrated.*] I tell you – I feel like pulling into town and catching a nice Pub Special at the Station Hotel. Lekker braaied steak on a roll. Tomato bredie. All the bladdy condiments you want.

JJ: What's happened to the turps?

PA: Worcester Sauce. Pickle Onions ...

JJ: These things all empty here.

PA: Where the days you could still swing a square meal for two rand twenty-five?

JJ: We running outa' turps.

PA: Take it easy with that. That's the last we got.

JJ: Bugger it.

CHRISTIAAN has wandered downstage, looking off.

CHRISTIAAN: There was also a house. Down by the gate. I'm sure there was a house ...

PA: How's it coming with the house?

JJ: What house?

PA: You didn't work on the house?

JJ: Where from? Had my hands full all day, man.

PA: Chopping down trees again?

JJ: I wasn't chopping trees ...

PA: We got to fix the house before we fix the fence. What's the point of having a smart-fancy fence and fok-all house to live in!?

JJ: I was fixing a' oke's car.

PA: Los all that shit! Where's a' priorities here? I'm busting my gat trying to coax a cabbage out the ground – you fiddling around with somebody's clutch!

JJ: We need the money.

PA: We need some order, that's what we need. We need some discipline. A plan of attack ... ! I got a team a' oxen here, all pulling in different bladdy directions! What about that alarm? You sort out that alarm on the packing shed?

JJ: Ja, ja ...

PA: Windows? Doors? Trip-wires all connected?

JJ: Trip-wires don't work.

PA: What d'you mean, trip-wires don't work? It works on bladdy trip-wires!

JJ: Not anymore.

PA: Jissus. I'm pissing against the wind with you people! How d'you expect the bladdy alarm to go off!?

JJ: Don't worry about it.

PA: I worry about it all the time ... !

JJ: It's organised. I'm handling it.

PA: Ja, like you handle the bladdy house ... ! [*JJ turns and moves off around the downstage side of the caravan.*] Hey-hey, you don't walk away from me when I am talking to you, young man! I'll klap you from here to kingdombladdy come!

JJ reappears, tossing a Hyperama bag at his father. It contains a large, battery-operated loud hailer.

JJ: Here, man.

PA: And now! What's this?

JJ: New system.

PA squeezes a button beside the trigger, causing a short, sharp siren-type whoop. He flinches.

PA: You wire it up to this, or what?

JJ: No, man. You get a kaffir*.

PA: I get a kaffir?

JJ: You get a kaffir to stand there.

PA [*a beat*]: And where am I gonna find this kaffir? You think kaffirs grow on trees?

JJ: Gideon can do it.

PA: Gideon's gone. He's not here anymore.

JJ approaches GIDEON, intent on having some fun.

JJ: What's this? His shadow? [*Barking like a dog, to GIDEON.*] Woof-woof! What you doing here? [*to PA.*] What's he doing here?

PA: I know what he's trying to do, but he can forget it.

---

* This word is offensive but has been retained because it is an accurate reflection of the character and the historical era in which this play is set.

JJ: Looking for a handout, hey, Gideon? Huh? You want a pasela? Woofwoof!!

PA: Hey. Answer my bladdy question now, man. You actually expect a oke to parade up and down by the work shed, lugging this thing?

JJ: Why not?

PA: Jissus, poephol. We trying to set up a bladdy alarm system down there. Alarm's supposed to work twenty-four hours a day – round the bladdy clock. The way I look at it, that's three shifts – eight hours each. Three shifts – three kaffirs. A) where am I gonna find the money for three kaffirs when I can't even afford *one* kaffir – and B) even if I *had* three kaffirs, what's to stop the kaffirs breaking in and helping themselves? Tell me that! *[An~ then system that steals ... Brilliant! JJ has moved off in search of cleaning liquid.]* Sometimes I think you were born with your brains in your backside. Every time you go to the kakhuis, it's bye-bye some more brain cells! *[Raising the loud hailer to his lips]* POEPHOL ... ! DOOS ... ! *[Lowering the hailer, shaking his head.]* Yissus, it's not fair, hey, Gideon? The tricks the Good Lord plays on you? Three sons. One dies on the Border. One runs away. And I'm left with this ... ! *[Shouting off again.]* Wynand would've sorted it out! Wynand would've fixed that alarm chop-chop – trip-wires, the lot ... !

JJ returns, carrying a plastic bottle of used turps.

JJ: Wynand's dead.

PA: I know that. But you wait 'til Michael gets back.

JJ: Where from? Australia!?

PA: He's coming home. He's my son. Who do you think's going to run this bladdy farm ten years from now?

JJ: I am.

PA: You!?

JJ: S'right, ja.

PA: You couldn't run from here to the chicken-hok, you want to run a farm ... !?

JJ: It's not a farm, anyway. It's a vrot-stinking smallholding that's fucked-out finish!

PA: Whose fault is that!?

JJ: Things'll be different when I'm in charge.

PA: You'll be in charge over my dead body, ou boeta!

JJ: I can wait.

PA: Oh, ja ... !?

JJ: Wait 'til you peg. Wait 'til you croak. Drop off the bladdy tree ...

PA: Izatso, hey? How about trying for it now? Come on – you want it so bad ... !

JJ *[turning away]*: Ag ...

PA: Ka-maan ... ! I dare you! Come! *[Shoving him, pushing for a fight.]* You fulla' such big talk! You reckon you can take over ... ?

JJ: Voetsek, man ... !

PA: I'll kill you before you take over, you good for nothing piece a' bladdy bokdrol!

JJ: Piss-off, man ...

PA: Jislaaik ... !

PA is stung into action, trapping JJ against the side of the caravan as he tries to escape.

JJ: Hey, take it easy ... !

PA: You been looking for a bladdy good klap and, boy, you gonna get it now ... !

JJ tries to scramble away but is tackled. PA kicks him on the ground and dives on to him as the youngster tries to crawl beneath the caravan.

EVIE comes out of the caravan. A young woman in her mid-twenties, she wears high-heels, slacks and a fancy top – her 'going out' clothes.

PA is laying into JJ. She does her best to separate them, but they roll about like a couple of wild dogs.

EVIE: What's going on here ... !? Stop it! Stop it, man! When you gonna bladdy grow up!?

PA [*panting heavily*]: Think you can take on your old top, hey? No, my boy. I'm sorry ... !

JJ [*struggling*]: Bugger you, man!

While the struggle goes on, EVIE moves to the tap beside the caravan and grabs a half-empty bucket of water. She hurls it over PA, who is by this time astride JJ, his hands on his throat. The cold shower forces PA to jerk bolt upright.

PA: Waaaaaaah!!

JJ: Shit ... !

JJ uses the opportunity to roll clear and charge into the caravan, locking the door behind him.

PA [*to EVIE*]: Bitch! You bladdy ... ! Jissus! Where's he gone!? [*Heads for the caravan door, hammering on it.*] Come outa' there, you little bliksem!

JJ: Up yours!

PA [*battering the door*]: Blikskottel!

JJ: One day I'm gonna get you! One day you gonna be dead ... !

PA: Never ... !

JJ: Vrek! Finish! Pushing up fucken daisies!

PA: Who's gonna kill me? You and what nuclear heat-seeking atomic bladdy warhead ... !!

EVIE: For God-sake, man ... !

PA: I fought a leopard with my bare hands! With these bare bladdy hands, boy!

JJ: Talk kak, man!

PA sneezes powerfully and looks down at his soaked clothing.

PA: Jissus! Look at me. I'm drenched! A person could catch his death of pneu-bladdy-monia, man!

EVIE: I'm sorry, but you asked for it.

PA: Thanks a lot. I'll invoice you for the funeral. [*He looks her up and down for the first time since she emerged from the caravan.*] And now? What's this?

EVIE: What's what?

PA: This!

EVIE: This?

PA: This, ja! That!

She looks down at her clothes.

EVIE: I'm not in tonight.

PA: And where the bladdy-hell you think you going?

EVIE: Out.

PA: Out? [*to GIDEON.*] She's going out. [*to EVIE.*] In trousers?

EVIE: What's wrong with that?

PA: Since when does a lady wear trousers?

EVIE: I'm taking the bakkie, okay?

PA: Since when does a young woman put on pants?

EVIE: I'll be back before twelve.

PA: Your mother never wore pants!

EVIE: They not pants. They tights.

PA: They what?

EVIE: They slacks.

PA: Slacks ... !?

EVIE: Helencas. Body-tights. Fashion-fits.

PA: Don't give me any fancy names! They trousers. They pants. Dis 'n blerrie broek, man!

EVIE: Can I take this bakkie now, or what?

PA: How on earth do you expect to catch any man, dressed like that?

EVIE: I'm not trying to 'catch' any man ... !

PA: Of course you are. Why do you think you go into town all the time? You looking for a husband to father your children.

EVIE: Oh, God ...

PA: Ha-haa ... ! I know young girls, jong. They squirt that stuff under their ears. They dress up to the nines. They shout – look at me, I'm up for grabs.

EVIE: Hell, but you can talk some shit, sometimes.

PA: Language! Language ... !

EVIE: Stick your stupid bladdy bakkie, man!

PA: Hey-hey-hey ... !

EVIE: I'll stay at home.

PA: Bladdy hell. You better pull yourself together, my girl. It's just as well your poor mother's no longer alive. The way you been behaving lately, your conduct would've killed her.

EVIE: I'm gonna go crazy here.

PA: You put on something respectable. You put on something that upholds the good name of this family – that honours the memory of your dear departed mother, may she rest in peace – I'll think about it. Until then, the subject is closed. [*He heads for the car seat where his plate is, stopping to address* GIDEON *again.*] And you!? What the bladdy hell d'you want now, Gideon? You beginning to irritate the hell outa' me!

EVIE: Maybe he wants a lift into town.

PA: Ja, well – nobody's going into town, are they? And since nobody's going into town, he can't have a lift, can he? [*to* GIDEON.] Now, bugger off, Gideon. I'm not going to tell you again. [*Rattling the caravan door.*] JJ! Open up! I wanna get outa' these wet clothes here. [*He sneezes. Then, to* EVIE.] You see? You see!? Bladdy bronchitis ... !

He moves around the back of the caravan. EVIE *and* GIDEON *exchange glances, there is an unspoken communication between them.* CHRISTIAAN *picks this up immediately.*

CHRISTIAAN: Now, if I imagined that – why did I? Maybe if he had gone, like they were trying to force him to ... ? But he never did. But then again, there was a whole story before I 'stumbled upon this heartland I never knew existed ...' [*Turning to leave.*] Me and my empty petrol can ...

He moves off slowly, stopping as though he is considering saying something else. He decides against it, disappearing along the route by which he entered.

PA is still out of sight, at the rear of the caravan. JJ *emerges tentatively, peeking out of the door. He munches at a chicken drumstick.*

JJ [*to* EVIE]: Shhh.

PA [*behind caravan, banging*]: Somebody's looking for it, boy. Looking for it very hard.

He comes around to the front again in time to see JJ *skip safely to the other side of* EVIE. *The youth grins, taunting his father.*

PA [*to* JJ]: You still gonna see your gat, ou boeta.

JJ: Please! From you? You're like yesterday's dry fart. All noise – no voema!

PA: Jissus! Little bliksem!

PA hares off after him. JJ *cackles away like a demented reprobate.*

EVIE and GIDEON watch each other. She is on the car seat – angry, hurt, trying to control her emotions.

EVIE: Have you eaten today? You want me to go get you something? [*She looks at him.*] No? If you don't want any chicken, there's – no?

She turns away again. There is an awkward pause.

EVIE: So. [*She looks at him. Looks away.*] I think it's just stupid, that's what I think … !

He makes a swift, emphatic gesture. Placing one fist on top of the other. She knows immediately what he means.

EVIE: Ja, but it's not going to work, can't you see that? It's not going to get them to change their minds!

He punches his chest. Again, her response is immediate. She jumps up, striking him.

EVIE: Ag, you're so stupid, man! Okay, do it your way … !

GIDEON gesticulates with great passion, dropping to the ground, scooping up the earth and rubbing it into his face.

EVIE: Ja, but you know they don't care! They don't give a damn that your ancestors are buried here! [*She shrugs, hopelessly.*] I thought of it again today, you know – down at the farm stall. How easy it would be to just stand there at the side of the road – jump out when a car comes past. It's very quick.

GIDEON makes a slight move towards her. PA returns. He is panting heavily, his limp more pronounced now.

PA: Only when I run. Only then does it hurt. Little bit. Otherwise it's fine. First Class. [*He stops and stares at GIDEON, then turns to EVIE.*] Come inside, Evie. We watch ol' whatsisname, man – on the TV. Lotsa' laughs.

EVIE: Stick your laughs. Thanks all the same.

PA: You're just cross 'cause I won't let you go into town. [*She darts a look at him. He beams, begins crooning.*] 'Is your heart filled with pain? Will you come back again? Pah-pah-pee-pah-pah-pah-pah-pah-paaah … ' [*He heads for the caravan, his jaw set.*] Don't let me start counting, Gideon. Because if I start counting, you in big trouble, my boy. [*Entering the caravan, he pulls off his wet shirt, replacing it.*] No, man. You don't want to go into town, man. You hate town. What's in town, anyway? Drink. Drugs. Lazy bastards who got nothing better to do than hang around bladdy discos, boozing all night.

EVIE [*half to herself*]: Home from home.

There is an angry cry from inside the caravan.

PA: Hey … ! What the bladdy-hell … !? [*He emerges with a half-empty bottle of*

Klipdrift, highly indignant.] Where's my line?

EVIE [*not happy to see him drinking*]: What line?

He is eyeing GIDEON, *suspiciously.*

PA: I put lines on my bottles. It tells me if people have been into them or not ... !

EVIE: I thought you weren't supposed to be drinking anymore?

PA: That is not the answer to my question ... !

EVIE: You go through your bottles so fast, you don't have *time* to put lines on them.

He stares at her, caught out. He plunges back into the caravan, pouring himself a tot.

PA: Jissus ...

EVIE: You were stopping. You said so.

PA: My last one. My very last one. Let's call this a toast to my last one. [*He comes out of the caravan and stops on the top step, raising his glass.* EVIE *is far from amused.* PA's *eyes are on* GIDEON *now. His voice is cold – a slow burn.*] It seems all I do around here is spend my time talking to brick walls. [*to* GIDEON.] You getting deaf now, Gideon? Huh? You deaf now as well as dumb? Okay. Orraight. For the last and final time. Bye-bye. Totsiens. Hamba kahle. [*He looks to* EVIE. *She watches* GIDEON *with a thrill of expectation at what promises to be some kind of a showdown.* PA *looks to* GIDEON *and back to* EVIE.] Is there something the matter here?

EVIE: He's not moving.

PA: I can see that.

EVIE: In case you hadn't noticed, he's been standing there all day.

PA: All day, has he? I can think of better ways of spending the day when you should be out looking for work.

EVIE: He obviously doesn't think so.

PA: And you? What about you?

EVIE: What do you mean?

PA: You know very well what I mean! You read his mind? Or do you two have some secret code nobody else understands?

She darts a look at GIDEON *before replying.*

EVIE: We talk.

PA: Oh, you 'talk'? To you, he talks? He talks to my daughter. My slet of a daughter. Who behaves like a hoer and wears men's clothing! To her, he talks! [*Bearing down on her.*] Maybe you'd be so kind as to explain to me how a man with no voice manages to talk! Or are you the one who does all the talking!?

EVIE: Why you so cross all of a sudden?

PA: He's been fired! I've fired him! As from twelve o'clock last night. What did I tell him? Sweetfontein is not a retirement village. It's not a home for the handicap. He wants to stay here – he works here!

EVIE: He's got no problem working here ...

PA: Then let him work.

EVIE: Fine. Then it's just a question of paying him.

PA: He gets his pay! He gets his pap. He gets his meat. He gets his ...

EVIE: That's not pay.

PA: I pay him in kind.

EVIE: He doesn't want it in kind. He wants it in money.

PA: Money!? Hah! What do I look like? A bank!? Huh? Barclays? Volkskas? I look
like the First Standard National bladdy Trust Bank!? How many times do I have
to tell you, there's a campaign against me! A vicious, orchestrated campaign to
bring me to my knees!

EVIE: Ag, ja, Pa. That's a bit tired now ...

PA: Tell me they didn't build that new road on purpose, cutting off my farm stall!
And the dam! Those bastards who put up the dam so my river gets no water ... ?
I'm surrounded by enemies who want to destroy me!

He turns to the tap to add water to his brandy.

EVIE: I don't see what all this has got to do with Gideon? All he wants is his share.

PA: Me too, ja.

EVIE: What he was promised ... !

PA: Hey-hey-hey ... ! What's this 'share' now, all of a sudden!?

EVIE: You promised Ma. The day she died. You said he'd always have a home here.

PA: Never ... !

EVIE: I heard you. I was there.

PA: She was dying. She was on her death bed. What else you expect me to say!?

EVIE: So you lied?

PA: It was a totally unreasonable request. I loved your mother, bless her heart, but
the English are mad. They want to give the world away!

EVIE: You lied to a dying woman.

PA [*heavenward*]: Emily, forgive me! [*to* EVIE.] I said it. But I didn't mean it like that.

EVIE: Then you admit it?

PA: Yes. No! You confusing me! I struggle. I suffer. Look at me – [*He lifts his trouser
leg, revealing his suppurating shin to* GIDEON.] Forty-eight years old! Jissus!
When my father was fifty, he was like a tree ... ! [*Pausing to gather his strength
for a final, calculated attack.*] Your father never wanted money. He never spoke
of his 'share'. He was satisfied with the roof over his head, the shirt on his
back and food – food in his belly. Shelter from the wind and the rain, and a
protecting – helpful hand. Voetsek! Out of my sight! Gagga!

JJ returns. A spent, exhausted PA *looks across at him. The youth senses the tension.
Perhaps he was watching.*

JJ: What's going on here?

PA: Him. He doesn't want to go away.

JJ: Don't make me laugh. He's gone long time orready.

PA [*to* GIDEON]: You hear that? You gone long time orready.

EVIE: No, he's not.

PA [*to* EVIE]: You keep out of this.

JJ: He's finish and klaar.

EVIE: Ma said he can stay here as long as he likes.

JJ: Ma said – Ma's not here anymore.

PA: I say he's gone. And if I say he's gone …

JJ: She's always on his side.

EVIE: It's not a question of sides.

PA: Who the bladdy hell's in charge here!?

JJ: You watch. Just now she's gonna come with that crap about his ancestors grazing here with their cows.

PA: Kakstories!

JJ: How they were here before us!

PA: Strond! Kak! Rubbish!

JJ: She always comes with that.

EVIE: Maybe it's true …

PA: I don't wanna hear it! I don't wanna hear it!

During the course of all this, GIDEON *quietly takes his leave – no-one should notice it, hopefully not even the audience.*

JJ *is not letting up on* EVIE.

JJ: Why don't you tell him, hey? [*to* PA.] When they drive in the bakkie – when they go into town – she lets him sit in the front!

PA: She does what?

EVIE: Only when it rains.

JJ: I've seen her. I've seen him.

PA: In the front!?

JJ: In the bakkie.

PA: My bakkie!?

JJ: Next thing, she's gonna let him drive.

EVIE: Why not? He drives better than you do.

JJ [*to* PA]: She sells those shoes he makes! Those kaffir-takkies! In the farm stall … !

PA: Jissus … !

JJ: Sells more shoes than bladdy vegetables … !

PA: How long's this been going on behind my … !? [*He spins around and sees that* GIDEON *has gone.*] Bladdy hell … ! Where's he gone? Gideon … !?

JJ, pumped up, is on the move.

JJ: Jislaaik! The bastard ... !

PA: Don't moer him! Don't kill him!

JJ darts this way and that, before plunging off into the darkness at full tilt.

JJ: Fok-it ... !

PA [*turning on* EVIE]: You see now? You see!? If that poor kaffir gets a hiding now, it's thanks to you. [*Looking off, anxiously.*] This is what comes of all your talk. You fill their heads with all sorts of nonsense, and then they don't know where they stand anymore. Now I'm not gonna tell you again. I'm the one who gives the orders around here, otherwise it's a total bladdy gemors.

He digs around in a pocket and contemptuously tosses the bakkie keys at her.

PA: Now, here. Go to your bladdy disco. Take the bladdy bakkie. You made me very sad tonight.

He enters the caravan, switching on the fairy lights as evening falls. EVIE *is left with her own thoughts – 'Trekliedjie' filters in with the mood change.*

From inside the caravan, we hear the heavy static of an unhealthy television set. Blows and curses from a disgruntled PA.

PA *emerges from the caravan and stands looking up at the TV aerial.*

PA: Now, why am I getting bugger all reception?

He looks around for something to throw at the aerial. Finds a battered, empty milk carton and various other potential projectiles. Begins tossing them. When he scores a direct hit, he goes inside to check the results. A muffled 'shit!' is heard. The static snaps off.

JJ blasts by, out of breath, brandishing an iron pipe. He charges off in another direction, spitting fire.

PA *emerges holding a pair of homemade bunny ears – three metal coat hangers stuck together with copper wire and tape – and spots* EVIE *staring up into the night sky. He moves to join her on the car seat.*

PA [*after a pause*]: Penny for your thoughts. [*She looks at him, then back at the night sky.*] What you looking, Evie? Huh? What you looking ... ? Oh, yes – I can see it. Up there in the sky. One of those shuttlecock things. Americans. Incredible, you know. Man's quest. First they sent up a dog. Then they sent up a monkey. And then they sent up a Kommunis. [*She looks at him.*] Before your time. I was sitting outside with Wynand. Down there by the house. He was still tiny, man. Still a baby. I pointed up into the sky, I said – look, Wynand. There goes Yuri

Gagarin. You know what he did? He kotched all over my shoulder. [*EVIE is not responding the way* PA *feels she should. He takes the bakkie keys from her lap and pockets them.*] So. You're not going into town? Wise girl. And you mustn't worry. Your mother came to me. I can feel it in my bones. It's any day now.

EVIE: What's any day now?

PA smiles. It is the dream that keeps him alive.

PA [*pointing out front*]: He's going to come riding up here, over the bult. A white Mercedes. Tinted windscreens. Air conditioning. He's going to pull up in front here and climb out. A tall man. Blond. Brown with the sun. He's going to come across to me and put out his hand. Pa, he's going to say, Pa – he's not going to call me mister or meneer or sir, anything like that. Pa, he's going to say – I've come for your daughter. And I'm going to lead you out and present you to him. And there's going to be this huge big wedding. The church is going to be stampvol – people coming from all around. Ox braai. Lamb on the spit. Singing and dancing and carrying on. And you going to come back here, the two of you, and move into the farmhouse. And he's going to take over this place. Build it up again. Make it like it was before. Before they started with all their nonsense.

She stares at him long and hard, getting up.

EVIE: You been watching too much TV.

PA: Uh-uh. Aikona. You see, your mother spoke to me. I heard her voice loud and clear. It's been ordained in the eyes of the Lord. [*He leans forward and kisses her gently on her forehead, before turning to enter the caravan.*] Everything's going to be fine again, Evie. Everything's going to be okay. You'll see.

JJ arrives, more composed now. He smiles smugly at EVIE.

JJ: He's gone. Looks like the bastard finally saw the light. Pity, actually. I was looking forward to kicking a bit a' black gat.

As he enters the caravan, closing the door behind him, we hear him and PA *laughing raucously.*

EVIE *is not alone for long. The laughter has barely started when* GIDEON *crawls out from under the caravan. He moves to the lounge chair, rolling a homemade smoke. 'Trekliedjie' swells to cover the fade to black and scene change.*

Scene Two

Late afternoon. JJ is perched atop the caravan, repositioning the TV aerial. He conducts a conversation with PA, who is inside the caravan, fiddling with the control panel. The tone of their voices suggests they have been at it for some time.

JJ: Now? Now ... !?

PA: No.

JJ [*adjusting aerial*]: Now?

PA: No. [*JJ moves it again.*] Wait-wait-wait ... ! Wait!!

JJ: What?

PA: You moved it!

JJ: I'm s'posed to be moving it.

PA: Well, *don't* move it!

JJ: Don't move it. Okay.

PA [*a beat*]: Okay. Move it.

JJ: Move it?

PA: Move it!

     JJ tentatively moves it.

JJ: How's that?

PA: No.

JJ: Now?

PA: Uh-uh.

JJ: Nothing at all!?

PA: Just a whole lota' zig-zags. Scrambled eggs.

JJ: What frequency you got?

PA: What d'you mean – frequency?

JJ: On the channel.

PA: Which channel?

JJ: The channel that it's on.

PA: Ah, wait – there's a little sort of a thinga-ma-jig ... !

JJ: A knob?

PA: No, sorta' whatjoo-macallit ...

JJ: Button?

PA: No, man! Sort of dingamalerie thing with a whole lota' junk written here – thirteen and a four. And then sixty-eight and a ...

JJ: You gotta look for the button with a little knob next to it ...

PA: Knob?

JJ: Or a button.

PA: A button ... !?

JJ: Kind of switch.

PA: Make up your bladdy mind, man!

JJ: It's either set on UHF or VHF.

PA: VHF ... ?

JJ: You not using that bunny ears again!?

PA appears in the doorway, holding the homemade aerial.

PA [*highly indignant*]: You sat on my bunny ears!

JJ: Los a' bunny ears – you bugger up the signal.

PA: Shaddap. I know what I'm doing here. Squeeze the orange.

JJ: Squeeze a' orange?

PA: Squeeze the bladdy orange, man ... !

JJ: What for?

PA: Why you think I got the orange up there – decoration!? [*JJ squeezes the orange.* PA *looks back into the caravan.*] You see! We got a picture!

JJ: We gotta picture!?

PA: Beautiful picture – only it's green!

JJ: Green? What d'you mean – green?

PA: Green, man – green! Fokken Martians all over the bladdy screen!

JJ: Give it a klap ...

PA: I don't mind a green Joan Collins, but bladdy Magnum PI!

JJ: Give it a bit of a smack.

PA: Magnum Pea Soup.

EVIE enters. She carries a battered money tin and the farm stall keys. She sits down on the car seat.

EVIE: God, you still at it?

The menfolk ignore her completely. PA *tries to get a signal by moving the bunny ears around.*

PA: Aaag, jislaaik ... !

EVIE has opened her tin and started checking cash slips and so on.

EVIE: Get rid of it. More trouble than it's worth.

PA [*reappearing, to EVIE*]: Hey! Enough a' your snide comments. You get any customers today?

EVIE: Three or four.

PA: Is that all!?

EVIE: No, wait a minute, I lie. Two, to be exact. Or rather, two and a half.

PA gives the bunny ears cord a hefty yank, unplugging it.

PA: Hey! There's a' luck! It's working!

JJ: What's on? Pumpkin Patch?

JJ proceeds to tighten the aerial in place. PA begins winding up the cord.

PA: At last! Fantastic, man.

EVIE: Mad, if you'll spend as much time on people woek as you do on the TV!

PA [*coming out*]: Hey, this is critical, hey. I got a feeling they gonna kill Bobby
    tonight.

EVIE: All my life.

PA: JR's got something up his sleeve.

JJ: Cliff Barnes.

PA [*to JJ*]: You think so?

JJ: Charlene Tilton.

EVIE: Haven't they already killed Bobby?

PA: Are you mad!?

JJ: They tried to kill him, but he wasn't properly dead.

PA: He was properly dead, but he wasn't physically dead because the whole thing
    was actually a dream.

EVIE: A dream?

PA: Ja. But now I got a feeling they *really* gonna actually kill him, like they killed
    Pam the last time.

EVIE: Pam's dead, is she?

PA [*to JJ*]: 'Pam's dead' – listen to this.

EVIE: I thought maybe that was also a dream?

PA: Listen, my girl. You can't distinguish between reality and fantasy in this world –
    you in deep trouble. Moer of a deep.

JJ [*back on terra firma now*]: The one person they should really wipe out is Mizellie.
    She's a total pain in the gat.

He enters the caravan, PA following him.

PA: No-no-no, she's okay. I tell you where the real kak started. It started when Bobby
    left Jenna. Bobby leaves Jenna, Jenna shacks up with Ray Krebbs, and then all of
    a sudden everyone's shacking up with everyone else.

EVIE starts reading a magazine.

JJ: Where my beers?

He emerges from the caravan, PA *following.*

PA: Ray Krebs must leave Jenna. Jenna must go back to Bobby. And Bobby must forget about Pam. Finish and klaar.

JJ is scratching around the braai area.

JJ: There's nothing wrong with Ray Krebs, hey?

PA: Ray Krebs is okay.

JJ: I like Ray Krebs.

PA: Same here. But Ray should rather sort of – be on his own.

JJ [*opening outside stove, cupboard, and so on*]: What if he doesn't wanna be on his own?

PA: He's much better on his own, man. He's a bachelor-type. He should stay with his horses. Home on the Range.

JJ [*to* EVIE]: You seen the beers?

EVIE [*staring daggers at him*]: There no beers.

JJ: What d'you mean – there no beers?

EVIE jerks out a foot, catching him on the shin.

JJ: Eina!

PA [*rambling on*]: As for that bitch, Sue Ellen, JR must put her against a bladdy wall and shoot her. That's the only answer.

JJ [*to* EVIE, *rubbing his leg*]: What's your case?

EVIE [*hissing*]: Do I have to spell it out for you?

PA [*going back into the caravan*]: His biggest mistake was to marry her again. First time he divorced her, he shoulda' kicked her out for good. Alcoholic slet!
[*Abruptly.*] Hey! Where's my booze?

EVIE [*to* JJ]: You *see* now!?

PA: Who the hell's taken my bladdy bottle!?

EVIE [*trying to change the subject, loudly*]: JJ's fixed the power-saw, Pa!

PA [*sticking his head out*]: What?

EVIE: Your power-saw. JJ's fixed it.

PA [*a beat*]: I didn't know it was broken.

EVIE: Ja, well. I'm just telling you. It was broken – now it's fixed.

PA: Until he breaks it again. Where is it?

JJ [*glaring at his sister*]: It's fixed.

PA: Where is it!? [*JJ picks it up from behind the box of cabbage leaves – begins to activate it.*] Jislaaik! look how you chew the blade here.

JJ: Blade's still okay.

PA: That was a new blade!

JJ: There's nothing wrong with it. I mean, look. Check here, man ...

With the power-saw working, he searches for something on which to demonstrate its effectiveness. EVIE *and her magazine provide a wonderful opportunity to extract some sort of revenge.* JJ *moves around in front of her and reduces the magazine to confetti as she hurls it at him.* EVIE *freaks out completely.*

EVIE: Jesus Christ! Are you ... !? Are you totally out of your ... !? You coulda' chopped my bladdy – shit!

Both JJ *and* PA *are helpless with laughter.*

JJ: Shredded Wheat!

PA: Instant bladdy snow-storm ...

EVIE runs into the caravan.

EVIE: To hell with you!

PA [*trying not to laugh*]: Evie, wait ... !

JJ: Check this thing ...

PA: I shouldn't laugh but, jislaaik, that was funny ... !

JJ: Use it for braai paper.

PA: Confetti ...

Music is banged on in the caravan ('Stagger Lee' – Vinnie and the Viscounts).

JJ: She's woes now.

PA: Now she's woes.

JJ: No supper tonight.

PA: Bread and water.

JJ: Fantastic, man. Fantastic.

PA approaches the door, knocks on it.

PA: Evie ... !?

The music is banged up even louder. JJ *lets rip with the power-saw for good measure, and saunters off.*

PA [*shouting after him*]: Hey, take it easy with that thing now!

PA dances to the music, highly amused. He moves to the braai area and surreptitiously opens a storage box. Digs into it. He pulls out a half-empty bottle of Klipdrift, and begins unscrewing the bottle top eagerly.

A sound at the caravan door causes him to spin around, holding the bottle behind him. EVIE *is glaring at him from the top step.*

PA [*sheepishly*]: Evie ... ?

She goes back inside to switch off the ultra-loud music. PA *uses the diversion to hastily replace the bottle and cup in the box.* EVIE *re-emerges.*

EVIE: What you got there?

PA [*butter wouldn't melt ...*]: Nothing. No. I thought maybe we should have a braai tonight. Sort of – you know? Sort of –

EVIE: Let me help you.

PA: No-no, it's okay. I'll do it later. Really. It's okay ...

EVIE: Allow me.

She fishes the brandy bottle out of the box. PA *is forced to backtrack for all he is worth.*

PA: Hey, look at that! So *there* it is! How did that get in there ... ? [*He knows he cannot pull the wool over her eyes.*] Gideon was stealing the stuff. I had to sort of –

EVIE: Gideon doesn't drink.

PA [*a beat*]: Ha-haa! That's a good one. Show me a houtkop that doesn't drink, I show you –

He knows it is not working.

EVIE: How many more times we going to go through all this?

PA [*demonstrating*]: Just a little tot, man. Just so much ...

EVIE: What it's doing to your leg, Pa ...

She turns away from him, clutching the bottle.

PA: Look, I know what you thinking. You thinking, ja – whatsa' bet he's got dozens a' bottles hidden all over the place here? But that's not true ... !

EVIE: Pa, I got to talk to you.

PA: There's no problem, I promise. It's all under control ...

EVIE: It's about something else, Pa.

PA: I'm turning over a new leaf.

EVIE: I can't go on anymore!

PA [*a beat*]: What you talking?

EVIE: I'm talking *me*, Pa. Here. In this place. We live like animals. In a hok ...

PA: Everything's going to be okay ...

EVIE: I can't breathe ...

PA: When he comes, he'll make it right ...

EVIE: Don't look to someone else, Pa – look at *us!* You don't see it any more.

PA: Ever since your ma died – I know it – you been everything here. You been mother, daughter, house-meid, everything ...

EVIE: When I'm down at the farm stall ...

PA: No, wait a minute. Not mother. Not wife and mother. You going to be that soon ...

EVIE: Pa ...

PA: Your mother came to me ...

EVIE: You're not listening to me, Pa!

PA: You want to get out of the farm stall, just tell me. I get a kaffir ...

EVIE: It's not the farm stall – and don't call them kaffirs ... !

PA: You wanna go back to the Building Society, is that it?

EVIE: I'm not going back there.

PA: Then what is it?

EVIE: This is no life, Pa. Sometimes I'm sick. I get sick to my stomach! I wake up in the morning, I want to vomit!

PA [*quickly*]: You not in trouble? Don't tell me you in trouble!

EVIE: How would I be in trouble, Pa?

PA: You wouldn't do that to me! To our name ... !

EVIE: What name? Our name stinks orready – to High Heaven ...

PA: Don't you *ever* say that!

EVIE: I feel dirty – all the time. Every time I wash, it's like ... moving the dirt – my skin – my hair – my – my clothes –

PA: You got nice clothes. You look lovely in your clothes when you don't wear those – pants.

EVIE: Oh, God – I can't talk to you.

PA: Is that all you worried? You worried from your hair? You got nice hair – you got your mother's hair. Nicer even than Jenna Wade! [*Trying to make light of it by singing a television jingle.*] 'Sometimes you need a little Finesse – Sometimes you need a lot ... '

EVIE: It's okay, Pa – forget it.

PA: Are you a pretty girl, is that what you asking?

EVIE: I'm asking someone to hear me, Pa ...

PA: I hear you. I'm trying to help ... [*Pacing about, ill at ease.*] Evie. Listen. Whenever your mother wanted to talk ladies' talk, she used to phone your Auntie Winifred in Hazyview.

EVIE [*a beat*]: Ladies' talk?

PA: Ja. They used to go on for hours. Talking.

EVIE: What is ladies' talk, Pa?

PA: Don't ask me. It's the talk ladies talk when they want to talk about, sort of you know – ladies' things. [*EVIE rises slowly and enters the caravan. PA bumbles on.*] You want to go into town, there's a tickey-box by the Station Hotel. You can go phone her from there.

EVIE [*distracted*]: Ja.

PA: You can take the bakkie. Here the keys ...

EVIE: It's okay.

PA: No. Here you are. Come on.

EVIE: Just – leave me alone. Please.

PA: Okay. Fine. But I'm gonna put the keys here by the trellis, okay? Just in case. They on the hook. Anytime you want to go talk to your Auntie Winifred, you just – you know – feel free. [*He hangs the keys on the trellis. He moves to the sawn-off Sasol drum and removes the lid, pleased at being able to change the subject.*] Hell. It's coming on here, Evie. We winning. You must come see it. [*Tossing fresh cabbage leaves into it. Shaking up his solution and pouring it in.*] Soon be ready. [*Spotting* JJ *approaching.*] Hey, JJ … ! It's brewing here. It's cooking up a storm.

JJ is pumped up.

JJ: You're not gonna believe this. The bastard is still around. He slept in the pondok last night.

PA [*a beat*]: How do you know?

JJ: All his food. His pots and pans still inside there. [*He turns for the caravan.*]

PA: What you going to do?

JJ: Wait for him. Wait up all night, if I have to.

PA [*anxious*]: JJ!

JJ: What?

PA: Don't tell Evie.

JJ: Why not?

PA [*lowering his voice*]: Whatever you got to do, do it quietly. Don't make a fuss.

JJ: That's up to him, isn't it?

JJ enters the caravan. PA *continues working on the contents of his drum. He lays more cabbage leaves inside it, sprinkling salt and sour milk into it.*

Inside the caravan, we hear JJ *barging about, cursing angrily.*

EVIE: What you looking for?

JJ: Jissus, *there* they are! In future, you wanna hide my beers, you tell me where you put them.

EVIE: Hey! What you doing? What you want *that* for!?

JJ: Let go, man!

JJ emerges, struggling with EVIE *over a lethal-looking sjambok. He rips it from her grasp. Under his arm is a stick of biltong and a six-pack. He exits purposefully.*

EVIE: Pa … ! He's got the sjambok!

PA *is inspecting an old thermometer*

PA: Beautiful. Temperature's perfect.

EVIE: You said no more sjambok! You said never again!

PA: This is the batch, Evie. No question ...

EVIE: Leave that stupid stuff alone, for God-sake! [*Half going after* JJ.]

PA: This 'stupid stuff' as you call it, is going to make us rich beyond our wildest dreams.

EVIE: You know what he's going to do if he finds him, don't you!?

PA: So what?

EVIE: You said he could stay here!

PA: Who?

EVIE: You told me this morning. You said he could ... !

PA: I said he could leave his things here 'til he finds a new place!

EVIE: Then why you letting JJ take the sjambok!?

PA: Jissus, if it makes him happy to take the sjambok, then let him take the bladdy ...

EVIE: I don't believe this ... !

PA: [*exploding*]: Bladdy hell! Have you any idea what it's like trying to keep everybody happy around here!?

EVIE: Who the hell's happy ... !?

PA [*bearing down on her*]: Now listen to me! And listen very carefully. Gideon is gone. He's past history. He's water under the bladdy bridge ...

EVIE: He doesn't see it like that ...

PA: I don't care *how* he sees it. It's got nothing to do with him! [*Easing off.*] I never wanted it to end like this, but that's the way it has to be. From now on, I'm using cheap labour from the veld. I'm using people who do as they are told and give me no problems. I got enough problems as it is.

EVIE stares at her father in stunned disbelief while he meanders back to his 'processing plant'.

EVIE: God, it's no wonder he hates you.

PA: I know why he hates me. It's my own fault. I should've left him that time when he was three years old with the dogs.

EVIE: It's not the dogs ...

PA: It's the dogs! Guaranteed! I couldn't sleep last night, thinking about it. He knows he owes me, and he hates me for owing me.

EVIE: He *owes* you ... !?

PA: He owes me! He bladdy-well owes me ... !

EVIE: Because you threw some water on some dogs?

PA: Jissus, I risked my bladdy life! They nearly tore my hands to pieces! [*Looking at his hands, back at her.*] Shit. Ninety-seven stitches, the doctor gave him. I put in a few more myself. Fishing-gut nogal. Jissus, when we looked at his throat we couldn't tell what was meat and what was flesh. There was just this blood. Everywhere.

He turns back to his cabbage-culture.

EVIE: So you think because you saved his life, you have the right to run it?

PA: I'm not running anybody's life. He runs his own life. That's why I'm letting him go.

She moves to the caravan. He knows she is unimpressed by his argument.

PA: You think it's easy for me, hey? He was a good boy. He *used* to be a good
boy ... ! [*She has disappeared into the caravan.*] His father was a good boy! Old
Amos was one of the best. Old Amos will always have a place in my heart. A
very special place that you could never possibly understand ... [*She has emerged
from the caravan with her handbag, heading for the bakkie keys.*] What you
doing?

EVIE: Sort out your own supper tonight.

PA: You going into town?

EVIE [*taking the keys and leaving*]: Don't wait up for me.

PA [*shouting after her*]: Give my regards to your Auntie Winifred, hey. And reverse
the charges! She's got pots a' bladdy money. [*Shouting after her.*] And tell her
to remember us out here in the sticks! We still family! [*Turning away, half to
himself.*] Haregat English bitch ... [*Looking heavenward, quickly.*] Excuse a'
company, Emily, but – she was never one of my favourites, your sister. [*He turns
back to his cabbage-leaf culture.*] She always thought you pulled a raw one with
me. Well, we'll show them, jong. They be laughing on the other side of their
faces when we riding high and back on top again. [*Looking out towards the
road.*] But send him quick, Emily. That plume of dust. I mos know what a cloud
of dust from a Mercedes looks like ...

*He performs the pouring, stirring ritual in his Sasol drum, with all the tender care
and attention of someone absolutely convinced that 'alles sal regkom'.*

*As he hums happily to himself, 'Trekliedjie' folds in and the lights fade to black for
the scene change.*

Scene Three

As the lights fade up, 'Trekliedjie' gives way to the sound of a minister intoning the tail end of the Epilogue on television. It is beyond midnight. There is evidence of a one-man party – plates, bottles, photo albums lying open, a general mess. PA has passed out on the car seat, facing the audience. The television is positioned on a small table, set downstage, the aerial and battery wires leading into the caravan. The image flickers on his drunken, slumbering features. An empty Klipdrift bottle is held in his right hand that hangs limply to the floor.

Off stage, we hear the frenzied sounds of someone being whipped by a sjambok. In stark counterpoint, the minister's voice drones on.

JJ enters, carrying his sjambok (most of his beers and biltong long since finished). He breathes heavily, polishing off the final beer. He tosses the can away before entering the caravan and pulling the door closed behind him.

A couple of beats later, just as the Epilogue gives way to the National Anthem, GIDEON emerges from the shadows. He walks around to face the sleeping PA. The back of his shirt is torn, and we see the blood seeping through. He watches PA for a moment before moving to the Sasol drum. He removes the lid and – with 'Die Stem' still droning on – whips out his cock and begins pissing into it. Having relieved himself, he zips up, replaces the lid and casually saunters over to the rear of the TV. He jerks the cord from its socket, causing the anthem to snap off abruptly. He flexes the cord in his hands, moving towards PA. The sudden silence gives the moment added intensity. Almost as soon as we have guessed his intentions, he drops the cord and moves to the door of the caravan ... Is he going to go inside? He knocks boldly on the door. Nothing happens. He repeats the procedure. JJ's tired voice is heard from within.

JJ [lazily]: It's open, Evie. I'm not kaalgat. [GIDEON impishly knocks again, this time more loudly.] It's bladdy-well open, man!

GIDEON knocks at the door again and ducks away just in time to avoid being seen by JJ as he angrily swings open the door.

JJ [to his dead-to-the-world father]: Ha-ha! Big joke! You think I'm a poephol?

He storms back inside, slamming the door behind him. Yet again GIDEON repeats the action and disappears before JJ tears out of the caravan and unceremoniously dumps PA out of the car seat, sending him sprawling.

PA: Wha – !? What the ... !?

He flounders like a beached whale.

JJ: Wasn't born yesterday! [*He steps on the live TV cable*] Ei-naaa ... ! [*Hopping around on one leg, to* PA.] It's bladdy live, man! Think it's clever ... !? Coulda' killed me!

PA appears distressed, but by something far more serious than being dumped on the ground.

PA: Jissus ... ! JJ ... !? Where's my – where's my dop ... !? Jissus ... ! No ... !

He crawls around on his hands and knees, knocking plates, albums, and so on, aside in his search for a bottle with some alcohol in it.

EVIE enters, back from town, and stops in her tracks.

EVIE: What on earth – !?
PA: Evie ... ! Jislaaik!
EVIE: What's been going on here ... !? [*EVIE wanders around, aghast.*] [*to* JJ.] Who's responsible for all this?
JJ [*to* EVIE]: How the fok must I know?
PA: Tell me it's not true ... !
JJ [*to* EVIE]: Don't look at *me*!
PA: Jissus. JJ ... ! Evie ... !

EVIE starts to clear the debris.

EVIE: I go away for a coupla' bladdy hours ...
PA: Evie – JJ – ?
JJ: Don't try blame *me* now!
PA: There's no more ...
JJ: Shit ...

PA tops them both with an almighty scream that hangs in the air.

PA: THERE'S NO MORE COCA-COLA ... !!!

His cry serves to shut them up. They stare at him.

PA: I'm driving into town for my usual dop in the pub ...
EVIE [*barely audible*]: Pa ...
PA [*gritting his teeth, determined to tell it*]: But it's not there anymore! The Station Hotel is gone! And now I'm digging in the rubble like a bladdy baboon in a mishoop. I don't even know what it is I'm looking for – and then I find it ... ! It's the last bottle a' Klipdrift and it's the only one left ... ! [*Snatching up one of his own empty Klipdrift bottles.*] [*to* JJ.] But the bottle's fulla' cracks and the brandy's

sommer leaking out. The Greek! The Corner Greek ... ! I charge down to the Corner Greek and, thank God, he's still there. A Coke, I say to him. Coca-Cola! To go with my Klipdrift. He just looks at me! He's never heard of it!! And all the time the brandy's just seeping away onto the floor a' that cafe until there's bugger all left. And now I know it's true. No more Coke. No more Klipdrift. No more Nothing. [*He sobs, face to the ground.*]

JJ and EVIE *have entirely different attitudes to* PA'*s story. There is a pause before* JJ *breaks the silence.*

JJ [*unimpressed*]. And that's it ... ?
EVIE [*concerned*]: Come inside, Pa. It's bedtime.
JJ: Now, if that was Carling Black Label –

EVIE *tries to help* PA *to his feet. He shrugs her off.*

EVIE: What you doing?
PA: I'm going for a walk.
EVIE: A walk!?
PA: You kids go to sleep.
EVIE: You can't go walking this hour of the night!

He sits down, taking his shoes off.

PA: Bit a' fresh air, that's all. I want to look over my land.
EVIE: But it's dark. You won't see a thing!
PA [*rising to his full height, passionately*]: Who needs to see anything!? I can smell my land. I can feel it between my toes. I mos know my land!

They watch him move off into the gloom, a pathetic, broken man. EVIE'*s concern for him is outweighed by her anger.* JJ *is mildly amused by it all.*

EVIE: It's starting all over again. I can just see it. [*Turning on* JJ.] How could you let him get like that?
JJ: He gets like that himself.

She begins collecting debris.

EVIE [*in a cold, controlled fury, barely held in check*]: I thought we agreed to watch him?
JJ: You're the one who's watching him, not me. As far as I'm concerned, he can drown in the stuff.
EVIE: Meantime, I must carry on wiping up the kotch, changing his clothes, putting him to bed ... ?
JJ: You don't have to do anything. You can just sommer leave.
EVIE: Oh, wouldn't you just *love* that?
JJ: I thought that's what you were doing anyway?

The intensity of her anger takes him by surprise.

EVIE: Ja, well – think again!

JJ: But what about all the talk? How much you hate it here?

EVIE: You think because Michael left, I must also leave?

JJ: Michael left because *you* were leaving. You wanted to go more than *he* did!

EVIE: Your little plan's not working, so you might as well give it up.

JJ: What plan?

EVIE [*stopping her clearing up. Looking him straight in the eye*]: Don't think I don't know what you're doing. You been doing it all the time. Making it so lousy to live here that one by one, we all go away and leave you on your own. [*She knows he knows it is true.*] That's why the house never gets fixed. You don't want to fix it. It might just get too comfortable and you stuck with us for good.

JJ: What kak you talking now?

EVIE: It's true. Every time Gideon got started on the house, you always found some problem ...

JJ: That's 'cos he kept ballsing up.

EVIE: You just made it look that way.

JJ: Stupid poephol didn't know his arse from his elbow.

EVIE: You can talk! Leaving those bags of cement to go hard in the water.

JJ: That wasn't me!

EVIE: It wasn't Gideon either.

JJ: What is it with you and that kaffir, anyway!?

EVIE [*helpless in the face of this*]: Are you never gonna stop?

JJ: No. Not 'til he's gone. Gone for good! Too fulla' shit for his own bladdy good! [*Pointing off.*] If that old fart out there had listened to me in the first place, I'd of got this joint back on its feet long time oready. We need a clean out here. From the bottom, up. And you right – I'm glad Michael's buggered off. You must all bugger off. Everybody who keeps moaning all the time, must all bugger off. Leave it to those that know.

EVIE: Meaning you, I suppose?

JJ: I don't know how many times I said it. We build the fence. We put up the razor-wire. We kick out every bastard troublemaker and get on with our lives. It's so bladdy simple, it's a joke!

She stares at him as if at a stranger.

EVIE: What is it with you?

JJ: What?

EVIE: Sometimes I look at you, I wonder what's happened to my brother?

JJ: You want your brother – run to Michael.

EVIE: If anyone's running anywhere, it's you.

JJ: I'm staying right where I am ... !

EVIE: Oh, ja? Then why you so scared?

JJ [*aghast*]: Who the hell's scared!?

EVIE: The barbed-wire ... ? The fences ... ? I'd call that scared.

JJ: Security. That's what it is. Protection.

EVIE: Protection from what?

JJ [*staring at her*]: Typical woman.

EVIE: Protection from what?

JJ: From the dangers. There all sorts of dangers. Ask Pa. They come in the night. They come rape you!

She shakes her head, giving up on him.

EVIE: What a mess.

She begins clearing up again. He crouches beside her.

JJ: You don't see it. You let them suck up to you. And then – when you go to sleep – they kill you in your bed. [*Reaching out to her.*] But not while I'm here. With me here, you safe.

She pulls away from him.

JJ: No-one's gonna hurt you, Evie.

EVIE: Except you.

JJ: I would never hurt you. Never.

EVIE: What you doing ... ?

JJ: You my sister. I kill anyone who touches you ... [*He paws at her.*]

EVIE: What you trying to ... ? [*She cuffs him.*]

JJ: I'm sorry.

EVIE: I warned you ...

JJ: I'm sorry.

EVIE: I told you before. I tell Pa.

JJ: I haven't done nothing wrong!

EVIE: I'll tell him how you watch me.

JJ: I just want to look after you ...

EVIE: I look after myself!

JJ: Soon he'll be gone. Then what you do? That leg's poisoning him. I've seen it before with the cattle. When it gets like that, they slag them.

EVIE: You want to kill your own father now, do you?

JJ [*deadly earnest*]: You gonna need me. I warn you.

He turns and lumbers off toward the caravan.

EVIE [a *sardonic chuckle*]: Huh. If you're thinking of calling this place your own one day, you better make sure it's yours in writing.

She gathers the box of photos and heads for the caravan.

JJ: What d'you mean?

EVIE [*enjoying the moment*]: You haven't done your homework, have you? It doesn't just drop into your lap. There's papers involved. Things handed over.

JJ [*a beat*]: I know that.

EVIE [*turning away*]: You do? Good for you.

JJ: It's all cut and dry. I'm the only one left.

EVIE: Only one what? He could leave it to anybody.

JJ: He's not gonna leave it to *you!*

EVIE: No, but then what about Ma?

JJ: Ma!? Ma's a pile of ashes in the bottom of a storm lantern!

EVIE: That's right. Ashes to Ashes. Dust to Dust. [*She chuckles.*] That'd be something, hey? Ma's Revenge. [*Entering the caravan.*] Paying him back for forcing her to live in a dump she always hated. I like that. There's something right about that ...

She closes the door behind her. JJ looks distinctly ill at ease. He considers entering the caravan then stops. Looks off in the direction PA took. Mooches about.

Presently PA enters. He fondles a small red tomato.

PA: Is this now a tomato, or is this not now a tomato? [*Showing it to JJ.*] There's nothing like the feel of the first bladdy tomato.

JJ [*preoccupied*]: Ja.

PA: Where's Evie?

JJ: Gone to bed.

PA: Lemme go show her.

JJ: Pa ... ?

PA: No, wait a minute. She'll just want to stick it in a stew or something. [*Inspecting it, lovingly.*] What-the-hell? Take the bladdy plunge. [*to JJ.*] You want some?

JJ: No thanks.

PA bites into the tomato – pure bliss.

PA: Mmmmm-mm ... ! Ait-sa! [*Wiping a hand on his shirt, moving to grab the TV.*] Okay. Time to hit the feathers. You coming in?

JJ sits on the car seat. He shows no sign of budging.

JJ: What exactly did you mean last night? That argument we had?

PA: When?

JJ: Last night.

PA: We had a argument?

PA is preoccupied with the loose TV cable.

JJ: Ja. Suppertime. You said I'm not – what you said was – I'm not fit to run this place.

PA [*a beat*]: I said that!?

JJ: You said it right here.

PA: Ag. Ja. Well. Heat a' the moment.

JJ: So you didn't mean it?

PA: What you worrying! Still a long time from now, man. [*Keen to change the subject.*] Come help me take this stuff inside. [*He is almost afraid to look at the youth, whose eyes are boring into him. He gathers his wits before continuing. The sequence that follows starts quietly enough, but builds to an inevitable climax.*] One thing, JJ. You got to understand. There's more to running a farm than charging around with a moersa-fat power-saw, chopping down blue gums.

JJ: Okay. So a tree hit the tractor. I'm sorry.

PA: Did I say tractor ... ?

JJ: I didn't mean to hit the tractor ...

PA: Who said anything about the tractor? Tractor was the last thing on my mind ...

JJ: I apologise. I'm sorry. I'll pay it off.

PA: While we're on the subject, you also rolled my Cortina.

JJ: Your Cortina!?

PA: But we won't talk about that ...

JJ: That was three bladdy years ago!

PA: Was it? Jissus. Seems like yesterday.

JJ: How the hell can you bring up the Cortina!?

PA: Easy. You turned my Cortina into a *conce-tina!*

JJ: That was a accident!

PA: Your whole bladdy life's a accident! You a Living Bliksemse Bulldozer. Fokken Human Tornado. You remind me of that King. King Whatsisname – only in reverse.

JJ: What king?

PA: King Dingamalerie, man. Whatjoo-macallit ... ! Everything he touched turned to gold. You the same, only opposite. Everything you touch falls apart.

JJ: You calling me a doos?

PA: Midas ... ! That's it. King Midas.

JJ: I work my bladdy gat off here!

PA: I know that. I'm not saying you don't ...

JJ: And now you calling me a doos!?

PA: I'm trying to get it into your head that it's farm management. The simple things. Like twelve times six.

JJ: Twelve times six?

PA: Twelve times six.

JJ: What the fuck is twelve times six!?

PA: That's what I'm asking you.

JJ: Oh. Great. So now I must know my twelve times table to run a fucken farm!?

PA: I should bladdy-well hope so. Twelve boxes. Six cabbages in each box ...

JJ: Jissus ...

PA: How many cabbages altogether?

JJ: You always come with this addition–subtraction shit.

PA: Multiplication. Something times something is multiplication. Addition–
subtraction is something else ...

JJ: Ja, man, fuck ...

PA: It's something your mother used to try on you after school, to no avail. Except
she used matches ...

JJ: Okay, okay, man ... !

PA: Here we are, JJ, I got twelve matches in this hand, I got six in this ...

JJ: Look, man – everybody knows – you wanna do all that kak, you use a bladdy
calculator!

PA: Calculator?

JJ: All you do is punch a' bladdy buttons.

PA: Fine. Let's have a demonstration.

JJ [a beat]: Hey?

PA: Let's have a demonstration. Go fetch it. [JJ is de-balled.] You can't, can you? And
why not? Because it's broken. And who broke it? Hey? [Bearing down on him.]
Who broke the only bladdy calculator this family possesses!?

JJ: What you got against me?

PA: Tell me I'm lying!

JJ: What is it with me? You never moaned at Michael!

PA: Yes, I did.

JJ: How come you never shat on Michael? Or Wynand ... !?

PA: Each man according to his merits.

JJ: That's the way it's always been, isn't it? Wynand was the Hero, Michael was the
Brains and I'm the Total Stuff Up ... !

PA: No ...

JJ: I'm the one you kick around!

PA: Not true. I love my children. All of them.

JJ: Oh, so you love me now, do you?

PA: You're my son. You're mos my own flesh and blood.

JJ: Then prove it. Put your cards on the table – and your money where your mouth
is, and lemme see exactly what it is I got to look forward to ... !

PA: JJ ... ! [*He breaks off, turns away. It is the most difficult thing he has ever had to say to him.*] I couldn't give you Sweetfontein even if I wanted to.

JJ [*incredulous*]: Why not?

PA [*a beat*]: It's been ordained. [*JJ simply stares at him.*] It's out of my hands. [*He lets this sink in.*] But we'll still be here. *All* of us. And we'll have everything we could ever wish for. Your brother-in-law will see to that.

JJ: Brother-in-law ... ?

PA: He's going to fix this place up something incredible.

JJ: What brother-in-law?

PA: Evie's husband. Isn't that wonderful!

JJ: Since when she getting married?

PA: I been waiting for this since – hell, man ...

JJ: I didn't know she was getting married!

PA: It's on the cards.

JJ: When?

PA: Soon.

JJ: How soon?

PA: Soon-soon.

JJ [*on the boil now*]: Who is this guy? What's his name? Where's he from?

> *EVIE, who has been listening to the last little sequence, chips in from the top of the caravan steps.*

EVIE: Some smart-fancy place somewhere, far away. [*PA spins around.*] He's going to come riding up along here one morning in a big-fat BMW.

PA: Mercedes Benz! A white Mercedes with tinted windscreens ... !

JJ: How come I don't know anything about all this!?

EVIE: Because it's all a load of junk.

PA: Don't listen to her ...

EVIE: Total rubbish.

PA: Don't listen to a word she says!

JJ: I wanna meet this oke!

EVIE: He saw it all on TV. Jumbled up somewhere between his Dallas–Dynasty and his brandy and Coke.

JJ [*not even listening anymore*]: Jissus ... !

PA [*to EVIE*]: Your mother came to me.

EVIE: Oh, ja – for sure ...

PA: She spoke to me.

EVIE: What – long-distance telephone?

PA: She came to me with a message.

EVIE: My mother's dead, for God-sake!

PA: A miracle is going to happen, Evie ...

EVIE: Jesus ... ! [*Plunging into the caravan.*]

PA: A mira – Evie ... ?

JJ: I'm gonna moer him. I'm gonna smash this guy's face so bad, he's gonna wish he never been born.

PA: JJ ... ! Wait. JJ, listen to me ... !

JJ [*moving off, into the night*]: I'll take him. One-on-one. Man to Man ... !

PA: JJ ... ! You don't understand. It's all going to be okay ... !

> PA *is powerless to stop JJ wandering off.* EVIE *appears, bearing the storm lantern containing Emily's ashes.*

EVIE: You want my mother – here she is!

PA: Evie ... !?

EVIE: You want your wife? You want her ... ?

PA: What in God's name ... !?

EVIE: Stay where you are! Stay right where you are ... !

PA: Evie. Give that ...

EVIE [*circling away, holding the lantern aloft*]: You come one step closer, I smash it.

PA: Okay. Orraight. Okay. Now, put your mother down!

EVIE [*keeping her distance*]: Take a good look.

PA: Evie ... !

EVIE: Are you looking?

PA: I'm looking. I'm looking.

EVIE: Don't move!

PA: I'm standing still. I'm sitting down.

EVIE: It's a chunk of glass with some dust in the bottom. That's all it is ...

PA: Yes.

EVIE: You see that?

PA: I see that ... !

EVIE: It doesn't talk to you and you can't talk to it.

PA: No.

EVIE: It's not a person. It's nothing living. It's what is called an inanimate object ...

PA: Yes! Okay! I see that – I know that ... ! Evie, what are you ... ? Why are you – jislaaik, man ... !

EVIE [*exploding*]: I'm sick to death of your drunk-stupid stories, your crackpot ideas ... !

PA: Be careful with that ... !

EVIE: Your never-ending bladdy Klipdrift dreams!

PA: I'm not drinking again ...

EVIE: You call yourselves farmers. You're not farmers ...

PA: Not properly, no ...

He holds his hand out, his eyes on the lantern.

EVIE: The only thing you ever did properly in your life was crash cars at Tarlton Race Track.

PA: Wembley. We raced at Wembley.

EVIE: Cars and drink. While they worked the land ...

PA: 1966. North-Eastern Transvaal Stock Car Racing Champ, that was me ...

EVIE: Are you listening to me?

PA: People want me back. They asking where's the Champ?

EVIE: You're not listening to me ...

PA: I was the best bladdy driver they ever had!

EVIE: Here. Here's a bladdy trophy for you ... !

Contemptuously she tosses the storm lantern at him. He lunges forward, saving it from hitting the ground and clutching it to his chest.

PA: Jissus, are you mad!? [*EVIE goes into the caravan, slamming the door behind her.*] You ought to hang your head in shame! Is there nothing sacred anymore!? [*Cradling the lantern.*] Forgive her, Emily. Forgive her. [*Looking about.*] Now, where is daddy's big boy?

He starts to move off, aimlessly.

PA [*calling out*]: Wynand! Wynand ... !?

From inside the caravan, we hear EVIE's voice.

EVIE: JJ!

PA [*moving off*]: Wynand!!

EVIE [*opening the door*]: His name is JJ!

PA: What?

EVIE: His name is JJ. You calling him Wynand.

He stares at her, long and hard.

PA: You're a bitter girl. A bitter, heartless girl. [*He slowly turns away, moving off.*] Now where's daddy's big boy ... ? JJ ... ? JJ ... !?

EVIE sinks down onto the top step, watching the confused, battered man limp off into the darkness. She lets her head drop onto her knees, a picture of utter helplessness and despair.

The haunting sound of GIDEON's Jew's harp is heard off-stage. He emerges from the shadows and stands in the centre of the patio area, watching her. When she looks up and sees him, she talks to him as though he has been there all the time, not the least bit shocked that he is still around.

EVIE: I'm leaving. I'm saying goodbye to this place. It's not so difficult. I've been over it thousands of times in my mind. I'll get up tomorrow morning, as usual. Go down to the farm stall and open up. But, instead of trying to sell something to the first person that stops, I'll ask for a lift. Doesn't matter where they're going. [*A beat.*] But, one thing I do know. Once I'm gone, I'm never coming back. [*GIDEON has not taken his eyes off her face. There is no reaction from him that suggests whether he believes her or not – or that he really cares one way or the other.*] It's the noise, you know. The noise that goes on and on and never seems to stop. Even at night. Even when I'm down by the road and on my own. Their voices. Their machines. All I want is a place without noise.

He slowly moves to her and puts out his hand. She takes it. He draws her to him as the lights begin to fade. They embrace. 'Trekliedjie' swells up as the lights fade to blackout.

ACT TWO

Scene One

A few days later. Afternoon. PA's *limp is more pronounced now, as if his leg is deteriorating all the time. He stands over a newly-completed wooden crate, axe in hand.*

PA: The time of reckoning has come. Now, let them come ... [*Looking skyward.*] I'm ready and waiting for any bliksemse bird who wants to come try. Any fool voël who wants to come tackle my tomatoes, feel free. Because why? Because I got your bladdy number, jong! Come, Emily, come look ...

He picks up the storm lantern from the little table beside the car seat.

PA: How you like? Clever, hey? [*Replacing the lantern and beginning to tie a length of rope to a stick.*] You see, the problem is tomatoes. Not tomatoes themselves, but the colour of tomatoes. 'Specially when they getting ripe and turning red. Not easy to hide. Now, you can throw in the towel, or you can fight them. But *how* to fight them? Well, you can paint your tomatoes. But that's not such a good idea, because you still got to eat them. Or, you can build some sort of machinery that will convince the little bliksems that tomatoes is not such a good idea after all. [*Setting up the trap – the box held up by the stick.*] Now. By placing a bright red tomato in full view of the birds that fly over, you let them know that *this* is where the party's at. Add a few titbits along the way, and – voepla! You got him!

Chuffed with himself, he feeds out the rope and gets down on his hands and knees beside the car seat. While he is doing this, CHRISTIAAN *enters. This time he is a character, a lot less sure of himself than when we saw him as narrator. He carries an empty five litre Trek petrol tin.*

PA [*in his own world*]: Right. Bird comes down. Piek-piek-piek ... piek-piek ...
CHRISTIAAN [*tentatively*]: Er – excuse me ...
PA: Piek-piek-piek ... bit further ... piek-piek-piek ...
CHRISTIAAN: Er – Oom ... ?
PA: Shhh ... ! Bird gets underneath – tries the tomato – [*Yanks the rope. The box drops.*] Got him! Ha-haa! [*Overjoyed, addressing the stranger.*] How's that ... !?
CHRISTIAAN: Ja, Oom.
PA: You like?
CHRISTIAAN: Ja, Oom.
PA: You know what it is?
CHRISTIAAN: Ja, Oom.
PA [*suspicious*]: You do?

CHRISTIAAN: It's a trap, Oom.

PA: A trap?

CHRISTIAAN: Ja, Oom. [*Demonstrating.*] You put the food in here with a little trail going along here and then you wait for whatever it is you waiting for. When whatever it is you waiting for comes along, it eats its way along the trail 'til it gets underneath. When it's properly underneath, you pull the string, it falls on top of him. You got him.

PA stares at him. He is not amused.

PA: You been watching me.

CHRISTIAAN: No, Oom.

PA: You been spying on me?

CHRISTIAAN: No, Oom. We used to do this when I was small. It's the way we used to catch pigeons on the front lawn.

PA [*slow smile*]: Man after my own heart. What did you say your name was?

CHRISTIAAN: Christiaan, Oom.

PA: Krisjan?

CHRISTIAAN: Ja, Oom. [*Showing him the tin*]: I ran out of petrol up on the road. I thought maybe Oom might be able to help me, Oom.

PA studies him.

PA: That's a nice suit you wearing.

CHRISTIAAN: Thank you, Oom.

PA: I like a man who wears a suit, and it's not even Sunday.

CHRISTIAAN: It *is* Sunday, Oom.

PA: It is?

CHRISTIAAN: Ja, Oom.

PA: Oh, yes – of course. Yesterday was Saturday.

CHRISTIAAN: That's right, Oom. Tomorrow's Monday.

PA: Monday. Funny. When a man works as hard as I do, one day seems the same as the next – if you know what I mean, Krisjan?

CHRISTIAAN: Ja, Oom.

PA: Time is like a thing with legs, Krisjan. It runs and runs. The older you get, the faster it runs. In the end, you just chasing 'til you drop.

CHRISTIAAN [*smiling*]: I've never seen it like that, Oom.

PA: That's because you still young. When you still young, you run past anything.

CHRISTIAAN: You not so old yourself, Oom.

PA: Not so old, no. Not so old I can't still do the vastrap, hey? Chikka-jei, chikka-jei ... ! Ou Charles Jacoby and the boys. You remember ou Charles?

CHRISTIAAN: Oom?

PA [*hopefully*]: Ou Charles. Chikka-jei, chikka-jei. Vastrap? Tiekiedraai? Ruk a' rol? [*He does a brief 'turn'. CHRISTIAAN looks quizzical.*] No? So. You stuck on the road?

CHRISTIAAN: Ja, Oom. [*Pointing off.*] I went to that house down there, but it was all sort of closed up.

PA: Ag, you won't find nothing by the house, man. We got hit by the floods. Flash floods. Condemned. When my family gets off its fat gat, we still might get it right. [*Almost as an afterthought.*] You got family, Krisjan?

CHRISTIAAN: Ja, Oom. I'm actually on my way home from seeing them. I try go see them at least once a month. After church on a Sunday.

PA: Good. That's good. I like that. Church and family. One must never lose sight of that.

CHRISTIAAN: No, Oom.

PA [*suddenly very sociable*]: How about a dop, Krisjan?

CHRISTIAAN: I don't drink, Oom.

PA: No?

CHRISTIAAN: No, Oom.

PA [*smiling*]: But you will have a cup of coffee with me?

CHRISTIAAN: That'd be nice, Oom. Thank you, Oom.

PA [*turning to caravan*]: Make yourself at home, Krisjan. We fix you up here, no problem.

CHRISTIAAN: Oom is very kind, Oom.

PA [*stopping on the steps*]: Tell me, Krisjan, you – er. You wouldn't by any chance drive a Mercedes, would you?

CHRISTIAAN: Mercedes, Oom?

PA: Ja. White Mercedes. Tinted windscreens – sort of, you know – air-conditioning?

CHRISTIAAN: I drive a Volksie, Oom.

PA: Aha.

CHRISTIAAN: White Volksie with a dent in the back. Petrol gauge is always on the blink. That's why I keep running out.

Trying not to let his disappointment show, PA enters the caravan.

PA: Don't knock a Volksie, Krisjan.

CHRISTIAAN: No, Oom.

PA: I had a Volkswagen before I had my Cortina.

CHRISTIAAN: They good cars, Oom, no question.

PA: Before that, was a Datsun Pulsar – Opel Rekord. Now I just sommer drive a bakkie.

CHRISTIAAN: Bakkies are nice too, Oom. Very nice.

PA: You take milk and sugar, Krisjan?

CHRISTIAAN: Ja, Oom. Thank you, Oom. Two sugars and a dash of milk.

> PA *whistles happily to himself inside the caravan.* CHRISTIAAN *looks about, taking in the fairy lights, the kudu horns. Intrigued by what he sees.*

CHRISTIAAN: Nice place you got here, Oom.

PA: Ag, ja. We do our best. It's no picnic living out here on the plots, I can tell you.

CHRISTIAAN: A lot quieter than living in town.

PA: You can say that again.

CHRISTIAAN: You should try visiting the Post Office some time. Up on the second floor, when all the machines are going flat out.

PA [*his head out*]: Post Office?

CHRISTIAAN: The sound stays ringing around inside your head long after you clock off.

PA: I didn't know you were a postman, Krisjan?

CHRISTIAAN: Post and Telecommunications, Oom. It's a different thing. Desk job. Computers. [*Shrugging.*] I wanted to be a writer, Oom. You know, newspapers – stories. Stuff like that. My father didn't approve. He said if I wanted to be a man of letters, I must rather go work by the Post Office. [*Removing the lid of the Sasol drum and peering in.*] But I won't give up the idea, Oom. The thing is to try find the right story.

> PA *re-emerges from the caravan.*

PA [*ticking him off*]: Hey-hey-hey, outa' there, boy.

CHRISTIAAN [*replacing the lid*]: Smells terrible.

PA: That's 'cos it's not processed yet. You wait 'til I start processing it.

CHRISTIAAN: What is it, Oom?

PA [*a beat, smiling*]: Play your cards right, I might just tell you. [*He plucks a bloom from one of the pot plants and inserts it in* CHRISTIAAN'S *button hole.*] You know, I can't tell you what it's like to meet a man who wears a suit and sits behind a desk, for a change. [*Removing the young man's jacket, he carefully places it on the car seat.*] Tell me, Krisjan, you do much paperwork? You know – twelve times six?

CHRISTIAAN: Oom?

PA: Facts? Figures? Things like that?

CHRISTIAAN: Oh, ja, Oom. From morning 'til night.

PA: Listen, Krisjan, I'm going to fetch a pipe to suck that petrol. You hear the kettle start boiling, just switch it off, okay?

CHRISTIAAN: Don't go to any trouble, Oom.

PA: No trouble at all, man. None. Bugger all. [*Scuttling off, highly enthusiastic.*] Evie … ? Evie … !?

CHRISTIAAN *continues his inspection of the property, the box containing the cabbage leaves, solution and so on. At one point, he picks up the storm lantern and, turning it over and semi-unscrewing it, causes some of Ma's ashes to stream to the floor. Not knowing what they are, he casually dusts his trousers, his shoes. He pokes his head into the caravan, entering it.*

He is moving around inside it, when JJ *enters. armed with the power-saw.* JJ *stops short when he sees the neatly folded jacket (buttonhole flower prominent) on the car seat. He is shaking the Trek tin when* CHRISTIAAN *emerges from the caravan.*

CHRISTIAAN [*caught out*]: Oh, hello. I was just – my car is – [*Ill at ease under JJ's unrelenting stare.*] I was checking the kettle. [*Weak laugh.*] You watch a kettle, it doesn't boil, hey? [*Putting out his hand.*] Sorry, my name is …

JJ: You must be the oke.

CHRISTIAAN: Sorry?

JJ: The oke. You're the oke.

CHRISTIAAN *takes him to mean 'the oke who wants petrol'.*

CHRISTIAAN: Oh. Ja. I s'pose I am.

JJ [*icily*]: Don't get any ideas.

CHRISTIAAN: Hey?

JJ *activates the power-saw and brings it up to* CHRISTIAAN'S *throat in one smooth, unhurried movement. He inches the visitor backward until his spine is pressed flat against the caravan. For a moment we must believe that* JJ *is going to lop his head off.* CHRISTIAAN *must certainly believe it.* JJ *switches it off and allows the whine to fade away.*

JJ: Just don't get any ideas.

CHRISTIAAN *is feeling his throat, wide-eyed.*

CHRISTIAAN: No. Okay. I won't.

JJ: You wanna talk to anybody, you talk to me. I'm the one you talk to. Not to him. Not to her. Not to nobody but me.

CHRISTIAAN: Ja, okay, I didn't know that. I'm sorry. It's not as if I didn't expect to pay for it. I mean …

JJ: Stick your bladdy money. It's not for sale.

He begins to move off.

CHRISTIAAN: Oh. I see. I didn't want a hell of a lot – [*Moving to the Trek tin, picking it up.*] Just enough to get me to – well, half-full if – if - even a *quarter*, I mean –

He looks up to where he expects JJ *to be. The violent intruder is gone.* PA *returns with a short length of hosepipe.*

PA: Here we go. This'll suck that petrol quick-sticks – [*Stopping short.*] Whatsa' matter? You okay?

CHRISTIAAN: Ja.

PA: You sure?

CHRISTIAAN: There was somebody here. I think there was a misunderstanding. Chap with a power-saw ...

PA: Ag, that'll be JJ. Chops down anything that's standing up. We lucky we got a tree left in the whole bladdy place.

CHRISTIAAN: Seems like he knows how to use it.

PA: Ja. About the only thing he *can* use. If he wasn't my own son, I'd kick him out, wraggies. [*Entering caravan.*] How's that coffee in there? Listen, Krisjan, how about staying for a meal, man? Have some food with us.

CHRISTIAAN [*suddenly not so keen anymore*]: Er – thank you, Oom, but – I think maybe I should be –

PA: We don't see many people from outside and, besides – I got a proposition for you.

CHRISTIAAN: Proposition, Oom?

PA: Two sugars, you say?

CHRISTIAAN: Two sugars, Oom. Two sugars and a – what kind of a proposition, Oom ... ?

PA comes out of the caravan, bearing two mugs of coffee.

PA: The Lord works in mysterious ways, Krisjan.

CHRISTIAAN [*taking a mug*]: Thank you, Oom.

PA: He is like the schoolteacher who plays games with his pupils. But the games are more like tests. Like those pictures in the comics. Inside the pictures, there all sorts of things you must find them. Only it's hard to find them, because they don't look the way you expect them to look.

CHRISTIAAN: The pictures?

PA: Ja. Like you looking for a Mercedes, orraight? Or a Mercedes is what you *think* you looking for. But when you find the Mercedes, it's not a Mercedes at all but a horse of a totally different colour.

CHRISTIAAN: The Mercedes?

PA: You follow me, Krisjan?

CHRISTIAAN: I'm trying to, Oom.

PA: Good. Now ...

There is a commotion off stage as EVIE shrieks for help and comes charging around the caravan, JJ in hot pursuit. She carries the power-saw – the obvious cause of the dispute.

EVIE: Pa ... ! Pa ... !!

JJ: Jislaaik! Come here, you little bitch!

EVIE: Voetsek ... !

JJ: Gimme that – fok it ... !

PA: What the – ?

EVIE: Pa ... !

She tries to dodge behind CHRISTIAAN. *JJ cuts her off, grabbing the power-saw. She refuses to let go of it and a screaming tug of war ensues.*

JJ: Let go!

EVIE: You not gonna do it!

PA: What the bladdy hell ... !?

EVIE: He's going to chop down the pondok!

JJ: Give here, man!

PA: Shaddap! Stop that!

JJ succeeds in ripping it from her grasp.

JJ: Bitch!

PA [*to JJ*]: Gimme that thing.

EVIE: Don't let him do it, Pa.

JJ: It's okay, Pa ...

PA: Give me that bliksemse thing right now!

JJ: But, Pa, I'm gonna ...

PA yanks the power-saw out of his hands, in no mood for this display.

EVIE [*to PA*]: He says you said he could do it!?

PA brushes the protests aside, composing himself.

PA: Evie, I'd like you to meet a young gentleman ...

EVIE: Did you say he could chop down Gideon's pondok ... ?

JJ: Lemme go do it, Pa ...

PA: Shaddap ... !

EVIE: Did you give him permission ... !?

JJ: It's a vrot-stinking kaffir-khaya, makes the place look like a ... !

EVIE: That's how *you* see it! You haven't even been inside it ... !

PA: Shaddap!! Jislaaik! Where's your respect? We got a guest here! And it's a bladdy Sunday, nogal!

EVIE [*calmer now*]: All I'm asking, Pa – did you say he could chop down Gideon's pondok ... ?

PA: Enough of Gideon ... !! [*Turning to the bemused* CHRISTIAAN.] Now, I've got a young gentleman here who's travelled a long, long way today to – [*Noticing* EVIE *stomping off without so much as a backward glance.*] Evie ... ? Evie ... !! [*PA comes back to* CHRISTIAAN, *trying to turn it to his advantage.*] Tough little koekie, that one. Mind of her own.

JJ: Pa ... ?

PA: She's got a real sense of – how d'you callit? Gentleman's agreements ...

JJ: Pa ... ?

PA: But is she good in the kitchen! Hell, man. Cooks like a bladdy dream ...

JJ: Pa, lemme go do it.

PA [*shoving him, angrily*]: Bugger off.

JJ: You said I could ...

PA: Get away, here, man! Just go ... ! Go! [*He has an idea.*] Wait a minute ... ! JJ ... ! Come here! [*JJ stops where he is.*] Come here, man. Quick. [*Signalling to* CHRISTIAAN.] Krisjan, gimme that tin ...

CHRISTIAAN: Oom?

PA: I must apologise. It's like a bladdy madhouse here today ...

CHRISTIAAN: That's okay, Oom.

CHRISTIAAN *hands* PA *the Trek tin.* PA *hands it to* JJ.

JJ: What's this?

PA: Never mind. Take this. Go down to the bakkie and suck this full for our guest.

He hands him the hose as well.

JJ: What for?

PA: Because I say so. Here – [*Digging in his pockets for the bakkie keys.*]

CHRISTIAAN: I can do it, Oom.

PA: You having coffee, Krisjan. [*Handing keys to* JJ.] Off you go. [*JJ stares at him. If looks could kill ...*] I said move it!

There is a moment between them before JJ *turns and moves off very slowly.* PA *shakes his head, more in sadness than in anger.*

PA: No respect for authority, these kids. Starts when they young. I warned the late wife. I told her. I said, you let a kaffir-meid take care of them when they growing up, this is what happens. If Emily was still alive, she'd turn in her grave, man. Which reminds me –

PA *picks up the storm lantern, showing it to* CHRISTIAAN.

PA: Krisjan, I'd like you to meet her. The late wife.

CHRISTIAAN [*horrified*]: Oom ... ?

PA: Her personal remains. She was a great woman.

PA *carries the lantern back into the caravan.* CHRISTIAAN *stoops hastily to remove the tell-tale ashes beside the car seat. When* PA *emerges again,* CHRISTIAAN *pretends to be tying a shoelace.*

PA: No, you know, Krisjan – she wanted to have her remains scattered over the ocean. But I couldn't find it in my waters to have her just sommer tossed to the impersonal fishes far from hearth and home.

PA picks up his coffee cup and sits on the car seat. CHRISTIAAN *is keen to change the subject.*

CHRISTIAAN: Oom? Who is this Gideon, Oom?

PA [*a beat*]: He's somebody we don't talk about, Krisjan.

CHRISTIAAN: Oh.

PA: He's a closed book around here.

CHRISTIAAN: So he's not the man I saw when I came in here?

PA: Man? What man?

CHRISTIAAN: Black man. When I came down there past the house ...

PA: You saw a black man down by the house!?

CHRISTIAAN: Ja, he was sort of standing there ...

PA leaps to his feet, looking off towards the house.

PA: Jissus ... ! Little bliksem!

CHRISTIAAN: I asked him if anybody lived here. Three times I asked him the same question.

PA: He didn't say nothing.

CHRISTIAAN: He didn't say anything.

PA: He never says anything. He's got no voice.

CHRISTIAAN: Oom?

PA is gritting his teeth.

PA: She's down there now. I take you a bet.

CHRISTIAAN: What you mean no voice, Oom? Is he deaf?

PA: I take you a bet she's skinnering with the little bastard right this very minute.

CHRISTIAAN: Oom?

PA [*absently*]: Hey?

CHRISTIAAN: How can a person have no voice, Oom?

PA [*miles away*]: My father had these dogs. Somebody left open the gate ...

[CHRISTIAAN *still does not follow*] They were trained to go for the throat.

CHRISTIAAN: They bite his throat, Oom?

It is a while before PA speaks, thinking aloud.

PA: Jislaaik. You live through droughts. You live through floods. You come out the other side, you think, fantastic, I can breathe again. But, no – they come with more stones to put on your back.

CHRISTIAAN: Who's this, Oom?

PA: All of them. The whole kaboodle. Even your own bladdy children. [*Smiling, wryly.*] Huh. I go to the bank the other day, you know what they do? They laugh at me.

CHRISTIAAN: It's tough for everybody, Oom.

PA: What is, Krisjan?

CHRISTIAAN: Everything, Oom. Life.

PA: Life?

CHRISTIAAN: Ja, Oom.

PA stares at him, unimpressed.

PA: Are you dying, Krisjan?

CHRISTIAAN: No, Oom.

PA: Come to me when you dying.

CHRISTIAAN: I don't understand, Oom.

PA: It doesn't strike as you as strange that three fully grown people are living in a caravan? That someone invites you to supper, you have to eat it outside – sommer alfredo ... ?

CHRISTIAAN: Maybe some people like it like that, Oom?

PA: Don't call me a fool to my face, Krisjan.

CHRISTIAAN: No, Oom, there are people who ...

PA: This is a proud family!

CHRISTIAAN: I can see that, Oom ...

PA: Over forty years we been running this place. First my father, then me. We built it up. We were selling things – buying things. Things were going better than ever before. Klop – as they say – bladdy disselboom. And then – I dunno. Something happened.

CHRIS [*a beat*]: What was that, Oom?

PA: I dunno. It's as if the Lord left us. He left the land. He left His people who had always been with Him. It was all happening so slowly none of us even knew what was going on until one day we woke up and, suddenly, we didn't have all the things we had before. All our friends had gone. Those same so-called friends we grew up side-by-side down the years. It cut deep inside. Sometimes it got so bad, I wanted to come home and just start shooting, you know. Shoot everybody. Shoot myself. I took my rifle, my Bible and my bakkie and I just drove. Didn't even know where I was driving. Away. But then I stopped. I said what you doing, man? You leaving family. You leaving children – maybe grandchildren! You leaving your future behind you! No man can do that. But I looked through that windscreen, and I could see it, man. That khakibos. That tall dry khakibos – standing all over my grave.

He stares as he may have stared on that day, the fear and loneliness still very much with him.

209

The silence between them is broken by the appearance of JJ, who enters carrying the filled Trek petrol tin. He tosses the bakkie keys and hosepipe at his father's feet. PA turns slowly away, retrieving his coffee cup.

CHRISTIAAN [*to JJ*]: Oh. Thanks. How much do I owe you?

JJ: Don't worry nothing. It's on the house. I see now I made a balls up when I buggered you around.

CHRISTIAAN: Oh. That's okay.

JJ: I thought you someone else.

CHRISTIAAN: Me? No, I was just –

JJ: Let's go stick this in your tank so you can be on your way.

PA [*one step ahead*]: What a good idea, JJ. We'll go find Evie to make some supper for our guest.

CHRISTIAAN: Oh. No supper for me thanks, Oom, I –

PA: It'll be our pleasure, Krisjan.

CHRISTIAAN: The coffee was very nice, Oom ...

PA: Supper will be even nicer ...

JJ: If he wants to get on the road, I think you should ...

PA: He's been invited to supper.

JJ: He doesn't want supper.

CHRISTIAAN: It's not that I don't want supper, it's just ...

PA: You see. He's fine for supper.

CHRISTIAAN: No, it's my lights. My headlights. I don't trust them when it gets dark.

PA: You come to the right place. JJ can fix them. He's good with cars. [*Pointedly.*] Broken cars are his best.

JJ: This oke wants to split. Can't you hear what he's saying?

PA [*not letting up*]: He's also got a problem, and we can help solve it. Where's your car, Krisjan?

CHRISTIAAN: It's okay, Oom.

PA: Where is your motor car!?

CHRISTIAAN [*giving in*]: About one kay from your gate. Other side of the farm stall.

PA: Give him your keys.

CHRISTIAAN looks to JJ, who is glaring at his father. He looks back to PA again, removing the keys from his jacket pocket.

PA: Evie makes one helluva stirfry. Her rattatoullie's something else.

JJ: Rattatoullie ... ? She's never made that in all her life.

PA [*determined not to be derailed now*]: There's always a first time.

JJ takes the keys slowly, stabbing a finger in CHRISTIAAN's face.

JJ: Don't get any ideas.

PA: Kay-sera-sera, boy. The Will of the Lord.

JJ: Don't push it, that's all.

PA: You threatening me?

JJ: Take it any way you like.

PA: Don't threaten me, boeta. Don't even try.

JJ moves off with the keys and the Trek tin. PA watches him go. Boere-Rambo still rules.

CHRISTIAAN: I don't want to cause any trouble here, Oom.

PA: You're a welcome guest here, Krisjan. I want you to know that.

CHRISTIAAN: I wish you'd let me pay for the petrol, I'd feel much better, Oom.

PA: I tell you what you can do, Krisjan. When I make Batch Number One, you can be the first person to test it ...

PA enjoys watching CHRISTIAAN's expression as he moves to the Sasol drum and scoops up his brew with a ladle.

PA: When times are tough, a Boer maak 'n plan. My Revitalising Cream.

CHRIS [*peering into the drum*]: Revitalising Cream?

PA: Ja. Cabbage leaves – sour milk. One or two other things, you know.

CHRISTIAAN: You put that on your face?

PA [*smiling*]: No-no-no, Krisjan. You make a culture. A fungus. From there you make the cream to put on your ...

CHRISTIAAN [*twigging*]: Oh, I see. Then you sell the culture so that anyone with cabbage leaves can do the same.

PA: There's it! Everyone's looking for the secret of youth, not so? Chikka-jei, chikka-jei! This stuff is going to make my face a household name all over the world.

CHRISTIAAN: Didn't somebody try that before, Oom?

PA carefully replaces the lid.

PA: Bladdy sharks, man. All of them. But this is the real thing. This is going to put Sweetfontein back on top again. [*Putting his arm around CHRISTIAAN's shoulders.*] Which brings me to my next question. What d'you think of farming, Krisjan?

CHRISTIAAN: Farming, Oom?

PA: Being a farmer? Working the land?

CHRISTIAAN: Everybody thinks of that, Oom.

PA: They do?

CHRJS: Ja, Oom. Every so now and then. But you soon put it out of your mind.

PA: Why's that?

CHRISTIAAN: You joking with me now, Oom.

PA: No, Krisjan. That's the trouble with people, you see. They convince themselves. They say no, no – I am good with my head. Or I am good with my hands. But it's not the head, nor the hands. It's what's in the heart ... !

CHRISTIAAN: I know what I can do, Oom. Also what I can't.

PA: Don't ever say that, Krisjan. I never thought I could fight a leopard, but I did.

CHRISTIAAN: You fought a leopard ... ?

PA: With these bare hands. And so could you.

CHRISTIAAN: No, Oom.

PA: What happens if you can't help it?

CHRISTIAAN: No, Oom. I'd run away, Oom.

PA: You meet him face to face in the bush!

CHRISTIAAN: I'd die of fright.

PA: Uh-uh, aikona. There's this rock, okay? Here, beside the path. [*Moving to the car seat.*]

CHRISTIAAN: You talking to the wrong person, Oom ...

While CHRISTIAAN *tries to wriggle out of it,* PA *sets up the scene, determined to put the youngster to the test.*

PA: Now, behind this rock, is this leopard, Okay? Okay, okay – I'll be the leopard ... [*Ducks behind the seat.*]

CHRISTIAAN [*nonplussed*]: Oom?

PA: Unless you want to be the leopard?

CHRISTIAAN: No, Oom, I –

PA: Yes, yes – you can be the leopard. I can show you what to do.

CHRISTIAAN: I don't want to do anything ...

PA: Come, come – get behind there ...

CHRISTIAAN [*pointing off*] Maybe he's finish with the petrol now, Oom ... ?

PA: Now, you this leopard, this very hungry leopard because you haven't eaten for four days ...

CHRISTIAAN: The petrol cap key's not the same as the ignition ...

PA [*ploughing on*]: What you see coming along the road here is lunch, okay? A three-course meal on two legs, strolling casually through the bush.

CHRISTIAAN: Oom –

PA: Come on. Buck down. I mustn't see you, otherwise I know you there. [*Reluctantly, very reluctantly,* CHRISTIAAN *disappears behind the car seat.*] Okay. You can smell me. Human scent. Here I come, ready or not.

He starts back near the caravan, hands in pockets, whistling away, strolling past the car seat. He is past it before CHRISTIAAN *rises – slowly, sheepishly.* PA *stops and turns around.*

PA: There's no second sitting here, Krisjan. I'm gone orready.

CHRISTIAAN: I don't know what I'm supposed to do, Oom.

PA: Okay, come. I'll be the leopard.

CHRISTIAAN: No, Oom. What I mean is –

PA: We must do this, young man. You will thank me for this in the long run!

PA hops down behind the car seat. A nervous CHRISTIAAN finally allows himself to contribute some positive action in the form of a hesitant stroll before the car seat. PA leaps out at him, doing his leopard impression. There is a brief. onesided struggle during which PA gets the better of a confused CHRISTIAAN.

CHRISTIAAN: Sorry, Oom.

PA: What d'you mean, sorry? Kill me.

CHRISTIAAN: Kill you ... ?

PA: Try kill me!

He tackles CHRISTIAAN again, letting out a tremendous growl. The reaction is not encouraging.

CHRISTIAAN: It's no use, Oom.

PA: Okay. Orraight. You be the leopard.

CHRISTIAAN: Oom ... !?

PA: You be the leopard ... !

CHRISTIAAN: I don't understand why we doing this, Oom!

PA is on a roll now, there is a manic quality about him.

PA: Maybe you should take off your glasses. [*Whipping them off.*]

CHRISTIAAN: I can't see properly without my ...

PA: Leopard doesn't wear glasses!

PA shoves him behind the car seat, placing the glasses on the armchair. The routine is repeated. But what happens next is not at all what we expect. Instead of CHRISTIAAN leaping over the car seat, GIDEON appears as if out of nowhere and tackles PA from behind.

At first, PA thinks it is CHRISTIAAN playing ball at last.

PA: That's it! Now we cooking with gas ...

A titanic struggle ensues and now PA really struggles for his life. CHRISTIAAN can only gape in stunned disbelief.

EVIE comes charging on in apparent pursuit of GIDEON.

EVIE: It's on fire ... ! Gideon's pondok! It's burning! I smelt the petrol ... !

During their struggle, GIDEON grabs the length of hose used for the petrol. He manages to get it around PA's throat.

PA: Ghhaaaaaaah!

CHRISTIAAN makes a feeble attempt to help PA.

CHRISTIAAN: No, man ... ! What you doing ... !?
EVIE: Come help ... !

She runs to the tap with the intention of filling a bucket. There is no water. ⟨⟨⟨⟨⟨⟨⟨⟨⟨⟨⟨⟨⟨⟨⟩⟩⟩⟩⟩⟩⟩⟩⟩⟩⟩⟩⟩⟩ *and, shoving EVIE aside, tries the tap. He hits it in frustration, and charges off. CHRISTIAAN is concerned for PA.*

CHRISTIAAN: Oom ... ?

The penny drops about the lack of water.

EVIE: JJ ... ! He's cut off the water! He's turned off the bladdy mains ... !
PA [*holding his throat*]: Aaaah-jislaaik ... !
EVIE [*to CHRISTIAAN*]: Don't just stand there ... ! His shack is on fire ... !
Everything he has is burning to the bladdy – ! Ah - shit, man ... !!

PA's voice is returning.

PA: I'm gonna kill him. Sowaar, I'm gonna kill him ... !

EVIE runs to the braai, snatching up a plastic bowl.

PA, on the ground, reaches up and grabs her.

EVIE [*tugging free*]: You're pigs, the lota' you ... !
PA: No ... !
EVIE: You worse than pigs!
PA: I forbid you to go there! I forbid you to go anywhere near that kaffir ... !
EVIE: Fuck you ... !

She spits at him. Full in the face.

PA: Jassaaaaasss ... !!

She is gone. PA tries to get to his feet, but his leg is well and truly damaged. With a cry of pain, he crumples to the ground. CHRISTIAAN half follows EVIE then comes back.

CHRISTIAAN: Where my glasses, Oom? Where you put my glasses?
PA [*trying to get up*]: Rifle ... ! My bladdy rifle ... !
CHRISTIAAN: Shouldn't we go help ...

PA [*buckling again*]: Aaah ... !

CHRISTIAAN: Is Oom orraight, Oom?

PA [*gritting his teeth*]: Go inside, Krisjan. Go get my gun.

CHRISTIAAN finds his glasses, then looks at PA's leg.

CHRISTIAAN: Oh, here they are.

PA: Eina ...

CHRISTIAAN: Shoe! This is bad, Oom.

PA: He tried to kill me. You saw what he did. You my witness.

CHRISTIAAN: You got to get this to a doctor ...

PA: Self-defence ... !

EVIE comes charging back, heading for the caravan.

EVIE: We had that fire extinguisher ... !

PA scrambles to his feet. He has a score to settle.

PA: Jissus ... !

EVIE is crashing around inside the caravan and thus cannot escape when PA corners her. We hear him laying into her in no uncertain fashion.

PA: Who grew you up ... !? Filthy bitch ... !

Somehow she manages to break free and scramble out of the door. PA grabs her and, shoving her onto the car seat, whacks her several times across the backside. He reprimands her as he beats her.

PA: This is what happens to naughty girls who don't listen to their fathers! [*Standing over her.*] Now, if his pondok is burning, let it burn. If it burns to the ground, maybe then he'll get the message.

He turns to CHRISTIAAN – his trump card!

PA: And if he doesn't – I got Krisjan here to help me.

CHRISTIAAN starts.

PA: Isn't that so, Krisjan? We going to fix this thing together – the two of us.

CHRISTIAAN: Oom – er –

PA: I want you to disregard all you have seen here. This is not normally what happens here during the normal course of events. She's a good girl. She's a hard worker. And most the time, she does what she is told.

He takes her hand and then reaches out for CHRISTIAAN's. His desperation is unashamedly transparent now.

PA: She'll make a great catch for the right man.

EVIE [*summons up all she has and flings in his face*]: I got a man orready. And he's been here all the time. And stop trying to kick him out. He's never going to go away – because why? Because we love each other!

She is on her way to the pondok. PA *is stunned. He can only stand as if turned to stone.*

PA: No. No. Evie ... ! Ei – na ... !

He clutches at his painful leg.

CHRISTIAAN: Oom? Is Oom orright, Oom?

PA [*unable to believe it*]: What was she saying? Was she saying what I think she was ... ?

CHRISTIAAN: Maybe I should go, Oom? I can stop by a telephone? Get some help.

PA [*lost in his own world*]: I should have seen it coming. I caught his mother feeding them when they were still small. I came into the kitchen and there they were – one on each black tet ...

PA *slowly gets to his feet, shrugging him off.*

CHRISTIAAN [*trying to help him*]: Oom ...

PA: Noooo ... !!

PA *cannot bring himself to look at the young man, so great is his shame. He drags himself into the caravan, closing the door behind him.*

CHRISTIAAN: I suppose that means supper is off ... ? Oom?

'Trekliedjie' swells to cover the scene change, as the lights fade to blackout.

Scene Two

A few hours later. It is early evening. GIDEON *sits on the car seat, his clothes covered in soot, his shirt scorched.* EVIE *bandages his hand.*

At their feet are a few possessions saved from the blaze.

EVIE: When I was little, I thought that's how it happened. God had this book with your name in it ... [GIDEON *grimaces.*] Sorry ... ! Too tight? [*Re-winding the cloth.*] Anyway, God had this book. Every time you were good, you got a 'good' tick. Every time you were bad, you got a 'bad' one. At the end of your life, He'd add up all the ticks. If the bad outnumbered the good, He'd stick you in this big lift and send you down to Hell. The Devil would grab you – chuck you in the fire – and you'd burn there forever ... [*Finishing his hand.*] That better? [*He nods.*] What worried me was not the number of ticks I had – I knew I had more good ones than bad ones – I was just scared to death God would go and lose the bladdy book.

He looks up at her, still able to smile.

EVIE [*suddenly serious*]: Hey. You sure?

GIDEON speaks to her in their 'language' – a series of signs – indicating their decision to stay and that it will be dangerous. Is she ready for it?

EVIE [*interjecting throughout*]: Ja. I know. Okay.

A distraught CHRISTIAAN wanders on, looking back in the direction of the road. EVIE lets go of GIDEON.

EVIE [*to CHRISTIAAN*]: Still no sign of him?

CHRISTIAAN: I walked right up the road. Back the other way too. I hope he hurries up. I got work first thing in the morning, and I've still got to find my way home.

EVIE helps GIDEON place his salvaged possessions in the middle of an African blanket, to be tied into a bundle. Books, bits of clothing and so on – all semi-destroyed.

CHRISTIAAN: How long can it take for a test drive? I didn't want anything fixed. All I wanted was a bit of petrol. Coupla' litres.

EVIE picks up a charred assegai, inspecting it.

EVIE: Oh, look. [*to* GIDEON.] I remember when you made this.

GIDEON, using his bandaged hand, indicates fifteen.

EVIE: You were younger than that. It was before Amos died. [*Looking around.*] How about the shield?

GIDEON indicates that it was destroyed and takes the assegai, dusting it off.

EVIE: It was beautiful, that shield.

CHRISTIAAN paces about, moves toward the caravan.

CHRISTIAAN: Maybe we should ask your father? You think maybe he might know where he is?

EVIE: I don't think my father knows where he is himself, right now. [*Taking pity on CHRISTIAAN.*] Maybe you should just go. Try and get a lift up on the road.

CHRISTIAAN: You mean – without my car!?

EVIE: It might not be such a good idea to be here when JJ gets back.

CHRISTIAAN: But he's got my Volksie! I can't go without my Volksie ... !

GIDEON carefully, almost lovingly, washes his assegai at the tap, which is working again.

EVIE: Why don't you take the bakkie? Fair exchange.

CHRISTIAAN: I can't do that!

EVIE: I would, if I were you. It's about the only way you're likely to come out of this with anything at all. JJ has been known to sort of – take a fancy to certain things.

CHRISTIAAN [*horrified*]: You're saying he'd – he'd steal my car ... !?

EVIE: He wouldn't see it as stealing it. More like – taking it over. It runs in the family.

CHRISTIAAN: This is crazy. I mean – who are you people!?

EVIE: Sometimes I ask myself the same question.

CHRISTIAAN: I want my car back.

The sound of the caravan door as it opens with a loud clatter, causes them to spin around. PA is propped up by a withered stick of a crutch. He holds an old rifle in his hand. He glares at GIDEON with a Boere-Rambo leer.

CHRISTIAAN: Oom? I have to go now, Oom!

PA: You have as long as it takes for my son to get back. When my son gets back, I am not responsible for what comes to pass.

PA moves slowly to the chair against the caravan.

CHRISTIAAN: Oom?

PA cannot look at his daughter. She moves to him and speaks the last words she will say to him.

EVIE: Pa. Pa – we staying. No matter what anyone says or does. We staying.

She folds the blanket, rolls it up, and enters the caravan, dumping it inside. She stands at the door, looking at GIDEON.

GIDEON has the assegai in his hand. He joins EVIE and they enter the caravan, closing the door behind them.

There is a moment of silence before PA speaks to CHRISTIAAN.

PA: I think you better be on your way, my boy. This is going to be no piekniek by the dam.

CHRISTIAAN: I want to go, Oom. But – my car ...

PA: You will forget everything you have seen here today, you understand? None of this has happened, is that clear?

CHRISTIAAN: Yes, Oom. No ... !

PA: Is that perfectly clear!?

CHRISTIAAN: Yes, Oom.

PA: Then I will bid you farewell.

CHRISTIAAN: I'd like to go, Oom ...

PA: Good-bye ... !

PA's rifle points dangerously in the direction of CHRISTIAAN's stomach. He begins to back away slowly.

CHRISTIAAN: But, Oom – my car ...

There is a moment when nothing happens. PA seems to have cut CHRISTIAAN out of his life to the extent that the young man feels he no longer exists. We become aware of a sound off stage. A dog howling? It is the sound PA made when we heard him for the first time.

CHRISTIAAN reacts to it the way he reacted to it at the beginning of the play and then turns around. PA looks up. Staggering on, wielding a virtually empty bottle of Klipdrift, is JJ. He is motherless.

JJ: Bowwwwwww ... ! How's this, how's this – [*Throwing back his head.*] Howwwwww-wauwwww!!

PA hoists himself up onto his crutch, the angry patriarch.

CHRISTIAAN, *for his part, moves to JJ and then, fearing the worst, hares off in the direction of the road.*

PA: What the bladdy-hell ... !?

JJ: How's this? Bowwwwww-wauwwwwww ... !

PA: How dare you ... !?

JJ [*cackling*]: You can't beat that, hey? Hauwwwwwwww ... !

PA: How dare you come in here drunk ... !

JJ: Who's drunk ... ?

PA: I'll have no son of mine a dronk-lap bastard!

JJ: Whatsa' matter? You the only one around here who's allowed to get pissed ... !?

PA: Shut your dirty mouth ... ! [*Taking a swing at him.*] We got a problem here. We in Groot Kak!

JJ: Stuff you, man.

PA: Jissus ... !!

JJ has been circling out of harm's way around the back of the car seat, PA crab-crabbing after him. Now the older man switches into overdrive, swinging his crutch and hitting out at him.

PA: I've had about as much as I can take from you! I'm going to teach you the lesson of your life ... !

JJ: What 'lesson', ou top? You got fok-all more lessons to teach ... !

PA hurls his crutch at him. Even in his present state, JJ is able to avoid being caught – a far different set of circumstances from the time they last clashed.

JJ: I'm in charge now. I'm putting you out to pasture. You in with the cows. You can go chew grass ...

PA: We'll see about that!

PA snatches up the power-saw, trying in vain to start it.

JJ: Pasture-time, granpa ... ! [*Cackling.*] 'Past-your-time ... !'

PA: Fok-it ... !

JJ: Give here, man ... !

JJ grabs the power-saw and swings PA around – hurling him to the ground. JJ bellows with laughter and kicks PA square in the face. The old man comes back – his pride at stake. JJ kicks him to the body – again and again, until there is no more fight left in the old dog.

JJ stands above his father and there is an eerie moment of silence. JJ moves to the bucket beneath the tap and pours the entire contents over his head. The sobering effect is instant. He shakes the water off, roaring like a lion.

He glances at his father before heading for the door to the caravan. He stops when he sees the rifle, moving to it and picking it up.

JJ: What's with the gun?

PA *lies in a crumpled heap, not responding.*

JJ: You had some trouble?

He plants himself on the car seat – in full control.

JJ: So. He didn't like it when I burned down his pondok? [*Smiling, savagely.*] I'd love to have seen his face.

PA [*hand to his bloodied nose*]: You might just do that. And sooner than you think.

JJ: Uh-uh, aikona – [*He has thought of it all.*] After I've flattened the house, he won't even have a tree to sleep under.

PA *starts laughing, a low gurgle. The irony of it all!*

PA: I hate to disappoint you, but – not only is he here to stay – he's shacked up with your sister.

JJ stares at him. PA *lets it sink in.*

PA: It's your baby now.

JJ's knuckles whiten as he clutches the gun, not knowing whether the old man is having him on or not.

JJ [*quietly*]: Don't bullshit me.

PA: Just what are you going to do about it, is what I want to know?

Just when we thought we would never see him again, CHRISTIAAN *appears – running on, out of breath. There is a self-righteous air about him. He addresses* JJ.

CHRISTIAAN: Okay. Now, don't tell me any stories because I've checked and double-checked. You took my parking meter money, you took my rear-view mirror and you took my Pioneer car radio.

JJ's eyes are still on his father. He slowly turns and disappears around the upstage side of the caravan. CHRISTIAAN *misreads his intentions, moving half way across the patio.*

CHRISTIAAN: Now, if you needed the money, that's okay. But if you don't mind, I'd like my car radio back, please.

JJ enters with the loud hailer, towering over his father.

JJ: Where are they?

He moves off, snatching up the rifle. CHRISTIAAN *turns to* PA.

CHRISTIAAN: Oom, I don't want to make a fuss or anything, but I paid over R500 for that radio ... !

In the distance, JJ *calls over the loud hailer.*

JJ [*muffled*]: Come out, wherever you are! This is a warning! A final warning! Evie ... ? Don't make me hurt you ... ! I don't want to hurt you ... !

CHRISTIAAN pauses to listen to JJ, then turns back to PA, who chortles away.

CHRISTIAAN: Oom? If I give you money for the petrol, Oom?

JJ [*off*]: Evie ... !? Where are you!?

CHRISTIAAN turns to the caravan in a futile attempt to get some attention.

CHRISTIAAN: All I want is some fair treatment here! Just give me my car radio and I'll go. Please, Oom. I won't make any fuss.

It is obvious that he is going to get no further joy from anyone. He turns out front. Very gently, 'Trekliedjie' begins playing underneath – an eerie adaptation which underscores CHRISTIAAN's words as he turns and speaks to the audience as he did at the start of the play. The follow spot picks him up, to stay with him.

CHRISTIAAN: It was as if he was looking straight through me. Like as if I wasn't there. I wasn't there for any of them anymore. All of a sudden, my car radio wasn't important. I knew I had to get out of there – as quickly as possible ...

As CHRISTIAAN turns to leave, he almost runs slap-bang into JJ who enters, lugging the rifle and dumping the bull-horn.

JJ: This is not the way to do it. You got to do it properly.

CHRISTIAAN: And yet, something held me back.

JJ: Go hunting like we used to go hunt with Oupa. Food. Torches. The whole kaboodle. When you go for big game, you go prepared. [*JJ, struggling with the rifle bolt, turns on PA.*] Why didn't you tell me the rifle was jammed?

CHRISTIAAN: I should've gone. I should've gone then ...

JJ: Rifle's supposed to be your best bladdy friend, man ... !

JJ turns to enter the caravan, ditching the rifle.

PA: JJ ... ! [*He stops.*] Where you going?

JJ: To fetch the oil. What you think?

PA: In the caravan!?

JJ: Why not?

PA: Why don't you take the power-saw?

JJ: Power-saw ... !? What for?

PA: While you're in there. Do them both.

JJ: Do them both?

PA: Two birds with one stone, man.

JJ [*smiling*]: You think I'm a poephol?

PA: I dunno. Time will tell.

JJ grins from ear to ear and, holding up a middle finger, gives him the cockiest of parting shots.

JJ: This is for you.

He turns away and enters the caravan.

CHRISTIAAN [*stepping forward and addressing the audience*]: And that's when I left. That's when I turned around and ran away. I must've driven all the way home in third, the car was smoking so much. It was only a couple of days later that the whole thing finally hit me. The whole – nightmare. And that's when I started making excuses. I'm still making excuses ... [*Turning to look at the caravan.*] But why? Is it because I was there, and I did nothing?

PA: I gotta fix that bladdy TV, man. It's the final episode, Tuesday night ...

CHRISTIAAN: Yes! That's what it is ... ! That's why it won't go away ... ! I should've stayed to see it ... !

PA: Call in Early Bird – Teljoy. Get it right.

CHRISTIAAN: I have to see for myself how it ends!

PA: It's building up to one hell of a climax!

CHRISTIAAN: But *how!?*

PA: Gotta watch it.

CHRISTIAAN: I wasn't *there!*

PA: Jenna goes back to Bobby.

CHRISTIAAN: But, wait! What am I thinking? There's only one possible way it can end! Isn't there?

PA: Ray Krebbs kicks the bucket!

CHRISTIAAN has moved back now. positioning himself to see the caravan door most effectively. He turns to PA. The musical sting snaps off abruptly. The door swings open – nothing happens.

PA: Wait-wait ... ! I've got it. There's this rodeo, okay? Big championship rodeo. Now Ray knows he's only the ex-champ of Texas, but he enters anyway ...

A blood-spattered JJ appears in the doorway. He carries the assegai, dripping with blood. His eyes have the 'thousand-mile stare'.

PA: Now, at first, everything goes lekker. He rides some big ones. But then – it happens! He gets thrown – a moersa shot!

JJ moves to the car seat and sits down.

PA: All the officials gather around – ja, it's true – he's broken his neck. He's well and truly kicked the bucket. [*CHRISTIAAN slowly, tentatively moves to the caravan.*] So there's this moersa funeral, okay? Southfork. Everyone's there. Ewings,

Barnses, you name it. Standing at the graveside is Jenna – crying on Clayton's shoulder. She looks across – she sees Bobby.

CHRISTIAAN *shudders at what he sees inside the caravan.*

PA: Now, all Bobby wants to do is pick her up and take her in his arms, but he knows – it's neither the time, nor the place ...

CHRISTIAAN: No!

PA [*to* CHRISTIAAN]: What d'you mean – no!?

CHRISTIAAN: It can't be ... !

PA: It's the only way!

CHRISTIAAN: This is *my* story, old man!

PA [*incensed*]: Rotate my crops ... !? [PA's *hold on sanity is fast slipping away. Propped against his beloved Sasol drum, he begins chuckling to himself.*] In order to rotate your crops, you got to have a crop to begin with. [*Taking in his domain, broken, pathetic.*] And the only crop I got – is sweet bugger all ... [*Starts to sing.*] 'I'm dreaming – of a white ... '

He breaks off, cackling dementedly, dropping his head on to his chest – the laughter giving way to tears.

'Trekliedjie' begins very quietly.

CHRISTIAAN, *still positioned near the door to the caravan, looks inside. The light comes up in the caravan – an ultra-bright light – turning the lace curtains gold. We hear* GIDEON *playing his Jew's harp, a heart-warming sound. And then* EVIE *begins laughing – there is a feeling of joy and hope.*

CHRISTIAAN *turns to the audience as 'Trekliedjie' swells to drown* GIDEON *and* EVIE's *bright laughter.*

The stage lights fade to blackout. The glowing light in the caravan fades to blackout. The follow spot on CHRISTIAAN *grows smaller and smaller – until we are back with the pin-spot we had on his face when the play began.*

Blackout.

Mooi Street Moves

A ONE-ACT PLAY IN THREE SCENES

Martin le Maitre as HENRY STONE and Zane Meas as STIX LETSEBE.
Photograph by Ruphin Coudyzer.

Cast

STIX LETSEBE, a city slick black dude in his mid-to-late twenties. Streetwise, charming-when-he-wants-to-be, but as dangerous as a sharpened bicycle spoke when the chips are down.

HENRY STONE, a white country bumpkin, also in his twenties. Slow and somewhat nerdish, he is out of his depth in *Jozi* and flat-broke.

The action takes place in a bachelor flat in a rundown Hillbrow (Johannesburg) tower block.
The time is 1993.

Mooi Street Moves was first performed at the Great Hall, Grahamstown Festival Fringe in June 1992, with Seputla Dan Sebogodi as Stix Letsebe and Martin le Maitre as Henry Stone. The production was directed by Paul Slabolepszy (assisted by Lara Foot). This final, full-length version was first performed at the Market Theatre, Johannesburg, on 27 January 1993, with the same cast. It was subsequently showcased at the Theatre der Welt festival in Munich in June 1993 and at the Glasgow Mayfest in 1994 with Zane Meas as Stix and Martin le Maitre as Henry Stone. The first American production of the play took place in September 1993 at MetroStage in Alexandria, Virginia. The production was produced and directed by Carolyn Griffin, with Doug Brown as Stix and Jeffrey Yates as Henry.

A large, sparse room. An old mattress lies on the floor. Around the room are pristine cardboard boxes, all shapes and sizes – marked Telefunken, Sanyo, Panasonic, and so on. Milk crates serve as chairs, there are pictures of Orlando Pirates on the walls. If the place resembles a squatter shack, so much the better. On lights up, we find a white man in his late twenties standing room centre. He is wearing an open shirt, slacks and well-worn shoes, and clutching to his breast a large brown paper bag with New York (or some such American logo) on it. Facing him, holding a tin plate of steaming pap, is a black man of the same age, flashily dressed. The black man silently offers the white man the food. There is no response.

STIX: Thata. [*Pause.*] Take it.
HENRY: It's okay.
STIX: Take it.
HENRY: It's okay.
STIX: For sure, it's okay.

> *STIX holds out the plate. HENRY clutches his paper-bag-suitcase. There is a pause – a frozen tableau.*

STIX: Thata.
HENRY: I don't like pap.
STIX: You don't like pap?
HENRY: No.
STIX: I make food. You don't want food?
HENRY: I've never liked pap.

> *STIX turns slowly and goes to his portable cooker – downstage – scooping the pap from the plate back into the pot on the flame.*

> *They study each other furtively during a long, awkward pause – STIX slowly stirring the pap with a metal coat hanger. The central light bulb flickers. They both look to the light. The white man is startled by the black man's angry cry.*

STIX [*shouting to the heavens*]: Ningazi ngama simba ... ! Si badala irent lana ... ! (Don't come with shit ... ! We paying rent here ... !)

> *Eventually STIX turns off the flame and, rising, moves to his mattress – still exchanging the odd wary glance with the white man. He sits down on his bed and begins to eat from the pot with his fingers, blowing at the food.*

> *HENRY mooches about, still clutching his paper bag. Every now and then, he looks towards STIX, who goes on eating.*

> *HENRY stares out of the window and sighs, perplexed.*

STIX: Sorry – ?

HENRY: Sorry – ?

STIX: You say something?

HENRY: No. I was just ...

STIX: Aha.

   Pause.

HENRY: I don't understand it.

STIX: Nami. (Me too)

   Pause.

HENRY: I don't ... I dunno. I'm ... I dunno.

STIX: Sekunjalo. (This is how it is)

HENRY: No, but, I mean – he didn't ... there was no ... why would he just ... ? [*Pause.*] Doesn't make sense.

   HENRY paces about, confused – unsure of his next move.

STIX [*to himself, in the vernacular*]: Stupid mugu. I make him pap and he doesn't want to eat it. How can a person not eat pap? Stupid mugu.

   HENRY stops his pacing.

HENRY: Unless ... unless he just ...

STIX [*in the vernacular*]: Be hungry. I don't care.

HENRY: Unless one day he just decided to – you know? [*Pause.*] But then why didn't he tell me?

STIX: Tell you?

HENRY: Yes. Why didn't he ... ? He could of written.

STIX: A letter?

HENRY: Yes. He could of said, listen – I'm – you know – I'm sort of ... I'm sort of ...

STIX: He didn't do that?

HENRY: No.

STIX: No letter?

HENRY: No. Unless ... unless he wrote me a letter and I didn't get it.

STIX: You didn't get it?

HENRY: Yes. No. That's if he wrote it, that is.

STIX: Yes. If he didn't write it, you wouldn't get it.

HENRY: No.

STIX: You have to write a letter and send it, for somebody to get it.

HENRY: Yes.

STIX: Write it. And then – ka-plak – in the post.

HENRY: I can't understand why he didn't do that.

Slight pause.

STIX: So this is what I'm saying, you see.

HENRY: What?

STIX: This is the story.

HENRY: What?

STJX: This.

HENRY: This?

STIX: Ja.

Pause.

HENRY: You think so?

STIX: This is what I'm thinking. Me, myself.

HENRY: That he just ... he just ... ?

STIX: Ja. [*Pause.*] Unless you got the wrong place.

HENRY: Oh, no – he lived here. This was his pozzie – no doubt about that. I remember exactly what it looked like ... I mean, here was the ... whatjoocallit? Right over here ... one a' those – um – I even slept on it ...

STIX: What ... ?

HENRY: One of those arm-chair-couch kinda' things that you – sort of – er – you do things to it and it ... and it ... sort of it ... and it becomes a sort of a ... it becomes a sort of a bed.

STIX: A bed?

HENRY: Yes. You sort of – [*Demonstrating.*] – up and out ... and it turns into a ... turns into a kind of a bed.

STIX: Aikona! Chair that says – hey, mfo! – I'm also a bed?

HENRY: You never seen them?

STIX [*vernacular*]: I must get me one of those.

HENRY: And then ... and then over there ... on that wall there – no, wait a minute – that wall over there – he had a TV unit.

STIX: TV unit?

HENRY: Yes. Except he had no TV. He was going to get a TV, but at the time he still didn't have one. Well, he had one, but it was a small one – little one – black and white. He got the unit first so that when he eventually got the new one, he'd have a place to put it, you see. He wouldn't have to worry about – you know ...

STIX: Where to put it ...

HENRY: That's right. And over here, he had a coffee table and a ... a gramtape-deck sorta' – radio. Carpet on the floor – pictures on the wall – smart – fancy lamp-stand ... all sorts of things.

STIX: All the mod cons.

HENRY: Sorry?

STIX: Modern appliances. You know – zabba-zabba – [*Whistles.*] Phee-phoo ... ?

HENRY: Ja, for sure. He had lots of those.

STIX: But no TV?

HENRY: He was planning to get one. New one. He had an old one, but he was gonna get another one. Nice one.

STIX: Too bad he's not still around, I could organise a very good colour TV. Easy terms. Codesa-desa, the price – no VAT! [*Takes his pot – collects plate.*] You not looking maybe for a good colour TV, huh? Philips? Telefunken? Remote Control? Zabba-zabba ... ! [*Looking him up and down.*] No? Too bad. [*He rinses off the plates in a plastic bowl filled with water. HENRY is staring at the bowl.*] Water is off, my bra. To get it, we must go to the river. [*He laughs at Henry's wide-eyed reaction.*] [*STIX crosses to his bed, patting his wet hands on HENRY's back. He grabs his newspaper (The Sowetan) and begins to read it. The lights flicker again and then snap off. In the darkness, STIX yells at the top of his voice.*] Bulala bathakathi ... !! (Kill the Whites ... !)

HENRY [*petrified*]: Juss-laaik ... !!

STIX guffaws and flicks a cigarette lighter, holding it close to his face. He shouts to the heavens yet again.

STIX: Hey! Madala ... ! Woza ... ! I-switch!

He begins singing a tribal song ('Impi ... ') – an eerie feel in the light of the flickering lighter.

Presently the lights come on again and STIX blows out the flame.

STIX: Aha! And Madala said – Let There Be Light!

HENRY could be forgiven for thinking he is slap-bang in the middle of a Third World lunatic asylum.

HENRY: How long you say you been staying here?

STIX: Me? Longtime.

HENRY: How long?

STIX: Long-long.

Pause.

HENRY: How long is that?

STIX: Too long.

HENRY stares at him – lost. He paces about.

HENRY: Wait a minute. I gotta do some thinking here, boy ... I got to do some quick bladdy thinking now.

STIX: Ja. Thinking is free, my bra. Coevert!

STIX watches HENRY as he mooches about. He takes a flashy tie from beside his mattress – inspects it.

HENRY: I'm sorry – I'm just trying to sort out sorta' … what I'm gonna do now. I'm a bit – I'm a bit …

STIX: Deurmekaar.

Pause.

HENRY: Okay, Look. Where can I find the caretaker?

STIX: Hah. Take care of what?

HENRY: How about a landlord?

STIX: You mean the owner?

HENRY: Man sort of – um … Man in Charge.

STIX laughs – thinly. Crosses to a clothing rail.

STIX: Last time I see guy like that is 1988. [*He holds up five fingers.*] Five years.

HENRY: That's bullshit …

STIX: Aikona. Is Hillbrow.

HENRY: Where do you go to pay the rent?

STIX [*hanging the tie on the clothing rail*]: Hah!

HENRY [*a beat*]: You saying to me – what you saying is, you don't pay rent … !?

STIX laughs. HENRY stares at him.

STIX: Hey! Where you from, my bra? Nothing is for mahala, jong. [*In the vernacular, tapping his head.*] Use your upstairs, white idiot – vuga wena! [*Back to English.*] He comes to collect once a month. N'kosi malanga. The Godfather.

HENRY: Godfather … ?

STIX: That's right, my bra … three rings – priiing-priinggg-prrriiinnggg … ! Lookout – big shit! Some people call him Comrade Kommissar-Chairman Mao. But, hey – this political shit, is safer just to call him – you know – like the top dog. He's the … he's the …

HENRY: The supervisor?

STIX: Aikona. He's the Godfather. But he's not like Al Pacino–Marlon Brando, uh-uh. He's like – er – George Foreman. George Foreman with a sore head. Mike Tyson. Mr T. You know Mr T … ? It's always – come, come – what you got, bra? – whatever you got – doesn't matter! Some bucks … Jack Daniels … Dulux Weatherguard.

HENRY is speechless. STIX crosses to his bed.

STIX: Whatever you got, bra. [*Clicks fingers.*] Come, come – Give Me Your Slice. Golden Banana.

HENRY [a *beat*]: He a painter, or what?

STIX: Who?

HENRY: What's he want with Dulux Weatherguard?

STIX guffaws and taps his head, mumbling to himself.

STIX: Why you not eat pap, my bra? [*HENRY cannot make head nor tail of this guy.*] Pap makes you big. Makes you strong.

HENRY stares at him long and hard, before turning on his heel and heading for the door.

STIX: Hey! Where you go now?

HENRY: Hey?

STIX: Where you go?

HENRY [a *beat*]: I gotta go find my brother ...

STIX: How you gonna do this? You know what the time it is now? Come. Sit down. Put down your bag. Have some food.

STIX leads him back in - sits him down.

HENRY [*quietly protesting*]: No, it's ...

STIX moves to the 'kitchen corner', picks up a fresh half-loaf of bread and a bottle of atjar - slaps them onto a plate - and offers it to HENRY.

STIX: Thata.

HENRY stares at him.

STIX: Bread. Fresh bread. White. [*Checking the jar.*] This ... ? This is atjar. [*HENRY stares at him, nonplussed.*] You don't know atjar? You don't know many things, wena? Don' worry. You come a long way and you don't know what's going on here. Is okay. [*He goes back to his paper.*]

HENRY: Where can I find the bloke who's in charge?

STIX stares at him, unable to believe this bloke.

STIX: There is no Bloke Who's in Charge, my bra!

HENRY: I gotta find someone who can ...

STIX: Listen to me! You not listening ... ! [*Patiently, spelling it out.*] Kyk. The building – okay? – this building – okay? – is run by the Action Committee representing the dwellers – that's all the peoples who's living here. But the Action Committee is in delicate negotiations with a representative of the owner who cannot be found right now because he is missing.

HENRY: The owner?

STIX: That's right. In Sandringham or Kensington or somewhere like that – nobody knows. Some guys are even talking Toronto.

HENRY [*a beat*]: Who's this now – the Godfather?

STIX: Aikona. Aikona. The Godfather is someone else. He is on the other side. There is another disagreement at present because the Action Committee is claiming that this Godfather is not representing THEM, but ANOTHER Action Group who is trying to sequestrate the building from the owner on behalf of ALL the peoples living in this area on the grounds of lack of adequate infrastructure – lights, running water, sewerage – things like that. Is a – whatjoo-call? – is what they call a two-prong breakdown on two fronts. Is a double dispute.

HENRY stares at him

STIX: In other words – it's a foggop. You understand a foggop … ?

HENRY: Yes.

STIX: Good. You understand something.

STIX takes out a knife, moves to cut the bread.

STIX: This explains, you see, why when you come in this building – you see some people are making fires in the electric stove. 'n Boer maak 'n plan, but a Black Man – he goes all the way, Lion Lager. [*He prepares a thick slice of bread with atjar.*] I know some guys who living here from longtime before. I ask them tomorrow, maybe they know where he's gone – your brother. They know everything – these guys. Everything. [*Plonking atjar-filled bread onto a plate.*] Okay. You eat this, my bra. You don't eat it, I give it to the street childrens – I'm not throwing it away.

HENRY does not budge.

HENRY: Can't we go find these guys now?

STIX: Is two o'clock in the morning, my bra. You knock on somebody's door this time, they kak on your head – throw you down the stairs. The only reason I'm not throw you down the stairs is that I'm a happy-go-lucky. I'm what they call a night bird. [*He makes for the door, plate in hand.*] Goodnight, bra.

HENRY: Where you going?

STIX: I'm going to find some hungry kids.

HENRY: Wait a minute –

STIX: Ah. You want it? Good –

He thrusts the plate into HENRY's hand. Henry is left standing holding his bag and the plate – still rooted to the spot. STIX stretches out on the mattress and picks up his copy of The Sowetan, *perusing the back page.*

STIX: Ai – ai – ai … ! Aikona – ! Fani Madida – ai! [*He 'scores' a goal.*] La-duuuuuuu-ma … ! [*Paraphrasing an article.*] Zane Moosa is unhappy with Sundowns … ! We waiting for him. Free Transfer. Ace Khuse – Ace Khuse scores again … hai!

What d'you think of Ace Khuse?

HENRY [*distracted*]: 'Scuse me?

STIX: Khuse? Ace Khuse? Kaiser Chiefs? [*He looks up from his paper for the first time.*] What's wrong, bra?

HENRY: Hey?

STIX: Hey? Hey? Your brain is gone on holiday, my bra. Is gone to Durban? What is wrong, my friend?

HENRY: No, I'm just ... if I don't find my brother tonight, I'll have no place to crash.

STIX: Crash? Where is this crash?

HENRY: Huh?

HENRY is at the window again, looking out over the Hillbrow flatland – lost – stranded.

STIX [*looking at him long and hard*]: What kind of malaka is this, huh? How can you come to a place after ten years and think everything, she will be the same?

HENRY: Six years ...

STIX: Mandela is free, my bra. Soweto has come to town. Things are different, jong.

HENRY: Ja, I know that.

STIX: You know that?

HENRY: I can see that.

STIX: What can you see?

HENRY: I've noticed.

STIX: You notice?

HENRY: Ja.

STIX: What you notice?

HENRY: Hey?

STIX: What you notice?

HENRY: No, that ... you know ... things are different.

STIX: Different?

HENRY: Things are different.

STIX: How are they different?

HENRY: Hey?

STIX: How are they different? In what way? You say things are different. What is this different?

HENRY [*a beat*]: What you trying to do here?

STIX: Where ... ?

HENRY: You trying to make me say something I don't wanna say ... !

STIX: Or is it who ... !?

HENRY: You trying to ... you tryna' put words into my mouth ... !

STIX: How can I put the words into your mouth, my bra? Words are not something you can eat – like bread!

STIX takes the plate from him, moves away. HENRY is about to leave. Not looking at him, STIX calls out.

STIX: I know where's your brother.

HENRY stops. Turns.

HENRY [*a beat*]: You know where my brother is?
STIX: I know someone who knows.

Pause.

HENRY: Since when?
STIX: Since longtime.
HENRY [*a beat*]: You lie.
STIX [*shrugs*]: Okay.

Pause.

HENRY: Where is he?
STIX: I don't know – but this guy – I know where to find him. We go find him tomorrow.
HENRY: Tomorrow?

STIX starts clearing away the pap pot and plates.

STIX: Don't worry about tonight. Tonight you stay here, tonight.
HENRY: Here ... ?
STIX: I've got blanket here. We can make place here. Is okay. [*Getting a place prepared.*]
HENRY: No, no – it's okay.
STIX: For sure, is okay.
HENRY: No, I'm saying – it's okay. I'm fixed up.
STIX: Where you fixed up?
HENRY: Hey?
STIX: Where's this place you fixed up?
HENRY: No, it's sort of ... [*Points off vaguely.*] It's okay. [*He hovers about.*] I'll come back tomorrow.
STIX: You come back?
HENRY: Ja. I gotta find my ... sheesh! [*He smiles, sheepishly – backing out.*] Thanks for the – um – [*Pulling up, abruptly.*] Oh, ja – er – what time?
STIX: Time?
HENRY: What time tomorrow?
STIX: Tomorrow.
HENRY: Ja, but what time? Eight o'clock? Nine o'clock? [*STIX stares at him.*] Okay, look I'll come ... I'll come sort of ... first thing. Um – okay. See you then.

HENRY goes. STIX mutters under his breath in the vernacular. He flicks at an orange with his foot – plays soccer with it, humming a tune. Goes back to his newspaper. Presently, HENRY reappears. He looks shocked, frightened.

STIX: Ja? What you want? If the lift, she's broken, you must use the stairs.

HENRY: There's a guy out there, he's got a knife ... !

STIX [*mock horror*]: A knife!?

HENRY: Outside there ... it's a big bladdy ... !

STIX grabs him, melodramatically.

STIX: Hey, wait – he's got one eye ... ?

HENRY: Ja, ja – it was all sort of white ...

STIX [*laughing*]: Ah, don't worry about him, my bra. That's Mashubane. He's in the business.

HENRY: Business ... ?

STIX: Ja. Thought he was gonna steek you? Come and have a dop. [*Turning away.*] Hey – they call him One Eye Jack. He's selling the girls from the building ...

HENRY: Girls ... !?

STIX: Hey, you wanna girl? Nice one? [*Indicates an ample figure.*] Electric blanket ... ?

HENRY: You mad, man ...

STIX [*laughing*]: Just checking. Come. Siddown.

He moves to the 'kitchen area', hauls out a bottle of whisky, pours a shot in a tin mug and offers it to HENRY.

HENRY: No, it's – er –

STIX: You want a glass?

HENRY: No, no – I don't ... I don't drink.

STIX: Hey-yob! You don't eat. You don't drink. Wena, you must say your prayers. He is coming to get you – that Big Makulu Boss in the Sky. The one with the white beard ... the white shirt ... sitting on the white cloud ... all the white little angels ... [*Afterthought.*] White maid ... [*Offers again.*] Thata.

HENRY: No thanks.

HENRY, nervous about going off down the passage, hovers about. STIX chuckles. watching the white man.

STIX: Hey, witgat. My broe. Tell me something. Do you think God is white?

HENRY: Hey?

STIX [*sipping at the whisky*]: God is not white. Uh-uh. The white people, they think God is white. But God is not white. God is the Bushman. On the other side of the moon. He comes in the night ... while you are sleeping. He shoots you in the gat. [*Indicating his backside.*] Ktoeeei ... ! If the arrow is the good one, things are good. If the arrow is the bad one ...

HENRY [*chortling*]: Huh.

STIX: You don't believe?

HENRY: Shoots you in the gat?

STIX: Right here. [*Indicating his rump.*] Tzak!

HENRY [*considering this*]: Nah ...

> STIX *laughs, shaking his head.* HENRY *laughs and then squirms, embarrassed at having dropped his guard in the black man's company. He approaches* STIX, *subserviently.*

HENRY: Um. Sorry. Listen. Can you help me out with a couple of ... ? Just 'til tomorrow ... [*Toying with an automatic teller Help-U card.*] I'm sort of ... um ...

STIX: You got no money?

HENRY: This is – um – this thing doesn't work.

STIX: What is that?

HENRY: No, this a Help-U card, but it's ...

STIX: Help-U card? [*Taking it from him.*] What good is Help-U card if it doesn't help you?

HENRY: No, I said to them in Richards Bay – before I left – I hate these things. I never wanted it in the first place. I said to them, I rather ... ag ... ! Gotta find my boet – my boet'll sort it out.

STIX: Ja, jong. Any man who puts his money in a video machine in the street is asking for trouble.

HENRY: Ten, twenty rand ...

STIX: Williams?

HENRY: Hey?

STIX: Your name is Peter?

HENRY: Henry. Henry Stone.

STIX [*staring at the card*]: Who is P Williams?

HENRY [*a beat*]: No, man – ag, it's a long story.

STIX: Ja, these things, jong. That's why God gave you socks. You put your bucks in your shoes. Or by your ballas. They see you with a big cock – [*Indicating running away.*] – psheeeow ... ! Zola Budd ... !

HENRY: Ja. Look. I pay you back when we find Steve. My boet. I promise.

> STIX *laughs at him, waving the card.*

STIX: Ha – haaa ... ! What's the story?

HENRY [*embarrassed*]: Ag ... please ...

STIX: Tell me the story. I like stories.

HENRY [*a beat, wearily*]: Ag, man. It was at the station. This bloke comes along and ...

STIX: Who is this?

HENRY stares at him, gloomily.

HENRY: Tonight. When I got off the train.

STIX: You rob this guy's card ... !?

HENRY: Are you mad? He took mine! Just talk, boy. All it is. Talk-talk-talk. [*STIX stares at him. HENRY cringes*] I thought he was trying to help me ...

STIX stares at him.

STIX: Help-U ... ?

HENRY [*this is not easy*]: I get off the train, and I haven't got any money, so ... so I'm trying to get some money outa' this machine ...

STIX: Ja ... ?

HENRY: So there's this man. He's dressed up all nice and smart and he kind of ... comes up to me ...

STIX: He says – let me help you ... ?

HENRY: No, he says – um – he says, are you saved?

STIX: Are you saved?

HENRY: Ja. But now I'm tired from all this time on the train and so I'm thinking – ja, well, he's talking about my savings and are they all sort of okay, you see – so I say, yes, yes – I'm saved, I'm fixed up. So then he says – Hallelujah, he says – Praise the Lord!

STIX: A – a – a – a ...

HENRY: So now he can see I'm having problems with my card, you see, so he says – are you having problems with your card? So I say, ja, well, I dunno – I'm not getting any bladdy joy here. He says – ah-ah-ah-ah – don't swear! Hey? I say – hell, I'm sorry, I mean ... jirre ... I'm not having any luck getting money outa' the machine. He says, ah-ha! He says he knows all about this because this is exactly what happened to him before he decided to invest with the Lord.

STIX: Invest with the Lord?

HENRY: Ja.

STIX: This is what he says?

HENRY: So he says let me show you. Then he takes out my card and then he sticks in his card and he starts punching all these numbers ... it comes out ... and then he says, look – look what the Lord has seen fit to give me since I turned my back on Evil.

STIX: A – a – a – a ...

HENRY: And it's written there, more than ten thousand rand.

STIX: Hau ... !

HENRY: No, so he says to me – how much do you want? So I say, no, it's okay – thank you very much – I only want my forty rand to see me through tonight. He, says – no, no – [*Mock preacher.*] Do You Believe? I say – ja, no, well ... we all mos believe, man.

STIX: Ja ... !

HENRY: So he says – Hallelujah – Praise the Lord, what's your number?

STIX: What's your number?

HENRY: What's my number ...

STIX: He wants your card number ... !?

HENRY: I didn't know what he was doing, so I ...

STJX: You give him your card number ... !?

HENRY: What else could I do ... ?

STIX: Hallelujah!

HENRY. Okay. Anyway. He takes out his card ... he puts back in my card. He punches away ... it comes out ... it's got eight thousand five hundred. He says – Hallelujah! The Lord loves you. I say, ja – fine, fixed up – can I please have my ... ? So he takes out the card, gives me the card – says, ja – I must go home and pray and then tomorrow if I want, I can go draw out as much money as I want.

STIX: And then he – pssshhhheeow! – Zola Budd?

HENRY: No, like an idiot ... ! [Hitting his head.] I waited for him to leave because I didn't want him coming back to worry me again.

STIX: He's got your card?

HENRY: I didn't know it until I sorta' – you know – had this thing spitting out all the time and I looked and saw the name.

STIX spits the card out of his mouth – highly amused.

HENRY: It's not actually very funny. I had all my money in that account – four hundred and eighty-five rand.

STIX: Not anymore, my bra. [He crosses to HENRY – laughing like a drain.] I see this guy, he comes in here – he's holding this bag. I say, why is he holding this bag like somebody is going to take it away from him all the time? Now I know. You been Saved once – you don't want to be Saved again. [He slaps HENRY on the back, falling about now.] 'Invest with the Lord ... Are you Saved ... ' [Sitting down, an afterthought.] The Lord Giveth and the Lord Taketh Away! [Packs up again.]

HENRY manages a brave smile, seeing the humour of it all. A brief pause.

HENRY looks about.

HENRY: Listen – um. You said ... it was okay ... if I kind of ... kip over.

STIX [a beat]: You mean ... crash?

HENRY: Dos down ...

STIX: Tiep?

HENRY: Stay the night.

STIX: Ja. You can sleep here, ja. [Smiling, enjoying this play on language.] La-la-panzi.

HENRY [getting with it]: Hit the sack.

STIX: S'coevert.

Pause.

HENRY: Hey, um … [*Heartfelt.*] Thanks.

STIX: No problem. No problem. Is not the Carlton.

HENRY: Sorry?

STIX: Is not the Carlton.

HENRY [*looking around*]: Roller-towel?

STIX: Hotel. Carlton Hotel.

HENRY: Oh. Ja.

Lights fade to blackout. Cross sound-light cue: 'Jericho' – from the Johnny Clegg/ Savuka album 'Cruel, Crazy, Beautiful World'.

On full lights up, it is the next morning. HENRY *sits at an upturned box eating bread and cheese, a blanket around his shoulders. Presently* STIX *enters – wearing a flashy pair of sunglasses and a leather cap, in addition to his fancy threads. He carries a number of new shoe boxes – an expensive haul. He stashes them on the pile of goods.*

HENRY: So? What happened … ?

STIX: Shhh … !

He tosses HENRY *a carton of cigarettes and shouts off – to some unseen person in the hallway.*

STIX: Manalapo … !!

HENRY [*staring at the carton*]: I only wanted one …

STIX *sticks his hand into his crotch area and hauls out his wad of notes. He counts them.*

STIX [*shouting off, in the vernacular*]: If you run away, I'll cut your balls off … !

He tucks the money back into his underpants and darts off – chatting animatedly to someone in the hallway. He reappears and immediately begins counting the shoe boxes.

HENRY: So. What's the story?

STIX: Huh?

HENRY: Ol' Steve?

STIX *spins around – pissed off.*

STIX: Hey! What day is it today?

HENRY: Hey?

STIX: What day is it today?

HENRY: Um. Tuesday.

STIX: Tuesday. Tuesday is a working day.

> *STIX does a recount of the shoe boxes, examining them one by one. HENRY watches him, intrigued.*

HENRY: What you doing?

> *STIX glances at him – back at the stuff.*

STIX [*a beat*]: Operation Hunger.

HENRY: You?

STIX: We are all hungry, my bra. Some people are more hungry than others. [*Placing the atjar jar before him.*] Try this. You like it. Coevert.

> *HENRY absently obeys him. STIX gets a small old suitcase. He opens it up and begins going through several piles of tickets, wrapped in elastic bands. He holds them up to the light, examining them. Throughout, he sings and hums.*

HENRY: Oh, ja. While you were out, I think he came. Three rings – triing- triing- triing! [*STIX stares at him, emotionless.*] I just – shaddap and pretended no-one was here.

> *STIX ignores him, comparing the tickets. HENRY looks on. STIX clearly does not like to be spied on.*

STIX: What you looking?

HENRY [*looking away*]: Sorry.

> *STIX selects several tickets and approaches HENRY. He slaps them onto the floor as if he is about to do some card trick – swapping and switching them around like a would-be magician.*

STIX: Okay, my bra – look sharp. Eat carrots. Which one is the right one?

HENRY: The right one?

STIX: The real one. Genuine article.

HENRY: Hey ... ?

STIX [*holding them up*]: Which one?

> *He swaps and switches like mad, con-trick time.*

HENRY [*taking a stab at it*]: That one.

STIX: This one?

HENRY [*confused*]: That one ...

STIX: That one ... ?

HENRY: This one.

STIX: You sure ... ?

HENRY: Wait ...

STIX: This one ... ?

HENRY: Wait, man – I can't see the numbers ...

STIX: Don't look at the numbers. Watch the birdie. Is like the Help-U card trick, heh? Tsak-tsak ... !

HENRY: What are they?

STIX thrusts one into his hand, pocketing the other.

STIX: For you. Don't thank me, thank the zabba-zabba ... ka-tshakka – ka tshakka ... ! When you the friend of the machine – you go where no man has never gone before.

HENRY [*reading*]: 'Ivory Coast ... ?'

STIX: Saturday. FNB Stadium. They lose one more time – pssht ... ! I never go again. Twenty-five bucks a seat. Daylight robbery. I want goals. I want six goals – six goals before half-time ... or they can all fok-off!

HENRY: Soccer-match?

STIX: Nigeria ... ! Phhht ... ! Zambia ... ! Phhht ... ! Zimbabwe! Phhht! Ons is kak, man. Orlando Pirates – we the only team that's beating Crystal Palace when they come to South Africa – but there's not one Buccaneer in the national squad! Not one! Instead, we got Philemon Masinga. [*Raving off, angrily.*] When Philemon Masinga is playing for South Africa, he doesn't know where is the goal. There is the goal – [*Imaginary goal.*] – Philemon Masinga is kicking all the way to Jabulani ... ! Kings Park Stadium! He thinks the crossbar, she's on top of the Brixton Tower! Boem! – Laduuuuuuuuuuuu-ma ... ! Ja. La-duma in Hartleyvale, Cape Town! [*He swears in the vernacular about useless arseholes who play for Sundowns.*] Bring back Screamer. We want Screamer. At least Screamer he's a Tshabalala and not a bladdy Portuguese from ... from Spain or wherever he comes from!

STIX whips up his tickets – back to his suitcase. Begins restacking them. HENRY watches him.

HENRY: So, did you manage to find him? This bloke?

STIX: What bloke?

HENRY: The bloke who knows where my boet is?

Irritated, STIX clumps the stacks of tickets in the suitcase, mumbling to himself – packing it away.

STIX [*in the vernacular*]: What must I do with this idiot? He comes here now and lands me in the shit just when I was getting organised. [*Back to English.*] Do this! Do that! Do this! Split focus!

HENRY changes tack – toys with his soccer ticket.

HENRY: Ja. Soccer. I'm not so mad for soccer myself, actually. Me, I like rugby.

STIX: What is this?

HENRY: Rugby.

STIX: What is this?

HENRY: Rugby, man. Rugby. You don't know rugby?

STIX: Is this the game they play, the ball she's like the banana?

HENRY: Banana ... ?

STIX: What is a ball, my bra? You know what is a ball ... ? [*Grabbing his orange.*] The ball, she's round. This is why they are calling it the ball. A ball is not like a banana – you run that side, the ball she's this side ... ga-dooiiingg ... ! You run this side, the ball she's – ga-doooiiinngg ... ! [*He runs around playing the dof whitey chasing a haphazardly bouncing rugby ball.*] Where's the ball ... ? Oh, there is the ball ... ! Where is the ball ... ? Oh, there is the ball ... ! Oh, no – the ball, she's – where is ... ? – ga-doooiiinngg ... !

HENRY: It's not like that, man ...

STIX: This running around is not something you can call a game. This is not something men with brains they are doing. This is a whole lot of boere – Afrikaner-monkeys – chasing the banana. [*Imitating a baboon.*] Hoh-hohhoh ... ! Hey, Fanie – ho-hoh – vat hom, Fanie ... hoh!

He is enjoying himself immensely, doing a fair impression of a baboon chasing a bouncing banana. He unscrews the cap of his Sparletta soft drink and takes a long drink, chortling to himself. He points at the large picture of the Orlando Pirates soccer team on the wall.

STIX: Me. Football, my bra ... soccer. Once a Pirate ... always a Pirate! Up the Bucs! [*He makes the crossbones sign. A pause.*] So you a fan of the Blue Bulls, hey? Naas Botha?

HENRY: No, uh-uh ... I like Faffa ... Faffa Knoetze. Western Province.

STIX [*disdainfully*]: Faffa ... !? [*Miming a man whistling, calling for his dog.*] Faffa ... phwee-phwoo ... Faffa, Faffa ... !

HENRY [*sheepishly*]: No, man ...

STIX: What kind of a name is Faffa ... !?

HENRY: It's a nickname, man. His mother called ...

STIX: No, bra. Now, soccer players ... soccer players, they have names. Guys like ... [*With great pride, these guys are gods.*] Doctor Khumalo ... Ace Ntsoelengoe ... John 'Shoes' Moshoeu ... [*His voice soaring.*] Augustine 'The Horse' Makalakalani ... ! Teenage Dladla ... ! Those ... are names, my bra.

HENRY: Ja. Um. Maak-a-kakkie who?

STIX looks at him – they exchange smiles.

STIX: Hey, wena!

HENRY [*chortling*]: Maak-a-kakkie …

STIX [*shaking his head*]: Faffa …

STIX sits down – playing with an orange – tossing it up, catching it – watching HENRY.

A short pause.

STIX [*a new tack*]: Tell me something, Harry …

HENRY: Henry.

STIX: Henry. Tell me, Henry. Your brother. Why you looking for him?

HENRY: What d'you mean? He's my boet. I want to see him. [*Smiling confidently.*] He's gonna sort me out. He's a businessman … own boss. No-one's gonna fire him. No, he'll fix me up – one-time. You check – I've got this plan. Got my eye on this drilling rig. To drill water.

STIX: Water?

HENRY: Ja. I read this ad in the paper. There's a guy down in Klerksdorp. Two thousand rand down – you pay the rest off in instalments.

STIX [*a beat*]: Your brother will buy this for you?

HENRY: Well, no – but we can – you know – make a plan. Maybe I work for him for a while. Maybe he gives me a loan. Maybe – I dunno – we'll see.

STIX: Uh-huh.

STIX gives nothing away. HENRY indicates the atjar.

HENRY: Hey, this stuffs quite nice, hey.

STIX: You like it?

HENRY [*mouth full, chewing*]: It's not bad.

STIX: Yes, atjar. Atjar is – er – is made from … how you say? – locust. [*HENRY freezes.*] Squash locust … brains of sheeps … [*HENRY looks ill. STIX guffaws.*] Aikona, man. Is okay … I'm joking … I'm joking …

They share a laugh. STIX drops his smile.

STIX: What happens if you don't find this brother of yours?

HENRY: No, I'll find him. [*He tries to swallow.*] Utcha … ?

STIX: Atjar.

HENRY: Atjar.

STIX watches him carefully.

STIX: So. Mister Henry Help-U card. You come now from where? Richards Bay?

HENRY: Huh. Dead loss. Kimberley, first of all.

STIX: Aha. Die Groot Gat. Big Hole. [*Laughs.*] In your stomach is also the big hole, huh? Not for long.

HENRY wolfs down his food, swigs at the coffee.

HENRY: Listen, I owe you one, hey?

STIX: One what?

HENRY [*indicating the fare*]: No, I see you right.

STIX: What? You gonna pay me with your Help-U card, bra?

HENRY: No, no – I'm serious. Me – I don't scrounge off nobody. 'Specially ...
'specially ... you know –

STIX: Underprivilege ...

HENRY: I see them right. [*He lights up a cigarette.*]

STIX [*mocking him*]: I'm very pleased to hear this, my bra – very pleased, because me, myself I was getting very worried ...

HENRY: Soon as I find my boet, I fix you up.

STIX: Ja. I'm sure. A man with such a smart suitcase as yours can fix up anyone. [*He lifts the New York paper bag.*]

HENRY [*the penny dropping*]: Oh, no – my suitcase fell apart. I was getting off the train and it – sort of ... splat! It was hellout old.

STIX: No problem. No problem. Maybe me, myself I can also do something for you. What is your fancy?

HENRY [*lost*]: Fancy ... ?

STIX: What's your preference, bra? I get you one cheap. You want a lock-bag? Sling-bag ... back-pack? Briefcase-satchel-moon-bag ... sun-bag ... starbag ... sporran ... !

HENRY [*lost*]: Sporran ... ?

STIX: I can organise. We Codesa-desa the price. Jus' say the word. [*HENRY laughs out loud.*] Hey, what's the matter with you? I'm offering you a good deal here.

HENRY: It's okay.

STIX: It's not okay, bra. You cannot walk around with a paper bag, even if it says New York. Shit is shit – doesn't matter what label you putting on.

HENRY [*smiling gauchely*]: You mad, man.

STIX: You the one who is mad, my bra. I make you a very sharp offer here. I know my job. I'm very good.

HENRY: Oh, ja? What you do?

STIX [*a beat*]: You don't know what I do? [*Aside.*] Makwerekwere. [*A pause.*] I'm a middle man.

HENRY [*a beat*]: What's that?

STIX: He's the man in the middle. There's the man on this side – there's the man on that side – there's the man in the middle. [*HENRY stares at him.*] I sell things.

HENRY: You sell things?

STIX: I'm a businessman. People sell to me. I sell to other people.

HENRY: What do you sell?

STIX: Everything.

HENRY: Everything?

STIX: Anything. What you want?

HENRY [*smiling*]: Nothing.

STIX: Nobody wants nothing. Everybody wants something. You tell me just now, you want a ... whatjoo-call ... ?

HENRY: What?

STIX: For the water ...

HENRY: Drilling rig?

STIX: I get you one.

HENRY: Where from?

STIX: Maybe I know somebody. This person, he knows somebody else ...

HENRY: A drilling rig?

STIX: If there is one somewhere, you can get it.

HENRY: It's not for nothing, hey ...

STIX: Nothing is mahala. You work for me, I make you rich.

HENRY: Me?

STIX: I make you rich.

HENRY: I work for you!?

STIX: What you say?

HENRY: Doing what?

STIX: Selling.

HENRY stares at him.

HENRY: You mad, man. I've never sold anything in my whole life ... !

STIX: You can learn. Anyone can learn. People will buy anything ... people will buy shit if you smile, wrap it up nice and do the right things.

HENRY: Uh-uh, no ... that's not right ...

STIX: You never bought shit?

HENRY: Never!

STIX: Nooit?

HENRY: Nooit ...

STIX: Ja? And last night this guy sells you a kak Help-U card for four hundred and eighty-five bucks ... ?

HENRY: No, no – that was ...

STIX grabs his arm – leads him to the merchandise.

STIX: Woza ...

HENRY: What you doing?

STIX grabs a brand new toaster box.

STIX: Come. You sell me this toaster.

HENRY: Hey ... ? Wha ... ? It's not mine.

STIX: Don' worry – come. Stand here. You in Mooi Street. This is Mooi Street. I'm walking down Mooi Street. You sell me that toaster.

HENRY: No, wait ...

STIX: Okay. Now, Mooi Street – it's a busy road ... one-way ... all the cars are going that way ... peak hour traffic, right ... I area' people on the pavement. There's a guy selling apples over there ... woman selling snuff here ... there's someone throwing up in the alley around the corner .... you get the picture ... ?

HENRY: Ja, no, but ... hang on ...

STIX ignores him, positions himself some distance away and launches boldly into his routine – in this case, a rap song – as he moves off down 'Mooi Street'. (It could also be a tribal song, a shebeen song).

STIX [*moving and rapping*]: 'Honking at the honey in fronta' you with the light on ... she turns around to see what you was beepin' at ... it seems the summer is a natr'l affrodisiac ... '

He peters out and turns to a dumbstruck HENRY.

STIX: Hey, mugu ... ! Sell it to me!

HENRY: You don't want to buy this.

STIX: How do you know? Come. Stand here. When I go past – sell it to me ... ! [*Over HENRY's protests.*] Come, bra. Get the situation here. The cars ... the people ... the woman selling snuff here ... the guy still 'round the corner, throwing up ...

HENRY: But, wha ... ? Uh ...

He repeats the exercise following the same routine. This time HENRY makes a pathetic attempt to part with it.

STIX [*with feeling*]: 'Honking at the honey in fronta' you with the light on ... she turns around to see what you was beeping at ... '

HENRY: Excuse me – um – do you want to buy a ... ?

STIX is long gone.

HENRY: You didn't stop.

STIX: You didn't stop me.

HENRY: Hey? Ag, no – this is stupid, man.

STIX: Aikona. Is not stupid. ls stupid to buy a kak Help-U card for four hundred and eighty rand ...

HENRY: Hey, look – will you just forget about that now ... ! That was robbery. It had nothing to do with buying or selling or ...

STIX: Come. I'm teach you. You want to stay in Jo'burg, you must know these things ...

HENRY: I'm not staying in Jo'burg. I hate Jo'burg.

STIX: Okay – you must beat Jo'burg.

HENRY: I don't have to beat Jo'burg. I'm not hanging around in Jo'burg. Soon as I got enough money, I'm going to go get that ... I'm gonna go drill for water.

STIX: But you must get the machine. And to get the machine, you must first get the bucks. And this is how you get the bucks. Woza ... woza ... sell it ...

HENRY: You not serious about this ... ?

STIX: Yes, yes – come ...

HENRY: This is a game, right ... ?

STIX: Sell it to me. Come. Be sell, feel sell ... you gotta feel the situation ...

HENRY: Yes, I mean – no ...

STIX: The cars ... the people ... the woman selling snuff ... the guy in the corner still throwing up ...

HENRY: Yes. Wait, I'm not ...

STIX [*going for it*]: 'Honking at the honey ... !'

HENRY [*only slightly better*]: Excuse me – um – look at this lekker toaster ... it's really nice ... it makes four slices and pops up ... ! [*He is unsuccessful yet again.*] You not playing the bladdy game here, man ... !

STIX: You not selling me, bra. [*Imitating* HENRY.] 'Excuse me, check this nice toaster ... it can make four slices and the four slices pop out the top ... '

HENRY [*grimly determined*]: Okay. Okay. You in trouble, my boy. Try ... come. Try again.

STIX [*enjoying himself*]: What ... ?

HENRY [*shoving him*]: Come ... come. Try again ...

STIX [*allowing himself to be shoved*]: What ... ?

HENRY: Let's go ... come ...

STIX [*beaming*]: You sure ... ?

HENRY: Come on orready, man. I show you ...

STIX: You sure ... ?

HENRY: Come.

STIX is about to start – breaks off.

STIX: You got the picture, hey? The cars ... the people ... the woman in the ... ?

HENRY: Look, are you going to ... !?

STIX: Right-right-right ... !

The procedure is repeated. This is the worst! HENRY *grabs him and thrusts the toaster into his face with a selling technique that borders on battery.*

STIX: 'Honking at the ... !'

HENRY [*grabbing him*]: Hey! Check this toaster! This is a fantastic toaster. It's cheap, man. It's got ... ! You must buy this! This is wonderful ... !

STIX struggles free, making a 'time-out' sign.

STIX: Wait ... ! Wait ... ! Wait ... !!

HENRY: What ... ?

STIX: Take your hands off me, witgat!

HENRY: Ag, no, man – jislaaik ... !

STIX: This is not selling! This is not ... ! You can't sell to me like that. That is not selling. That is assault. That is assault with a traditional weapon!

HENRY: You don't want to buy this!

STIX: No. That's right. You must convince me that a toaster is the one only thing I must have.

HENRY: Why are we doing this?

STIX: I already tell you ...

HENRY: I'm not doing this. This is ...

STIX: You going to get this right.

HENRY: No, I'm not going to ...

STIX: You must get this right ...

HENRY: To hell with you ...

STIX: Stand here. Kamaan ... !

HENRY: Kak, I'm not going to do this any more ...

STIX slaps him – hard across the face. HENRY is stunned into silence. There is a brief moment of 'anything could happen'.

HENRY: Hey ... !?

STIX: Come. Let me sell ... to you. Okay? [*Gently taking the toaster from HENRY.*] Come. Stand over there. [*Like a little puppy, HENRY complies.*] I'll stand here. You walk down the street ... down Mooi Street. Come. Let's go.

HENRY: I don't want a toaster.

STIX: We will see ...

HENRY [*with grim resolve*]: I'm not gonna buy it.

STIX: Come. Come. Walk down the road.

There is a brief pause. HENRY changes tack.

HENRY [*grimly*]: Okay. But you watch. There's no ways you going to sell it to me, boy – no ways ...

STIX: Okay. We'll see.

HENRY: Are you ready?

STIX: Come. Go.

HENRY [*copying STIX's tune*]: 'Hodgy at the ... '

STIX [*stopping him*]: Hold it. Hold it right there. What's that there? What's that?

HENRY: What ... ? Where ... ?

STIX: Let me see your shoe. Lift your foot.

HENRY: What ... ? Ag, no – they buggered ...

STIX: What size are you?

HENRY: Wha ... ? Hey ... !? No, I gotta get some new ones. What you doing now, man ... ?

STIX fetches a shoe box. HENRY is momentarily thrown.

STIX: Wait, wait. Have a look at these.

HENRY: No, no – it's okay – we ...

STIX: Let's try. Sit down. Come ...

HENRY: No, no, no ...

STIX: These are the best, my friend. The girls are gonna go mad for you in these. The best ... only the best. Imported from Italy. Made in Taiwan ...

STIX leads HENRY back to his breakfast box and makes him take off his shoe. He slips on the new shoe.

HENRY: Stix ...

STIX: How's that? What do you say?

HENRY flexes his foot.

HENRY: It fits. It's fine. [*He stands, trying it out – smiling now.*] It's actually quite lekker.

STIX [*a beat*]: Five bucks.

HENRY: Five bucks!?

STIX: Five bucks – special price.

HENRY: Fantastic. You gotta deal.

STIX: Coevert!

They shake hands and STIX goes into the double-handshake – Sowetan-style – ending with hands extended, hip-height. HENRY misunderstands this.

HENRY: No, no – I'll get you the money as soon as I see my boet. [*Turning away, admiring the shoe.*] Wow ...

STIX puts the toaster back, and plonks down on the mattress with his paper.

HENRY's back in 'Mooi Street'.

HENRY: Hey. What you doing? Come. Let's go.

STIX: Where?

HENRY: What about the toaster?

STIX: What toaster?

HENRY: You s'posed to try sell me the toaster!

STIX: I sell you the shoes.

HENRY: But ... you s'posed to sell me the toaster!

STIX: I made my sale, bra.

HENRY: But that's not the game ... !

STIX: A sale is a sale, my bra. Lesson Number One.

HENRY: Jeepers ... ! I don't believe this ... ! [*Pacing about, as* STIX *laughs.*] It's just talk, that's all it is. It's just talk-talk-talk. You worse than that bloke on the bladdy station, man. It's Crooks. Chancers. Snakes in the grass, man – whole lota' you ...

STIX: Man does not live by bread alone ...

HENRY: No, no – the whole town, man ... every comer you turn there's another bladdy shark ... ! [*Throwing off the new shoe, putting on the old.*] You ask me if this place is different. It's different, orraight. You can't even ... you can't even find this block of flats, because why ... ? Because they stolen the name off the front a' the building! What they want the bladdy name for .... ? I come here last night, hey ... I'm asking a bloke in the foyer downstairs if this is Cumberland Mansions – he's leaning against the door ... he's pissing in the pot plant ... !

STIX [*shocked*]: Yo ... !

HENRY: He doesn't even stop! I ask him – is this Cumberland Mansions? – he just – waha-aaeugh ... ! Sis ... !

STIX: Hai! No wonder that tree is always dying.

HENRY: This morning – when you gone out – I check outside here, there's this big noise ... they chopping up a sheep. On the stairs! All this blood and guts ... and they ... they selling it ... in chunks! In big ... chunks! Bladdy ... sacrifices ... !! No, I'm telling you – this place! As soon as I find old Steve and I got my money – I'm out of here, boy. I'm history. I get my rig. I go down to the farms and I deal with people you can ... you can talk to. Straight talk. I get them their water – and they pay me my money. That's a living. That's a life. Not the way people live in this place! It's not right, boy. Uh-uh. It's not right.

STIX has been watching him for some time. His words are like stones – ice cold. He virtually spells them out.

STIX: Hey, wena. N'gubani gamalako?

HENRY: Wha ... ?

STIX [*slowly*]: N'gubani gamalako? Wie is jy? What is your name? Ke-mangle bitso lehaho? [*He lets this sink* in.] You must know the play. You are never the same thing twice ... like a chameleon, you are what they want you to be, but – you make the sale. Lesson Number One. Sidewalking.

HENRY: Sidewalking?

STIX: Sidewalking.

HENRY: What's that?

STIX: That's how we live here in Jo'burg. Like the crab. [*He glides sideways.*] Ghwak-ghwak!

HENRY: Crab?

STIX: That's how I got my place. Downstairs. 1988.

HENRY: Bull, man. You didn't have a flat here in 1988, man – none of you chaps did. You weren't even allowed in here, man. The only way you could get in the building was if you worked here.

STIX: Ja. That's why you sidewalk, you see. Sideways.

HENRY stares at him.

HENRY: Sideways?

STIX: Is how you walk when in front of you is the big, high wall – broken bottles on top. You can't go forward. You don't want to go back, so you – ghwak-ghwak – you sidewalk. Sidewalking, bra. [*Dancing sideways.*] The walk of the people. Stix's Walk. Stix Letsebe. That's me. Creature with the hard shell.

HENRY: I thought your name was Sipho?

STIX: Sipho for some. Stix for others. [*He goes into reflective mode.* HENRY *watches him.*] Huh. 1988. Top Gun Outfitters. Nice pay. Nice people. Nice holidays. The best part of it all – it's in Hillbrow. Hai – Hillbrow! The Strip. The Sunset Strip. Manhattan ... ! [*Gear-change up.*] Yei ... ! I wake up one morning in the ghetto, I say – no, no – aikona, uh-uh ... ! Three hours to work. Three hours home. Three hours to sleep. Aikona! Hai sugga ... ! [*Angrily, in the vernacular.*] I was sick and tired of this bladdy nonsense ... ! Ek is die moer-in met die blerrie chandies ... ! All over the place, I see signs – vacancies ... vacancies ... vacancies! Furnished apartments! Rooms to let ... ! [*In the vernacular.*] I say – hey, fixed up – here we go! [*Back to English.*] I put on my tie ... my Florsheim shoes – two-tone – ziya-sparkela ... ! A dash of Brylcreem ... and my extra-special Colgate smile – [*He smiles toothily.*] I walk right straight up to the door – [*Demonstrating.*] Poem-poem-pa-doem-pa – tak-tak-tak ... ! [*Bowing and scraping.*] Excuse me, madam – if the madam would be so kind – [*Flashing his Colgate smile.*] My name is Sipho Letsebe and I am enquiring about the possibility of unfurnished accommodation ... [*Exploding in a high, squeaky voice.*] 'Voetsek! Hamba! Go away ... !' Hau. She didn't like me, that one. I try once more in Quartz Street. 'Goeie middag, meneer ... ' Goenk! [*The door is slammed.*] Try again in Kapteijn – [*He becomes the white landlady.*] 'I'm sorry, young man – not to say we discriminate – but, this year we are trying Indians and coloureds. Next year, we are trying blacks ... ' – But, madam – 'Don't you understand English? I said NEXT year, we are trying blacks ... !' – But, please ... ! [*He mimes stone throwing.*] 'Voetsek! Hamba! Go back to where you come from ... !'

HENRY [*smiling nervously*]: Voetsek ...

STIX: Ja. Didn't work. Not even the Colgate smile. These white people. No sense of adventure. Too many brick walls with broken bottles on top.

HENRY: So what you do?

STIX: I say to myself – forget it, bra – the white Boere have won. [*He swings around.*] And then it happens! OK Bazaars in Braamfontein – the shop next door! TV in the window – six o'clock news ... ! Mike Weaver arriving in South Africa to fight Johnny du Plooy. Heavyweight Boxing Clash of the Titans! There it was in full colour – the red carpet, Jan Smuts Airport. TV1, TV2, TV3 – Topsport, Supersport, M-Net – Bop ... ! [*He becomes a white TV newscaster.*] 'Hello, Mike. What do you think of South Africa? – Oh, you like it here? – Good. Lovely to have you back again. Any time ... !' [*He demonstrates a car pulling away.*] Vrrrroemm ... ! [*Police car sirens.*] Bee-boo-bee-boo – bee-boo-bee-boo ... ! Police escort – ja. Police escort ... ! Bee-boo-bee-boo ... ! Carlton – Sun City – champagne, blondes, brunettes – bikinis ... ! I look at this, I say – aikona! – Horror-nary White ... !? Horror-nary White se moer, man ... ! Time to change the tune, bra ... ! Time for a little show biz ... ! Time for some sidewalking! I go to my boss at the Top Gun. I say – come, Mr Weinstein – come, jong – emergency. I get a baseball cap – sharp jacket – USA – [*He indicates writing.*] Yale – UCLA ... ! Genuine Ray-bans – ten bucks! [*He sings.*] 'God Bless America ... !' [*'Sidewalking' along.*] Poem-poem-pa-doem-pa – Abel Road. Accommodation. Apply Within. I sidewalk up to the front door – takka-takka-tak-tak ... ! [*He becomes the expansive American.*] Howdy, ma'am ... ! Gimme Five ... ! [*He gives himself five – slapping hands and so on.*] Right on, right on, right on! My name is Leroy Strawberry, and – as you can see – I'm from the US of A ... ! [*Indicating his clothing.*] I'm a visitor in your bee-ooootiful country, and I'm lookin' for a place to stay ... ! Hau! She looks at me. Her mouth is like so – [*Demonstrating a dropped jaw.*] 'Excuse me – are you a NEGRO ... !?' You bet your cotton-pickin' Cincinnati Red Sox, ma'am ... ! Eddie Murphy ... ! Bill Cosby ... ! Sammy Davis Junior ... ! Louis Satchmo Armstrong ... ! One-two-three – she's got the contract – 'Sign along the dotted line, Mr. Strawberry ... !' [*He 'signs' while singing a spiritual.*] 'Nobody knows – the troubles I have seen. Nobody knows – but Jee-zuss ... ' I pay the deposit. First month – smokeless ... ! The same afternoon, I say – hello Hillbrow – bye-bye the train ... !

HENRY [*chuckling*]: Leroy Strawberry?

STIX: That's right, my bra. Gimme five!

STIX holds out a hand. HENRY tries to 'give him five' and STIX pulls his hand away. They freeze.

STIX: Too slow.

Snap blackout. Johnny Clegg's 'Jericho' as bridge music.

On lights up it is early evening and the flat is transformed. Another mattress is positioned near the boxes – another 'living space' – signalling that HENRY is well and truly ensconced, and has been for some time.

STIX squats on the floor in a similar attitude to the one in which we discovered him at the beginning of the play. He is working something out on a piece of paper – it is a crudely drawn map. He hums quietly to himself. Tap-taps on the map. Writes again. Gets up and paces about, checking his watch. Irritated, he returns to his map – tap-taps with the pencil – taps a tin mug, a plate. Pencil drum solo.

Presently, HENRY bursts into the room. He wears a suit and tie and is in a state of great excitement.

HENRY: Ta-ta-raaaah ... ! Ha-haaa ... ! [*He waves a wad of notes above his head.*] Eight hundred and fifty ... ! Cash! Hell, it was so ... like clockwork, man! Coevert! Gimme five! Okay. I park the bakkie where you said, hey – where it says Customers Only, okay ... ? I go round to the front. I'm standing outside and I'm scared, hey – I'm thinking, no – wait a minute – what if it all goes wrong? And then I remembered what you said ... Just ask the question and take it from there. So, I go in and I look for the oke with the powder blue safari suit with six pens in his top pocket. Zabba-zabba ... ! There he is. Right in fronta' me. Can't miss him. So I go up to the counter – exactly as you told me – 'Excuse me, could you tell me the way to Crown Mines. I'm looking for Madala ... '

STIX [*unimpressed*]: Mafuta.

HENRY: I know, I ...

STIX: Mafuta. You say – I'm looking for Mafuta ... !

HENRY ploughs on, nothing is going to stop him basking in the full glow of his moment of glory.

HENRY: Well, I said Madala and he still went along with it. So. We go outside ... I open up the bakkie ... he takes out the radios – one-two-three ... he gives me the cash ... there you go. Finish and Klaar ... ! Didn't even count them, man – [*Miming a soccer kick – STIX-style.*] La-duuuuuuumaaa ... ! Shoe! If Steve could see me now ...

STIX [*angrily*]: Mafuta. Not Madala. Is Mafuta!

HENRY: Ag, Mafuta – Madala – it's all the bladdy same. You should be pleased, man. I just scored my sale. I just scored my first big sale ... !

STIX: You must get it right.

The wind is a little out of HENRY's *sails.*

HENRY: Listen. You can be thankful it was me there and not you, hey. He doesn't like you, that guy. He said so. He tunes me – where's the cheeky kaffir* today?

STIX [*quietly, in the vernacular*]: White bastard ...

HENRY: I tell him you taking the day off.

STIX: You tell him I sit here on my gat ... !?

HENRY: What's wrong with you now, man? You should be thanking me for scoring the sale!

STIX: How can I be thanking a stupid mugu who doesn't know the difference between mafuta and madala ... !? How can I be thanking a stupid mugu who runs through the streets showing eight hundred bucks for the whole world to see ... !?

HENRY: I didn't run through the streets ...

STIX is getting charged up now.

STIX: And what is this, my bra? What is this ... !?

HENRY: What's it look like? It's a heater.

STIX: Is the goods, my bra. Is the merchandise. MY merchandise ... !

HENRY: I was cold. What must I do if I'm cold? We got all these things just sitting here ...

STIX: Nothing is just sitting here. It moves in and then it moves out. This is hard cash. Not something to play with ... !

HENRY: I dunno what's the matter with you sometimes. You got all these ... these things. Why not use some a' them, man? You ... you watch your soccer in that shitty little shebeen down the road, when you got the best bladdy sets in Johannesburg here ... !

STIX: Business is business and pleasure is pleasure. Don' get them mixed up. Is Lesson Number One.

HENRY: Lesson Number One ... ? Lesson Number One ... !? When you gonna get to Lesson Number Two? It's nothing but talk ... it's just talk-talk-talk ...

STIX: I talk, yes. Sometimes you must listen.

HENRY: You talk about finding my boet ... ! Every time we go look for this bloke who's s'posed to know where he is, he's not there ... !

STIX: You always in a big hurry ...

HENRY: Please! It's over three weeks now, my bra! It's like – ag, so what? Time means nothing to you okes ...

STIX: You not happy with the bucks, bra? You rather go out in the street?

---

* This word is offensive but has been retained because it is an accurate reflection of the character and the historical era in which this play is set.

HENRY: Get one thing straight. I'm only doing this to help you out, hey ...

STIX: You are helping me ... !?

HENRY: Soon as I find my boet, we quits ...

STIX: You are helping me? Mr Help-U card ... !?

HENRY: Okay, so we helping each other ...

STIX: What are we doing here – you and me?

HENRY [*a beat*]: No, it's okay. Los it ...

STIX: You work for me, my bra. You get a good deal. Fifty-fifty on what we sell. Accommodation – free of charge. Food – free of charge. Clothing – on the house ... ! [*Indicating HENRY's suit.*]

HENRY: Clothing? I didn't ask to wear this! Suit and bladdy ... ! I'm not a fancy bladdy smart-arse, man!

He whips off his jacket, rolls it into a ball and hurls it to the floor. STIX has had enough.

STIX [*matching his anger*]: Smart arse ... !? Okay ... ! Orraight ... ! Go ... ! Get out ... !

HENRY: I'm not a bladdy ... a bladdy ... !

STIX: Finish and Klaar! Finito! Is finish!

HENRY: I mean – hell, man ... jislaaik!

STIX picks up the suit, smoothes it out, puts it down. Returns to his piece of paper and pen.

STIX: Leave the bucks. Leave the clothes. Take your shit and don't come back ...

HENRY [*calmer now*]: You think it's easy, hey ... ? I mean – you think it's a piece a' piss to take a ... a whole buncha' radios in the back of a bakkie to a oke you never met in your whole bladdy life before and then ... and then ... ?

STIX: Hey – witgat ... ! [*Shoving him backwards.*] Something wrong in your ears? It's over for you, this job. No more Codesa-desa, you and me – Codesa's in its moer. Vat jou goed en trek, Van Vuuren! Hamba! Foggoff!

HENRY stares at him. A stunned pause.

HENRY: Okay. Okay. Okay. If that's the way you want it, then ... then ... okay. [*He backs away, looking about. Not ready for this.*] If you want me to ... okay. I mean – I help you out, hey ... ? I sort of ... hey? [*Indicating the boxes.*] I go places you can never go and then you just ... you just ... hey? I mean – what've we been doing these last few weeks, hey? You mean to tell me now you just gonna ... say bye-bye to three-and-a-half bladdy weeks of ... of ... of ... hey?

STIX: Those trousers are my trousers.

HENRY: Hey?

STIX: You look on the inside – what does it say? [*Jerking a thumb at himself.*] Man-About-Town.

HENRY: To hell with your bladdy Man-About-Town ... ! You want your ... ! You can stick your bladdy Man-About ... ! [*Hopping around on one leg, pulling them off.*] I couldn't care less if they Pierie-Pierie Whatsisname ... ! [*He hurls them at* STIX's *feet.*] Where's my pants ... ? [*He looks about, unable to find them.*] Where's my bladdy ... !?

STIX: They not your pants. They my pants. Your pants got a hole THIS big, my bra ...

HENRY [*turning on him*]: Okay, so I say Madala and not Mafuta – big bladdy deal, man ...

STIX [*folding the trousers*]: And it's Pierie Cardin, not Piri-piri Whatsisname ...

HENRY: You gonna tell me that some ... piss-face in a safari suit cares less if I say ... ma-shoe-shoe or ... ma-shwe-shwe or ma-ma-ma - whatever, man ... !?

HENRY cuts a pathetic figure in his tartan underwear.

STIX [*in the vernacular, smiling*]: Hey, witgat, you look stupid in your underpants, jong ...

HENRY: I mean – even *I* don't know what you charfing ninety percent a' the time, man. You hanna-hanna on at yourself in that stupid Fanagalo all the time and ... and – what – I'm supposed to smell what you saying ... ?

STIX: Fanagalo ... !?

HENRY: You talk to yourself one helluva lot, you know that? No, I'm serious. It's a major problem with you. People go to hospital for things like that.

STIX: Fanagalo?

HENRY: Zulu – Xhosa – whatever ...

STIX: Fanagalo is white man's language. I speak Swahili.

HENRY: Bull, man.

STIX: You don't know Swahili?

HENRY: You should learn to speak English.

STIX: I thought all clever Dutchmen, they can speak everything ...

HENRY: I'm not a Dutchman!

STIX: You a Dutchman, witgat. You the Afrikaner–Dutchman who runs around chasing the banana. And now – you slip on your banana! Hamba! Voetsek! Get out!

STIX leaves HENRY in no doubt that he is out in the cold. He stands room centre, a pathetic, broken figure.

HENRY: Stix ... how can I ... ? Where can I ... ? I can't go out into the ... [*as if in a dream.*] I need some bucks for my rig, man ...

STIX looks at him, does his best to stop himself from falling about with laughter and then bursts out laughing, covering his eyes with his hands.

HENRY: What ... ? [*STIX is in tears.*] What's so ... ?

STIX: Hey – please, my bra – put something over those legs. They hurting my eyes, man ... [*He hurls the trousers at* HENRY *and staggers about – helpless with mirth.*] You got whiter legs than Madonna, my bra ...

HENRY stares at him. The prime poephol.

HENRY: Jusslaaik ... ! Very funny, hey ... !

STIX [*mimicking himself*]: Hamba! Voetsek! 'Ag, please Stix. Don' send me in the street ... ' [*Apologising, or trying to.*] I'm sorry, my bra ... those underpants ...

HENRY picks up the trousers, unamused. He attacks STIX, whipping him. STIX ducks and dives, laughing again.

HENRY: Shit, you ... bastard ... !

STIX: Sunglasses ... help ... ! My eyes ... !

HENRY: Having me on all the bladdy time ... !

HENRY pursues STIX about the flat whipping and flicking at him with the trousers. STIX plays the 'subservient black', pleading for mercy and laughing at the same time.

STIX: Please, my boss ... ! I'm sorry, my boss ... ! Don't hurt me, my boss ... !

HENRY: Man-About-Town, se voet ... ! You shit ... !

STIX: Eina-aaaa ... ! Einaaa ... ! [*He freezes and points off.*] Behind you, Mashubane ... !

HENRY [*swinging around.*] Where ... ?

STIX hurls a pillow at him and HENRY drops the trousers and catches it. He advances on STIX.

HENRY: Now you gonna get it, boy ... now you gonna die a thousand deaths ...

STIX does a kung-fu pose. HENRY clucks like a chicken. HENRY clubs STIX with the pillow a few times and STIX pretends he has been badly hurt.

STIX [*clutching his finger*]: Ow – eina ... eeeh ... !

HENRY [*concerned*]: What ... ?

He approaches STIX to see what the problem is and STIX slowly uncurls his 'hurt' finger – showing him the sign.

They wrestle and struggle with each other, falling to the ground – a good natured scrap that clears the air.

STIX: Wait – don't tickle me ... !

HENRY: Say you sorry ... !

STIX: Don't tickle ... !

HENRY: Say you ... !

STIX: Aaaaah – sorry-sorry-sorry ... !

HENRY: Ja, my friend ... you must learn to play rugby. [*Cuffing him.*] It's not fair, man ...

They lie on the floor, out of breath, both laughing, sharing the moment. STIX *becomes 'serious' again.*

STIX: Mafuta.

HENRY: Mafuta.

STIX: Mafuta means fat and Madala means ...

HENRY: Old.

STIX: Old. Very good. Lesson Number One – Business is like soccer. You touch the ball with your hand in the penalty area – phhhsshht ... ! Line – down. [*He shoves the trousers at* HENRY.] Put on your trousers. Man-About-Town cannot discuss business kaalgat.

HENRY [*putting them on*]: Bastard ...

STIX [*getting up and going to his diagram*]: Okay. Now come. Sit. Tomorrow we do the Big One. I wait longtime for Pillay.

HENRY: Who is Pillay ... ?

STIX: Pillay is not easy, my bra. He's always got five or six guys and you must be watching all the time.

HENRY: Which guys are these ... ?

STIX: Pillay thinks because he's got these guys, he can Codesa-desa the price all the time. This time – he sees this white guy – he stops with the shit and he pays the bucks. [STIX *takes a pistol out of his table-box, placing it in front of him.* HENRY *just gawks at it.*] Okay. Now. Listen carefully. You take the gun and the gun is in your pocket. Your hand is on the gun all the time ...

HENRY [*nervously*]: Wait a minute ...

STIX: What ... ?

HENRY: No, no, no – hold it, hold it ...

STIX: What!?

HENRY: I'm not messing round with any ... guns ...

STIX: Don' worry. You won't need it.

HENRY: So why we taking it?

STIX: Insurance.

HENRY: Gsheesh ... ! [*He paces about.*]

STIX: Whatsa' problem?

HENRY: This is ... this is heavy shit, man.

STIX: That's right. Is heavy bucks.

HENRY: I don't wanna get involved in ... in ...

STIX: In what?

HENRY: No, in ... in ...

STIX: Business?

HENRY: No, man ... in ... in ... you know ... ?

STIX: You already involved, my bra ...

HENRY: Oh, no – ! Uh-uh – no ways ...

STIX: What you think you do with Sarel Safari Suit? You don't sell him ice cream, my bra. Is Criminal Offence ...

HENRY is shocked to the core.

HENRY: Hah! Listen. Don't get carried away, hey.

STIX: Who?

HENRY [*nervous laugh*]: Look. All I'm doing is ... I'm ... I'm helping you get rid a' some ... some soiled goods, that's all ...

STIX: Soil ... ?

HENRY [*lying through his teeth*]: I'm helping you sort of ... you know – move some of your factory sort of ... rejects. [*Petering out.*] Faulty sort of ... shitty stuff.

STIX: This is the best, my bra. This is Number One Shit. You won't get better anywhere ...

HENRY [*shutting him out*]: Okay. Okay ...

STIX: You know where this shit comes from?

HENRY: I don't wanna know, okay? You gave me this whole ... you came with this ... Operation Hunger thing, and let's leave it at that. Operation Hunger's fine by me.

STIX: What kak is this ... ?

HENRY: Jeepers ... ! [*He is struggling now, it's crunch time.*] We all have to close our eyes sometimes and, okay – orraight – I admit it – right now, that's what I'm doing ...

STIX: How can you close your eyes ... ?

HENRY: Two thousand down, that's all it is ...

STIX: Your eyes, they must be open ...

HENRY: There's this bloke in Klerksdorp ...

STIX: You think God's eyes are not open ... ?

HENRY: There's this ... God!? What's this got to do with God ... !?

STIX: You must KNOW what you do, and WHY you do it.

HENRY: Why are you doing this to me now ... ?

STIX: I know what I do. Eyes open, bra ... ! Open wide, all the time. I don't talk shit to my own brain ... !

HENRY [*flustered, anxious, trying to block him out*]: There's this bloke in Klerksdorp. It's two thousand down – that's all it is – and then you pay him off in monthly ...

HENRY paces about, trying desperately to justify his decidedly dicey job situation. STIX turns away – HENRY is after him like a dog with a bone.

HENRY: You pay the deposit. You take the rig – it's yours – okay? And then you go round from place to place, drilling for water. And then – as the money comes in – you pay him off. You pay your ... you pay your dues. It's honest work. Honest graft.

STIX [*in the vernacular*]: I'm wasting my time with this guy ...

HENRY: Two thousand rand. That's all I need. Once I got that, I can ... I can start. I can get money in and I can ... I can pay it back. I can pay you back. I can pay back whoever sort of ... whatever sort of ... I can work. I'm not scared a' work. [*Getting pretty het up.*] It's hard work. It's helluva hard work ... ! You slog your flippin' guts out, man ... !? [*There is a long pause.* HENRY *is spent.*]

HENRY: My own rig. That's all I want, man. That's all I ... that's all I want.

Another pause. STIX *toys with the piece of paper.*

STIX: Okay. Lomo. Pillay ...

HENRY [*quietly*]: What do YOU want?

STIX: I want to sell the stuff to Pillay ...

HENRY: No, no, no YOU! What do you want? You, yourself? For you? You got all this stuff ... all that bucks in your ballas. What's it ... what do you want?

STIX *looks at him long and hard.*

STIX [*matter-of-fact*]: I want to live, bra.

HENRY: No, boy ... it's not right ...

STIX: Take the gun.

HENRY: No, Stix, man ... we been through all that orready, man ... aikona ... !

STIX: Hey, mfo – thata!

HENRY: Those things got a mind of their own, jong ...

STIX: If you don't take the gun, we say bye-bye to Pillay ... ! Bye-bye to the bucks ... ! Bye-bye to everything!

HENRY: I can't do it, Stix. I can't point that thing at somebody like I know how to use it ...

STIX: What you going to use, white boy ... ? Huh!? You going to stand there holding your cock!? Look outside, mugu! Look downstairs! Look out in the street ... !

HENRY: There are guys who can ... you're okay. You and ... guys like Steve. Steve wasn't scared of guns, but then Steve wasn't scared of anything ...

STIX [*angrily, in the vernacular*]: To hell with Steve now, you idiot ... !

HENRY: You ask ol' Steve ... you ask my boet what happens when you ... hell, man – he's got some hair-raising bladdy ... 'Live by the gun – die by the ..' shit, man ... I gotta find my boet ... I gotta find ol' Steve ...

STIX: Steve ... Steve ... Steve ... !

HENRY: No, I'm gonna find him. Just 'cos you don't help me, doesn't mean to say I'm gonna stand around here and just forget about ...

STIX *explodes. He can't take it anymore.*

STIX: Steve is gone, my bra! Steve is finish! You won't see Steve no more – never again – so forget it ... ! For-jet ... ! For-jett . . .!! [*Thrown by his own outburst, he takes a while to calm down.* HENRY *is stunned into silence.*] Steve is on the Blue Train – pshweeow ... !

HENRY [*incredulous*]: Blue Train ... ?

STIX: Skokiaan. Purple Haze. First it was the coke. From the coke – to the kak! [*Vernacular.*] Why did he do that, man. No, man, bra Steve ... !

The depth of STIX's *concern shocks* HENRY.

HENRY: Hey, wait a minute ... what're you saying to me here ... ? You saying that you ... ?

STIX *walks away. The cat is out of the bag now. A pause.*

STIX: Steve, he was my Brother. McQueen. [*Pause.*] Steve and me, we work longtime together. [*Pause.*]

HENRY: Where is he?

STIX [*recollecting fondly*]: In the lift. Nineteen-eighty-eight. He says to me, ja – Stix – you can sell a pair of Levis and a three-piece suit, but can you sell a toaster ... ?

HENRY: A toaster!?

STIX [*smiling*]: Work for me, I make you rich ... [*Henry stares at him.*] Man does not live by bread alone ...

HENRY [*slow dawning*]: Of course – I shoulda ... man does not live by ... that was his favourite ... he said it right here. Right here in this chair ... [*He's just worked it out.*] You knew him ... !? You worked for him ... !?

STIX [*wryly*]: Ja. Toasters ... TVs ... everything. But TVs are not enough for Steve – aikona! One day – psheeeow! – he's gone to Zimbabwe – and then it's Botswana. Week after – Swaziland. And all of a sudden, it's the cars ...

HENRY: Cars ... ?

STIX: BMW. Mercedes. Only the best. And now he's got this big operation ... the cars are going out and the money's coming in.

HENRY: Wait a minute ... stick around ...

STIX: There other guys. Guys I don't know. Plenty – [*Sniff, sniff.*] – it's not the whisky anymore, it's the hard stuff. He moves out ... gone ... I hardly see him again.

HENRY: You trying to tell me he's running one a' those car-racket things ... ?

STIX: Cars are nothing, my bra. It's the Jet Set that got him ...

HENRY: Bullshit, man! You lie ... ! My boet was ... ! Steve was a ... ! My boet was a ... !

STIX: A businessman.

HENRY: A businessman, that's right ... !

STIX: A middle man who wanted to be top man.

HENRY: Bull, man!

STIX: In the kitchen, you can get burn. Bad ... !!

HENRY sits with his head in his hands. He knows this is true. A long pause.

STIX mumbles in the vernacular again, angry with the guy he fondly remembered as 'McQueen'.

STIX: I didn't want to tell you this, my bra. [*Vernacular.*] Oh, God – why? [*English.*] The day you walk in, it's like Steve's coming back. Small Steve. It's like the old times. The good times. Maybe if I can give something to you – in my heart, I can give it to Steve.

HENRY has had the wind well and truly knocked out of his sails. He stares ahead of him, distraught.

HENRY: And you don't know where he is?

STIX: Nobody knows where he is. The last guy who saw him says, ja – he went long time ago to Mozambique.

HENRY mouths the word – like it's the other side of Mars.

HENRY: Blue Train is ... Blue Train is meths ... !?

HENRY gasps. There is a long pause.

STIX: Come, my bra. Let's talk how we do this job. We finish this job – maybe one or two more – you buy this water machine and you free as the bird.

HENRY [*miles away*]: Morgan Bay. We always went there for holidays when we were kids. There was this little road that led down to the beach ... and Steve's got these shells. Hundreds of them. He makes a little gate kind of thing – toll gate kind of ... boom. Everyone who comes down to that beach has got to stop. You want me to open the gate, sir – you buy a shell. Only 20 cents. I'll give you two for thirty cents, ma'am – special price. [*Laughing.*] He got away with it too. People would stick their hands in their pockets and pay him. He'd open the boom and ... through they'd go. Wasn't even his shells or his beach, but everyone would pay up and everyone would be happy. [*Pause.*] He believed, you see. In himself. He just – puffed out his chest, made his voice kind of ... all official-like and ... looked like he was supposed to be there. Nobody ever asked him what he thought he was doing and he never explained why he did it. He just did it.

STIX: That's right, bra. He just did it. And now, we – we do it. Come, bra – come. Pillay ...

HENRY: This place ... ! This town ... ! He should never of come here, man. This Jo'burg is like ... like poison ... it's ...

STIX: Is terrible. Come ...

HENRY: The wrong crowd. He always got in with the wrong ... bastards like ... like ... !

STIX: Pillay. Shits ... !

HENRY: What d'you mean – Pillay? You, man ... ! You!

STIX: Yei! Get it right, bra! He came to me ... !

HENRY: But you were there ... !

STIX: One middle man goes – another one comes ...

Suddenly there is a ringing at the front door. The three long rings bring the argument to a sudden, dramatic halt.

STIX [*quietly*]: Shit ...

A pause. Three more rings. HENRY gives him a look to suggest they should pretend no-one's at home.

STIX: Not this time, my friend. This time, he breaks the door down.

STIX moves to the merchandise. Another three rings.

STIX: Ja, ja – I'm coming ... !

HENRY snaps – shouting, angrily.

HENRY [*shouting*]: Bugger off, man! Voetsek ... !

STIX: Shh! Uh-uh ... ! Aikona ... ! He hears you, then you must pay. All people staying here must pay.

HENRY : Bullshit! I'm not paying any ... ! I've paid enough bladdy ... spongers! Crooks! Con-men ... ! [*He moves towards the front hall.*] Fuck off – you parasite ... !!

STIX struggles to restrain him – the rings continue.

STIX: Mugu – shaddap ... ! That bastard will kill you for a fucken cigarette ... ! Witgat ... !

HENRY: That zot needs a stiff klap ... ! I'll kick his fat arse all the way down the fucken stairs ... !!

STIX: Voetsek, man ... ! Sit ... ! Sit ... !! Sit ... !!

He shoves HENRY back, grabs the toaster and moves off to the front door, swearing at the unseen intruder as he goes. For a second or two, HENRY does nothing. Then he gets up and begins getting together his things, dumping them into his 'New York' bag.

HENRY: Not right, man ... this is all ... not right ...

He stops, looks around, and lifts a pair of dripping black socks out of the wash bowl. He squeezes them out, sniffs at them and rolls them up, carefully – as if they were brand new Yves St Laurent.

During the following speech, STIX enters slowly. He staggers, but HENRY does not notice. STIX moves gingerly to his mattress and slumps down.

HENRY [*trying to sing*]: 'When she – e – epherds wash their socks – by – night ... '
Nursery School. [*He doesn't look at* STIX.] You ever sing that ... ? Primary
School? [*Pause.*] 'Si – i – lent Night ... Ho – o – ly Night ... ' [*Miles away.*] 'Sleep
in Hea – venly Pee – e – eace, slee – eep in Hea –venly ... ' [*Pause.*] I always
thought that Liepies was somebody's name. You know? 'Sleep in Heaven,
Liepies ...' I could never figure out what this Liepies bloke was doing in a song
about Bethlehem. [*Pause.*] And then, one year – one Christmas ... standing next
to Steve ... it was like I was hearing it for the first time – [*Singing.*] 'Slee – eep in
Hea – venly ... Peace ... ' I s'pose it's just the way you hear it, hey? Until the day
you hear it different. [*Pause.*] You shoulda' told me, Stix ... you should never
have ... you should've told me.

He finishes packing and approaches STIX. *The room is quite gloomy now in the
early evening twilight. It should grow darker, imperceptibly, right through to the
end of the play.*

HENRY: Here's your cash. Here's your bucks. [*He throws the money on to the bed.*] I
don't owe you nothing.
STIX: You won't find him, my bra.
HENRY: We quits. It's over.
STIX: There is nobody, my bra – only me.
HENRY: We all square. Leave it alone ...
STIX: Your eyes are open, bra. God's also ...
HENRY: Ja. Ja.

HENRY *moves to the door.* STIX *makes a sound – an odd sound of pain.* HENRY
stops, looks at him.

HENRY: Whatsa' matter?
STIX [*very quietly*]: Ai ...
HENRY: Stix ... ?

STIX *has been working at dislodging a sharpened bicycle spoke from his stomach.
He lets it roll across the floor.*

STIX: Ah ... !
HENRY: Shit, no, man – why didn't you ... ? Stix ... !
STIX: Is okay.

HENRY *looks around for something with which to staunch the flow of blood. He
grabs the nearest thing – a shirt from his bag.*

HENRY: We gotta get you to the hospital ...
STIX: Aikona ... !
HENRY: You mad, man – we got to let somebody ... !

STIX: Drink. Get me a drink ...

HENRY: Drink ... ? [*He runs around.*] Stix ... !

STIX: Drink ... !

HENRY [*in a panic*]: Stix, listen ... ! [*He grabs the Coke bottle.*] We can't sit around here ... !

STIX: Aikona ... ! Whisky ... !

HENRY digs around for the whisky, finds it.

HENRY: We gotta try find a doctor ...

STIX: No. Nobody comes here ... !

HENRY: You going to bleed to bladdy ... ! It's a bladdy bicycle spoke, man ... !

STIX: Stay here. Sit here.

HENRY [*helpless*]: Bugger it, man ... !

HENRY puts the bottle to STIX's lips and STIX grabs him with his one free hand. After a long swig, STIX perks up.

STIX: Siddown here. Is okay.

HENRY: Shouldn't we just ... ?

STIX: Shh – I'm okay now ...

HENRY: But it's my fault, man ... !

STIX: Shhh ... I'm okay ... I'm ... okay ...

STIX smiles bravely and offers HENRY a sluk of whisky. HENRY hesitates and then knocks back a large shot.

HENRY [*indicating the wound*]: How's it feel?

STIX: Is okay.

HENRY: For sure, it's okay?

STIX: Sure-sure. [*Shaking his head.*] Stupid ... stupid ... break the rules ...

HENRY: Somebody should arrest that guy.

STIX: Next time, I shoot him like a dog.

HENRY: Somebody should call the police ...

STIX: No police. [*Pause.*]

HENRY [*concerned*]: You sure you okay, Stix. Shouldn't we just ... shouldn't we just ... ?

STIX: Tell me about this water.

HENRY: What water?

STIX: You say you want this ... machine ...

HENRY: Oh, the rig?

STIX: Why you want this? Why is all you want?

HENRY: Why?

STIX: Why you want to go round with this?

HENRY [*a beat*]: Ever since I was a kid. It's all I ever ... [*His voice fades out as he stares into the middle-distance.*] To see those looks on the peoples' faces. People who've forgotten what ... what water even looks like. [*Pause.*] I grew up on the plots, you check, and every year this guy came around ... towing this huge rig on the back of his truck. It was ... it was like magic how he ... he held this catty-branch in his hands and he'd walk ... and he'd walk ... and then he'd say – here – here it is ... !

STIX: The water?

HENRY: Ja.

STIX: He found the water?

HENRY: Sometimes they'd tell him where they thought it was and they'd be wrong ... but when HE said water was somewhere – water would be there orraight. And we used to watch him ... all the kids from all around – watching him with that huge pipe going into the ground – gonga-gonga-gonga ... ! Deeper and deeper, until ... there it was ...

STIX: Water?

HENRY: The farmers used to pay him and he'd pack up that rig. His tent. And then he'd trek off somewhere else. To some other place where people needed ...

STIX: Water ... I want this water ... [*The life is ebbing out of him.*] This is the water I want.

HENRY: Let's do it then, Stix. Los this stuff. We don't need it, man. [*STIX grits his teeth.*] Look. Look. We sell the bakkie, okay? We go down to Klerksdorp and we find this oke. We ask him for the rig. Maybe we can ... Codesa-desa the price a little bit. Maybe do a deal ... It's a life out there in the Karoo, Stix – there's this ... sky! You know that you're alive when you ... Stix ... ? Stix ... !? [*STIX hums quietly, his eyes closed. HENRY Looks about the room, pondering his future.*] Tomorrow, OK? Tomorrow we sell the bakkie ... we sell this stuff to Pillay... we... we... [*STIX still hums.*] We take the bucks, and then we... Klerksdorp ... Kimberley ... the Karoo ...! [*Awestruck.*] You must just see it, Stix. The sun goes down over the Karoo ... and in the morning ... in the morning ... it comes up again ...

STIX hums, a haunting tribal melody. Lights fade to blackout. Music bleeds in.

The Return
of Elvis du Pisanie

A MONOLOGUE

Paul Slabolepszy as EDDIE (ELVIS) DU PISANIE.
Photograph by Ruphin Coudyzer.

The Return of Elvis du Pisanie, with the author as Eddie, was first performed at the Great Hall, Grahamstown Festival Fringe, in July 1992. For almost a year thereafter, the play toured nationally. The author also gave performances by invitation in Chicago, Illinois, and Alexandria, Virginia, in the United States. The production was directed by Lara Foot who worked closely with the author/actor, honing and trimming the text from its original two and a half hours' playing time to its current 75 minutes.

The stage is bare, but for a solitary lamppost – the tall lamp arching diagonally out over the street. The post – slightly off-centre – stands on a pavement with the name 'Union Crescent' stencilled on the kerb. (Perhaps there is a section of fencing behind the lamppost, or a wall – a stretch of corrugated iron?) A stick lies in the gutter, a plastic milk crate to one side.

On lights up (a very long, gentle fade up), we discover Edward Cedric du Pisanie leaning against the pole, staring up into the night sky. He wears a dark, crumpled business suit, blue shirt, tie, slip-on black shoes and white socks. His slightly over-long hair on opt back in a style that is somewhat out of date; he is your basic, regular, middle class, forty-something-ish, bloke-next-door. There are four beers in a six-pack at the base of the pole.

Eddie begins to sing – very quietly, haltingly, he croons the first two verses of the classic Elvis Presley song 'Love me Tender'.

A pause. He stares out front, across the road, dead serious.

> There are people who swear they've seen him, you know. Seen him in the strangest places. Sometimes it seems there are more people who've seen him since he's supposed to have died than … than when he was still around. Like the bloke who saw him on a MossGas oil rig, sixty kays off the East Cape coast. Then that little waitress girlie who guaranteed spotted him at the pub of the Wagon Wheel Motel in Beaufort West, knocking back a double brandy and Coke. And still the other guy who, only last week, swears blind it was him – putting in an offer for a second hand Massey-Fergusson outside the Apostoliese Geloofsendingkerk in Marble Hall. Marble Hall. [*Laughing.*] Who'd want to be seen dead in Marble Hall?

Swinging slowly around the lamppost, he again sings quietly, haltingly. This time it is the Elvis song 'Are You Lonesome Tonight'. Beginning with the fourth line of the song, he sings until he gets to the second last line of the first verse, ending with … 'Shall I come back again … ?'

He breaks out of it. Squints across the road.

> Okay. Lemme see if I can still get this right. [*Pointing across the road.*] Carlton Bioscope. [*Pointing left of it.*] The Station Hotel. [*Pointing left of that.*] Main Street – [*Pointing to his feet.*] Union Crescent – [*Pointing up the road.*] President. President into King George the Fifth Park. [*Self-satisfied.*] Not bad. Not bad for … jeepers … is it really … thirty years … ? Thirty years ago. Tonight.

He looks up into the light of the lamp – speaking to the heavens.

So where are you, huh ... ! C'mon ... ! What's keeping you? See ... ? Look ... ! It's the right place, isn't it? The lamppost. 'Scopes across the road. I mean – look, look – it's even the right time a' night, hey. And this time I'm waiting, my friend. This time I'm not leaving 'til I get some answers ... and you got one helluva lot to answer for, my boy.

Highly agitated, he paces about, wrestling with his emotions.

I nearly did it tonight, you know. I nearly ... went the whole hog. In fact, I wouldna' even been here right now if it hadn't been for ... [*Looking up.*] – huh ... ! Whoever woulda' believed that a simple act of ... switching on a car radio could ... could ... change the course of your life? [*Angrily, to the heavens.*] But it's not the first time he's interfered – oh, no ... ! It's not the first time he's ... stepped in ... uninvited.

Pause.

She might even have found me by now. Phoned the cops. Called the ambulance. They'd be carting me off ... laying me out. Getting me ready for the funeral on Monday or Tuesday and, boy-oh-boy – what an Event that would be, hey? This pathetic little bunch, all gathering around my AVBOB discount coffin and sadly shaking their heads ...

He picks out a 'face' in the 'crowd'.

Hah! Father Vincent! Must be tough for you, hey, padre? No talk today of the Kingdom of Heaven, hey? You don't believe a man who takes his own life can ever join that Everlasting Party up there, do you? How do you know, Father? Huh? What makes you such an expert? You watch Heaven 'live' on CNN – twenty-four hours a day ... !?

He picks out another familiar face.

I don't believe it ... ! Braithwaite!? You got a cheek! I gave twelve a' the best years a' my life, selling your shitty product, and you showed me the door. You think coming to my funeral's gonna make up for it ... ?

To another 'face':

Oh, come on, Bob – dry those tears, man. It's not me you crying for – it's the bum golfing partner you're losing – the guy you cheated a few bucks off every odd Saturday afternoon. [*To his 'wife'*] Eunice ... Eunice. Sweetheart, please – please try to understand that it's more than just ... these things don't just happen ... overnight ...

He peters out – staring into the middle-distance, before snapping out of it.

This is crazy, man. What am I doing here?

Pats around for his smokes. Takes out a packet.

[*Under his breath.*] Bugger it ...

Tosses empty packet away. Feels around again. Takes out a Wicks bubble gum.
Unwraps it. Pops the gum into his mouth. Absently reads the believe-it-or-not wrapper.

Bullshit, man. [*Tossing wrapper away.*]

He leans against the pole, staring out front, chewing gum. Pulls gum out and stretches
it – plays with it. Sticks it on the pole – makes patterns with it. Coyly sticks the gum
behind the pole – addresses the audience.

This stuff isn't what it used to be, boy. Back in '62 you could chew a Wicks King
Size bubble gum ten hours solid before it lost the pink. Three long weeks stuck
under your desk at school ... ! Hard as a rock, maybe, but pink, boy – pink as
a pink carnation. A chunk of Wicks glued to the inside of your blazer pocket
was still pink two and a half years after your teacher had caught you by surprise
mid-way through 'The Lord is My Shepherd' in Bible Studies or Religious
Instruction or whatever it was they called it when you were a kid. And stretch!
You could stretch a single Wicks right around a Chev Bel-Air and a Vauxhall
Victor, standing nose to sharkfin tail and still have enough to stick behind your
ear and save for later. And they talk of progress! They talk of things improving!?
Hell, man – you don't even get Miniature Deep Sea Divers in your Corn Flakes
anymore – and whatever happened to Hubbly Bubbly, hey? Gobstoppers?
Eskimo Pies? Lucky Dips at the Saturday morning matinee? Come to think of
it, you don't even get the Saturday morning matinee anymore! Not with Lone
Ranger serials, anyway. Those cliff-hanging episodes that went on week after
week ... Gene Autry ... Audie Murphy. [*Posing.*] This town ain't big enough for
the both of us, pardner ... [*Last 'puff' on a cheroot and chucking it away.*] Go for
your guns! [*Spitting tobacco.*]

He smiles, trying to recall those far-off, carefree days.

And then ... my absolute favourite ... Dick Tracy and the G-Men. [*Saturday*
morning matinee serial music.] Dan-dan-dan-dan-dan – dan – dan-dan-dan-
daah – ! Dan-dan-dan-dan-dan – dan – dan-dan-dan-daah – that music, hey!?
Dan-dan-dan – daah – dish! It was amazing how they got the punches to come
in right at the end of the music every time. There'd be this massive fight with
the music in the background and then – every time there was a gap – [*Punches.*]
– dish! Sort of – [*Music.*] Dan-dan-dan-dan-dan – dan – dan-dan-dan-daah
– dish! Dan-dan-dan-dan-dan – dan – dan-dandan-daah – dish! Right there.

[*Pointing across the road.*] Right across the road. The Carlton Theatre. Bladdy betting house now, can you believe it? Sixpence on a Saturday morning. Sixpence ... sixpence ... sixpence ...

He steps forward into another area, circling around. The lights around the pole fade out as the new lights fade up on him. He is a child again, acting all the characters and telling the story as if it were happening right there and then.

'One please.'

'Here you go, young man. And don't lose your ticket for the lucky draw, hey .... '

Jeepers, what was she talking? You hung onto that ticket like your life depended on it. But you weren't worried about any plastic model Sopwith Camel kit or anything else, like ou Mickey Twigg. You just wanted to know what happened to Dick Tracy!

[*MICKEY TWIGG, with a stutter*] 'B – b – but, Eddie – l – l - last week, I w – w – won a giant packet a' S – S – Sunrise Toffees, e – e – extra cree-e-eam and butter ... !'

[*YOUNG EDDIE*] 'Ag, man ... !'

[*African Mirror music.*] Tarra-ta-tan-tan-tan-tarra-ta-tan – ta-tarra-ta-tan-tan-tan-tan-tan – tarra-ta-taaaah ... !! Front row. Sticky floors and squeaky seats. [*Moving along the 'row'.*] Tik-tak – tik-tak ... [*Squeaky seat, as he sits.*] Tsha-keeek ... !

He becomes the entire gang – arguing, bickering, and so on.

'Shhht ... ! Shht ... ! Sorry, okes! Sorry! [*Sniffing, disgusted.*] Who farted ... ? Who farted ... !? Shht ... ! Sis, man ... ! Siddown ... ! Shaddap! Shaddap yourself, man ... !'

Onscreen sting.

Pa-parra-paaah ... !! [*Eating popcorn, looking up at the 'screen'.*] Here he comes – in Cinemascope! Ten foot high and twenty foot wide –!

[*Dick Tracy – into wrist watch.*] 'Okay, boys, I'm on my way ... !'

They always saved the best fights for the end, hey! Dick Tracy and this whole buncha' gangsters. Moersa' big warehouse – petrol drums and Highly Inflammable Material! Dick Tracy –! [*Dramatic Dick Tracy music.*] Dandan-dan-dan-dan – dan – dan-dan-dan – daah – dish! Dan-dan-dan-dan dan – dan – dan-dan-dan – daah – dish! Gangsters –! Dan-dan-dan-dandan – dan – dan-dan-dan – daah – dish! Dan-dan-dan-dan-dan – dan – dan-dan-dan – daah – dish! This burning cigarette ... sort of – dish! – across the room. Kwa-dang! – this petrol drum hits the deck – kwadonggg ... ! Bloep-bloep-bloep-bloep!

Petrol-petrol-petrol! Cigarette-cigarette-cigarette! [*Dick Tracy.*] Dan-dan-dan-dan-dan – dan – dan-dan-dan – daah – dish! Dan-dan-dan-dan-dan – dan-dan-dan – daah – dish ... ! [*Three rapid punches.*] Dish-dish-dish! [*Three rapid reactions.*] Dish-dish-dish! [*Two rapid punches.*] Dish-dish! [*Two rapid reactions – Dick retreating.*] Dishdish! [*Punch/reaction.*] Dish -! Dish -! [*Punch/reaction.*] Dish -! Dish -! Petrol-petrol! Cigarette-cigarette! Petrol-petrol! Cigarette-cigarette! Dick Tracy – Going Bananas -! Dan-dan-dan – daah – [*Punch.*] – dish ... ! Dandan-dan – daah – [*Kick.*] – dish ... ! Dan-dan-dan – daah – [*Double-fisted uppercut/downcut/left-cut/right-cut.*] – dish –! dish –! dish –! Gangsters – from behind – [*Hitting Dick in the neck*.] – dish! Dick – nigh! [*Falling to the floor – stunned.*] Petrol-petrol! Cigarette-cigarette! Petrol-petrol! Cigarette-cigarette ... ! Petrol-cigarette! Petrol-cigarette! Voooeeschhh ... !! Flames ... !!! Gangsters –! [*Running for a window, diving out.*] Waaaah ... ! [*Delayed reaction.*] Dish! Flames-flames-flames! Drums-drums-drums! Dick-Dick-Dick! Flames-Dick-drums! Flames-Dick-drums ... !

[*YOUNG EDDIE*] 'Get up, Dick – get uuuup ... !!!!'

Bgggggghhhh-wrggghh ... !! Bgggggghhhhwwwaaaaaaahhhhh....!! The biggest explosion in the History of the World! [*Deep American accent.*] 'What happens to Dick Tracy ... ?' The whole week, you wandering around – biting your nails – kicking the dog – klapping your sister ... dish! [*Quick klap.*]

Next Saturday –

'One please.'

'Here you go, young man. And don't lose your ... '

[*Impatiently.*] 'Ja, ja – I know, I know ... !'

[*Going to seat, sitting down.*] Front row. Same seat.

'Shht ... ! Shhht .... ! Sorry, okes ...! Who farted ... ? Shaddap ... ! Sis, man ... ! Sorry ... ! Shht ... ! Sorry ... ! [*Pause.*] Shh ... !'

[*Movie sting.*] Bwa-daaaannggg ... ! [*Deep American accent.*] 'Last week on Dick Tracy ... !'

He squats down and eats popcorn, watching the same section he described previously – wolfing down the popcorn. The odd exclamation ('Dan-dan-dandanning' music too) escapes his lips until the moment the gangsters have escaped and the flames approach the drums –

'Get up, Dick – get uuuuup ... !!'

At which point, he re-enacts the final section.

Dick – on the deck ... ! [*Groggily, shaking his head.*] 'Where am I ... ?' [*Spotting the danger.*] 'Holy Smoke ... !' 'Haaaah ... !' [*Diving out of the window – followed by explosion.*] Bggghhhwrrraaaaaah ... !!! Bgggggghhhwwwaaaaaaaahhhhh ... !!! Bgggghhhhwwwrrrraaaagh ... !!! [*Spinning toward the lamppost in the cross-fade.*] Dick had lived to fight another day!

When the lights cross-fade to come up fully on him at the lamppost – it is as if he has not moved from the reflective pose he was in before the story began.

Those were the days when they made movies. Real movies.

Pause.

'The Hanging Tree'. 'Twelve Angry Men'. 'Jailhouse ... 'Jailhouse Rock' ...

He stops short on the indirect reference to Elvis, uncertain as to how he should proceed.

Listen – um ... I got a confession to make. There's a helluva good chance that he might not rock up here tonight. In fact, it's ninety-nine point nine-nine-nine percent certain he won't. Rock up, I mean. Genuine. For this oke to come along here tonight would be nothing short of a miracle. And that's ... basically what I'm waiting for. Some kind of ... you know. That's basically why I'm hanging around here in the middle of the night, opposite the ex-Carlton Bioscope doing this ... I dunno. The truth is, it's ... it's my Last Shot. It's ... it's Crunch Time. [*Struggling now.*] Jeepers, I'm not making sense. The point is – why? Why get in the car – why drive over two hundred kays to a town I haven't been back to in over a quarter of a century in the mad-crazy hope of maybe – just maybe meeting up with someone who's supposedly long gone to join that Great Rock 'n Roll Party in the Sky? The answer's quite simple. No, it's not simple. It would be simple to say, ja – it's Elvis. Elvis Lives. Elvis Is, Was and Always Will Be. But it's ... it's more than that. Much – much than that ...

He wrestles with his emotions. Takes a deep breath.

Things ... happen to you in life ... you don't know how or why or ... or even ... where they come from. Things ... creep up on you. Outa' the blue.

Pause.

It's like ... one day ... you're standing in the boss's office. Boem! He hits you with it.

'I'm sorry, my boy, but that's it. Cheers, bye-bye and toodle-doo.'

What d'you mean ... ? Twelve years! You can't turn round after twelve years and just –!'

He doesn't wanna know. You walk outa' that place in a dwaal. Three weeks later you're still in a dwaal as one place after another gives you the same old story –

'No, sorry, it's okay we looking for youngsters.'

'No-no, hey – but that's fine, that's okay, that's cool – I'm a youngster. I'm a youngster at heart … ! See? Look! Two arms. Two legs. I gotta brain. Left side – right side – zing-zing! Hey … ? Hey … ?'

And then they smile – they always smile – 'Thanks, but No Thanks … '

Ha! You don't believe it … ! It's tickets. Forty-six years old and it's … ! This is it. End of the road. How did it get to this? I've always … done my best. I played the game like anyone else. I mean – my life's the same as the next man's. How is it that he's okay – the oke next door? He was also a kid once. A laaitie. He had a laaitihood just like mine. Or did he? And then you realise that it's all … gone. Past. All behind you. It's like you just woken up from a long, long sleep and your whole life – your … your whole journey to this point is – is just a … just a blank. You can't … grab hold of … anything …

Pause.

I mean – I had it planned tonight, hey. Right down to the … to the last detail. All I hada' do was … go do it. Supper was over. The kids were in bed. I'm sitting in fronta' the TV watching Rescue 911 and then – almost as if I planned that too – the wife comes across and says – okay, doll – I'm going to bed. Before I can say anything – she's gone.

As he gets to 'sitting in fronta' the TV, the lighting change happens again. Lights up down front, lights down around the lamppost.

Okay. So this is it. I look around. I'm wondering … where am I gonna put the note? I've written it and rewritten it about five hundred times and now I just … got to get rid of it. But where … ? I can't put it on top of the TV because the kids watch the cartoon in the morning and you can't have a sort of a … bye-bye – I'll love you forever, in the middla' sort of, you know – Popeye–Mickey Mouse–Loopy de Loop – it's not sort of … dignified. The mantelpiece? I can't put it on the mantelpiece, man! What if she goes out to the car before she goes to the mantelpiece? Well, does it matter? Of course it matters! Does she find you first or the note first? What if she finds neither? What if the kids go off to school – she thinks you gone off in the car to look for another job and doesn't even go into the garage? She doesn't go to the garage for a week? Two weeks … !? Three weeks later, she goes to the garage – finds the car – finds you in the car and you're … you're … you orready going green! 'Walla-walla-walla' – there's Captain Kirk, on the TV – trying to rescue this little kid stuck in a pipe. Letter, man! Letter … ! But – hang on – this is riveting stuff, man. Fire engines, ambulances – they tryina' save this little kid stuck in a pipe twenty feet under the ground. I'm wandering down the passage now – look in at the kids. They're asleep. Wife's asleep too – open book on the bed next to her. The passage! Bookshelf in the passage! It's there. [*The note.*] She finds it when she finds it. Okay. Back into the lounge. They pulling the kid outa' the pipe. Kid's all blue. At least he's okay. Keys … ! Keys … ! Where the car keys? Buggerit, she's always picking them up and putting them down and then you can never find them when you need them! I'm throwing cushions all over the place and now the bladdy dog's behind me – tail going flick-flack – flack-flack – he knows something's on the go. Where the bladdy keys … ! Wake her up! I can't wake her up. I wake her up, she asks me where I'm going – I say, no – don't worry – I'm just gonna go sit in the car and gas myself!

Making like the dog, excitedly panting around his heels.

'Hoha-haha – hoha-haha – hoha-haha … !' Bladdy dog's beginning to irritate the hell outa' me now! Stupid brak sees me looking for the keys this time a' night, he thinks we going on holiday – 'Mamzimtoti – the beach! – Dog loves the beach! Bladdy sea-sand in the car – Takes me a year to get the bladdy carpets clean! 'Voetsek … ! Down, Caesar, down … ! No, no – uh-uh – we not going anywhere now!' Ah – the keys! – at last! 'Trringtring … !' Buggerit. [*Picking up phone.*] 'Bob … ! Hi, Bob. Golf on Saturday? Fine. Yes. Nothing planned. No, no. Good. Okay. Right. See you then.' [*Dog noises.*] 'Hwah-hoha-haha-hoha-haha-hoha … !' – 'No, man!' Give him a steak. Out the kitchen door. Boem. Thank God …

Moving into another area and going into the 'garage'.

Okay. Into the garage. Plastic pipe from the broken Kreepy Krauly – in place. Okay. Beers on the seat. Doors. Gotta put something under the doors. Dammit. Hadn't thought a' that. Blankets? No blankets. Towels? Okay – towels. Back into the house – [*Dog sounds.*] 'Hwah-hoha-haha-hoha-haha hoha-haha … !' Buggerit, bladdy dog's bladdy vomited all over the kitchen floor! [*Step over vomit.*] Into the bathroom – grab the towels. Right. Back through the kitchen – [*Dog noises.*] 'Hwah-hoha-haha-hoha-haha-hoha … !' [*Step over vomit.*] Out the door. [*Whimpering noises.*] 'Oaw-oaw-oaw-ooaawooo … !' Dammit! Bladdy dog! Maybe I should put him in the car? Teach him a lesson! Dog crap in the kitchen – dog crap on the lawn! Spend more time on the bladdy weekend with pooper-scooper-spade in my hand than a bladdy Castle Lager … ! [*Whimpering noises.*] 'Oaw-oaw-oaw-oaw oawwww … !' Back into the kitchen. Open the fridge door. Okay – go for it. Feel free! Hope you choke on the bladdy stuff! Out the door. Into the garage. Okay. Pipe's in place. Towels under the door. Okay. This is it! Pipe in the window. All windows up. Okay. Turn on the engine. Hope she doesn't hear it. Wonder if it hurts … ? [*Sniffs.*] Smells kinda' … funny. Have a

beer ... OK ... ! [*Cracks one open.*] Pssst ...! [*Drinks, then shudders.*] Huh-huh ...!
Turn the car radio on, man ... !

He freezes in the act of switching on the radio, a pause.

[*Singing.*] 'Is your heart filled with pain ... ? Shall I come back again... ?' I don't
believe it. It's him! [*The 'story' lights fade down and the 'lamp' lights come up. We
are back in the 'now'.*] Is my heart filled with pain ... ? [*Looking up, angrily.*] Of
course it's filled with pain ... ! Why you think I'm doing this ... ? For fun ... !? 'Shall
I come back again ... ?' I dunno. Where were you the last time? Where were you
the last time I came to this spot, thirty years ago — and waited and waited and
waited ... !?

*Sits on the pavement and cracks open a beer – knocking it back. He takes off one shoe.
Knocks it on the pavement.*

Who bought these shoes? [*Studying them.*] They're not shoes – they moccasins.
Moccasins. Mock ... mock ... moccasins ... [*Puts a hand in the shoe, makes a
'walking' movement with it.*]

Puts the shoe back on again. Stares out front, lost. A pause.

Those guys who've ... who've had near-death experiences. They say – before you
die – it's like your whole life kinda – pshew! – flashes before you. But is that
now your whole life or ... or just parts of it? And if it's only parts of it – is it the
best parts or the worst parts ... ?

Pause.

What happens if your whole life has been one big balls up – from beginning to
end? One big ... gemors? Well, I s'pose if that's the case, you just ... you just lag.
You just ... die laughing ... ! [*Laughing.*]

Pause.

Uncle Albert, in the shit. Story of my life. [*Smiling.*] I mean – what kind of
a life is it where one of your earliest memories is that of a kleinhuis ... in the
agterplaas? An outside lavatory in a place called Italy Village?

Pause.

I think they called it Italy Village because that was the section of Modderfontein
where the Italian POWs were given cheap housing at the end of the war. They
were these – corrugated iron jobs – little white picket fences in front – stoeps
that ran right the way around to the back – wide open veld on either side
and a long dirt road that ran all the way down to the dam. The nice thing
about having a long dirt road leading up to your house was that you could see
someone come from a long way off ...

He gets up, moves downstage as if looking down the dirt road. Cross-fade effect from pole to flashback area – as EDDIE turns and becomes UNCLE ALBERT.

'Ag, no, man – life is a bastard ... !'

[*YOUNG EDDIE*] 'Ma – ma – look who's coming ... !'

[*UNCLE ALBERT*] 'Where's the lavvy, man ... ? Where's the lavvy! Ag, no, man – jislaaik ... ! You still got this Long Drop – twenty-five miles from the bladdy house ... !? You people must get rid of it! We got rid of ours before the bladdy war, man. We had to. Going for a quick piss at two o'clock in the morning in the middle of winter was a real Antarctic Exhibition. It was this cold, man – [*Showing an inch.*]. Bladdy ballas turn to ice – ice balls! [*Pissing, knock-kneed.*] Ha-ghu-ghughu ... ! It was so cold, you had to keep a can of anti-freeze under the bogroll to defrost your hindquarters before you sank down onto the woodwork. It got to the point where you'd be holding your bum against the coal stove at the kitchen door as long as you could before taking a lightning-quick dash across the back yard. Ghwhhhhooo-aaah ... !' [*'Pulling down' pants and squatting.*] No, man. You people must get yourself some modern appliances, man. You get outside pondoks inside these days, man – with chains. Big shiny chains. You pull them – [*Pulling chain twice – enjoying it.*] Grrrrrwwoooesch ... ! All gone. No gagga. No gedoentes. No nothing.'

Uncle Albert – our boilermaker from down in PE.

[*YOUNG EDDIE*] 'Ag, he's never boiled anything in his whole life, man. He's a bulldustmaker – always fulla' stupid stories ... !'

[*UNCLE ALBERT*] 'Have I ever told you about the time I shot that buffalo and the bladdy thing gored me right through to my spinal column ... ?'

[*EDDIE'S DAD*] 'Yes, Albert, yes – you got the horns hanging on your yacht in the Bahamas ... '

My Dad. Huh. He wasn't very impressed with his second cousin – twice removed. He always wished he'd remove himself permanently and never come back. As for my big boet, Nigel – he always prayed that the ground would open up and swallow him whole.

[*NIGEL*] 'Why does he come here all the time, man? Can't he see there's no room for him to stay ... ?'

[*UNCLE ALBERT*] 'Ag, don't worry about me, man. I'm a Child of Nature. I got my tent. I can sleep under a bladdy tree if needs be.'

Only problem was – the only okes who slept under the tree were my boet and me – while he stank out our room with his smelly feet and his big fat pipe.

[*YOUNG EDDIE*] 'How we gonna get rid of him, man ... ? Apple pie-ing his bed didn't work! Putting Brooklax in his breakfast only made him poep across the garden! And when we stuck that mamba in his trousers all he did was grab it behind the head and chuck it outa' the window ... !'

[*NIGEL*] 'We gotta do something, man. I can't take this anymore!'

Three or four days later and Uncle Albert is STILL complaining about the outside pondok –

[*Zipping up his fly.*] 'Ag, no, man – sis ,,, ! Throwing leyes fluid en wat ook al down that stinkgat is not going to help. It's a cesspool, man. If you people don't make a plan, I'm going to have to seriously consider what family members I decide to visit in future.'

'Woo-hooo ... !'

Nigel and I knew exactly what to do. We charged down to the Lakeside Cafe –

'You got any old tomato-boxes, Mr Moosa ... ?'

[*Indian accent.*] 'Tomato-box? For vy you vant a tomato-box ... !?'

[*Sawing, hammering.*] Zzzzit-zzzit-zzzzit-zzit ... ! Bang-bang-bang ... ! Bangbang-bang ... ! Bang-bang-bang... !

A lavatory seat the likes of which Modderfontein had never seen before ... ! Once we got the new seat in place, the next step was to make sure nobody used the pondok before Uncle Albert –

[*YOUNG EDDIE*] 'Er – um – where you going, dad?'

'Whatsa' matter, you wanna hold my hand ... ?'

[*NIGEL*] 'Use the potty, ma – use the potty ... !'

Five o' clock, and Uncle Albert at long last lifts himself slowly out of the deck chair on the back stoep.

'Ja – [*stretch, yawn*] – time to press a coil.'

He was going to press a helluva lot more than a coil and I suddenly got incredibly cold feet.

'Hey, Nigel – what if ... what if ... ?'

'Leave him, man. Leave him ... !'

[*UNCLE ALBERT, walking to pondok.*] 'It's a long road to Tipperary, a long road to go ... '

Five – four – three – two – one – Gwa-daaaaah ... !! [*Wood breaking.*]

'Waaaaaaaaaaaa-aaah ... !!' [*Long dropping sounds.*]

Pffffrrrrtsch ... ! Pflfrrrrtsch . . .! [*Squelching sounds.*]

The shit hit the fan in more ways than one ... !

[*EDDIE'S DAD*] 'What's going on ... !? O, jislaaik ... !! Get a rope – get a rope ... !!'

[*EDDIE'S MUM*] 'Oh, my God ... !'

[*EDDIE'S DAD*] 'Someone call the police ... !'

The police ... !? Ooh, I knew it – they were going to chuck us in jail and throw away the key ... !

[*EDDIE'S DAD*] 'OK, Albert – hold on tight ... !'

EDDIE'S DAD tosses a rope down and six men grab hold of it – gritting their teeth.

Half an hour – and six fully-grown men to haul Uncle Albert outa' that pit. But not because he was so heavy, but because he'd been transformed into a giant, swollen, Lunch Bar ... !

[*Tugging him out.*] 'Heave ... !' – Schlurp! – 'Heave ... !' – Schlurp! – 'Heave ... !' – Schhlllluuuurrrrp... !!

[*Horrified reaction.*] 'Waaaaaahhh ... !!!'

Jislaaik – talk about the Monster From the Bog! He looked like the Creature the World Forgot ... ! Everybody wanted to forget him, orraight – running off in all directions and grabbing hosepipes, pots, pans – anything to wash away this ... this Invasion of the Body Snatchers ... !!

[*Water-spray.*] Wrrrooooooeschhh ... !! Wrrrooooeesch ... !!

[*UNCLE ALBERT flailing about*] 'Waaaa-arghugh ... !!' Wwwwrooooesch ... !!

'Waaaaaa-uuugh ... !!'

[*YOUNG EDDIE*] 'Hey, Uncle Albert ... ! What about your stuff ... !?'

[*UNCLE ALBERT spinning off*] 'Ow-aaaaaargh ... !!'

EDDIE watches him off, smiling sadly.

Shame. We never ever saw Uncle Albert again. Not even so much as a ... Christmas Card. I often wonder ... what happened to him. What ... eventually became of him. The Creature the World ... Forgot.

EDDIE moves back to the lamppost. Cross-fade as before. Once again, it is as if the whole thing has happened inside his head.

Still. Who's to say his life was all downhill, hey? One thing's for sure – he never had to try sell underfloor heating at the arse-end of a recession. At least he never had to try convince a bone-headed boss that you can still outperform some smart-fancy windgat just outa' school – all smiles, goodlooks and hey-howzit-my-mate? Experience ... ! Hey ... !? Doesn't that count for anything any more ... !? Track-record ... ? Okay, okay – so you come short a coupla' times! But that's got nothing to do with outmoded selling techniques or ... or deal-making skills. It's the market, man ... ! It's what people want! If your product's not moving, it's not moving ... ! You don't turn around to someone who's been covering your back for you for twelve bladdy years and then ... and then ... !

Pause.

Who's gonna look after my kids, huh ... !? Who's gonna put them through school ... !? Who's gonna put them to bed at night and tell them stories about ... about ... ?

Pause.

I don't tell them stories. Not about their family, anyway. I just tell them ... lies ...

Pause.

[*EDDIE'S MUM*] 'Chin up, luv. Chin up. Look on the bright side ... '

Pause.

She was always telling me to do that – my ma. Even when it seemed my whole world had ended. Like that Easter-time ... [*Smiling.*] That bunny rabbit Easter egg. It was the nicest Easter egg I'd ever received. Long ears and buck teeth. It was wrapped in shiny crinkle paper with green and gold dots. My boet and sis ate theirs straight away, but I hung onto mine. I wanted to keep mine as long as I could. I put him on top of the washing-line pole so that I could watch him all day. And he could watch me – playing cops and robbers, cowboys and crooks, Lone Ranger-Lone Ranger. My boet always made me play Tonto ...

Turning into the game and becoming Tonto – war-whoops and all. Gunshots and arrows – a real cowboy movie!

'You're dead, man ... ! What d'you mean I missed ... !? S'not fair, man – every time you shoot me, I'm s'posed to die – but when I shoot you, you never die ... ! Ag, I'm not playing with you anymore, man – I'm gonna go eat my Easter egg ... '

He moves to the washing-line and stops short. There is no sign of his Easter egg. Cries like a four-year old – letter-box mouth.

'Waaaaaaaaaaaaaaaa – [*Catch breath.*] – ugh – waaaaaaaah ... !'

[*EDDIE'S MUM*] 'What's the matter, luv? Why all those tears?' [*Spotting ex Easter egg.*] Oh, good gracious me ... ! Your Easter egg's melted ... !'

[*Letter-box mouth*] 'Waaaaaaaaaaa – aaaagh ... !'

[*Comforting EDDIE*] 'There, there, luv – chin up. I'll get you another one.'

And she did too. She walked that whole neighbourhood up and down 'til she found a bunny rabbit Easter egg exactly like the one I'd lost. My ma. Delicate English Rose maybe, boy – but when she put her mind to something ... ! Like leaving home on the Southampton Castle ... never going back.

Pause.

There were times when she wished she had. Plenty times. I'd come home from playing with my mates and find her sobbing her heart out in that little outside pondok – those picture postcards from the folks back home ... Kensington Gardens ... Westminster Abbey ...

Singing, as MUM, à la Vera Lynn.

'We'll meet again
Don't know where
Don't know ... when ...'

She never properly – 'transplanted', my mother. Africa was always this dark, violent place that started just outside the window. [*Mine dance sounds.*] Ha-hum! Ga-doenk-gadoenk-gadoenk-gadoenk-gadoenk! Ha-hum! Ga-doenk-gadoenk-gadoenk-gadoenk -! The Zulu Mine Dances – the Bantu Compound across the dam.

Pause.

Right up until the day we left that place, she always believed those Zulus were gearing up to avenge the Battle of Blood River. [*Mine dance beat.*] Ha-hum gadoenk-gadoenk-gadoenk-gadoenk! Ha-hum – gadoenk-gadoenk-gadoenk-gadoenk-gadoenk!

'That's a War Dance, isn't it? They work themselves up, don't they? Into some sort of uncontrollable frenzy?'

'That's right, Doris – they sharpening their spears and then they going to come down here and chop us all to pieces. Bulalah! Bulalah bathaka thi ... !' [*Laughter.*]

Pause.

My dad. I s'pose he was sort of okay. In those early days, anyway. A fitter-and-turner at the local dynamite factory – served in the war in the North African Campaign. Tobruk. El Alamein. All those other ... funny names.

[*EDDIE'S DAD*] 'I fought Rommel ... !'

Huh. He was always saying that. 'I fought Rommel!' Like it was just him and Rommel for the vacant Heavyweight Championship of the World – [*American ring-announcer.*] 'On my left, and weighing in at a hundred and ninety-eight pounds – !' It was only later on we realised something must've happened to him out there in the desert. Maybe it was the sun? My ma always said it was the sun.

Pause.

Coek-cooeer-koek –! Coek-cooeer-koek –! Coek-cooeer-koek –! [*Turtledove call.*]

Pause.

How do you tell your wife that you can't go on? How d'you tell your kids that it's all been a mistake? That you shouldn't even ... be here ... ? That you have no right to be here ... ? How do you try to get them to ... try to understand when even you don't ... understand?

Turtle dove call again, more desperate this time.

Coek-cooeer-koek –! Coek-cooeer-koek –! Coek-cooeer-koek –!

Pause.

[*Hugely upbeat.*] It was great living near the dam. It was all a kid could ever want. Sliding down the dam wall on broken cardboard boxes – bits a' corrugated iron. Making kleilats with the willow branches and zhukking your mates with big, fat lumps a' clay. Zzzzzzhuk ... !

'Eina – you bliksem ... !'

Pietie Boshoff! No, no – wait a minute – Mossie Boshoff. That's right. Mossie Boshoff – the son of Oom Piet. Oom Piet ran a car painting business in his back yard and sometimes we'd help him sand down those cars when we had nothing else to do.

[*OOM PIET*] 'Howzabowrit, boys? Huh? A tickey or a farthing, depending on whether or not you're slapgat.'

We'd sand those big cars down 'til they looked like giant, shiny tin cans – waiting for their labels. Dodge and Studebaker ... Pontiac, Packard, Plymouth. [*Writing it in the air.*] ... Chrysler. The days when cars still had names. Proper names. When cars sounded like cars and not ... Thai ... Sushi ... Chinese takeaways.

For a moment Eddie stares into the middle distance, lost in that time of hope and happiness, then he slowly moves back to the lamppost – looks up to the light, takes off his jacket, drops it to the pavement and has a sip of his beer. He paces about, mumbling 'The sun ... the sun ... ma always said it was the sun ...' before snatching up the stick in the gutter and slamming the pole, hitting the milk crate. He leopard-crawls across the floor, becoming his dad and using the stick as a rifle. Flashback lights bang up.

'Get down! Get down! Get down! [*In great distress.*] Get down ...! Get down ...!!' [*Hurling the stick away.*]

Dad's nightmares and freak-outs were getting worse and worse. Sometimes I think that's why they transferred him. Just to get rid of him.

'What d'you mean you don't want to go, Doris ...? I been transferred – promoted ...!'

'You can't go anywhere, Stefanus – you're not well ...'

'Not well? I'm not well ...? This coming from someone who dives under the kitchen table every time a piss-will little thunderstorm comes along ...!'

My big boet, Nigel – to the rescue –

'They do coal mining in Witbank. They produce half the coal in the Union.'

'They got any good schools?'

'No, Doris – they send the kids to work in the coal mines as soon as they can walk!'

We laid the Caltex road map across the kitchen table to look for our new home, but I'd already seen it.

'I know where it is ...! I know where it is ...! It's a little black dot on the road to Lourenço Marques ...!'

It was more than a little black dot. It was a big black splodge. Coal mines and slag heaps as far as the eye could see. But at least it was a change. And, as far as us kids were concerned, a whole new, exciting experience. Chickens in almost every back yard – cocopans on the mine-dumps and down at the station – huge big steam trains – Gwoe-ghoe-gwoe-ghoe – gwoeghoe-gwoe-ghoe ...! Wooo-ah-wooooh-hooh ...! Shhu-sh – shhu-sh – shhush ...!

He watches the train disappear in the distance and turns at the lamppost. The lights cross-fade to 'present'.

And the best discovery of all – the Carlton Bioscope and the Saturday morning matinee. [*That music, dead quiet.*] 'Dan-dan-dan-dan-dan – dan – dan-dan-dan – dah ...!'

He stares at the movie house across the road, lost for a moment.

How they can turn a bioscope into a betting house? Trying to get people to throw away their hard-earned money on ... on gambling. That's one thing I tell my kids, it's – look after your money. Work hard and you can never go wrong. Well ... almost never.

Unable to hide his bitterness.

Purpose to everything. Huh. 'There is a purpose to everything ... ' Bullshit ... ! What was the purpose, Father Vincent ... ? What was the purpose me coming to this lamppost that night – thirty years ago – if my whole life since has been such a stuff up? [*Looking out.*] The way I look at it, there's bugger-all purpose to anything ... ! Like those two guys who built that boat ... ! That boat that never sailed!

As he steps forward, cross-fade to story-telling setting.

Joseph's Ark, as we called it. The boat in the neighbours' backyard. But it wasn't just an ordinary boat. It was this ... this huge, big ... ocean-going thing that took up more than half the agterplaas.

Pause.

It seemed that everyone in Witbank knew about the boat in Van Deventer Street. People would drive past slowly on a Sunday afternoon and then ... zoom away quickly before they were spotted by these two ... huh ... these two land-locked sea-dogs. Old Joseph, with his hammer – seventy-five if he was a day – all muscle and sinew. His brown body glistening in the sun. Oom Carel joining him after his shift on the coal-face and the two of them – working way into the night.

'Shaddap, man! Some people want to sleep ... !'

My dad ... huh ... [*shaking his head.*]

'You five hundred miles from the bladdy sea, man! How you going to get that thing to sail ... !?'

Father watching disapprovingly for a couple of beats.

'Look at those bladdy poephols. A cement bottom! How you going to sail a boat with a cement bottom ... !? It's like trying to jump out of a aeroplane with a concrete bladdy parachute, man!'

Back in Italy Village, he would've laughed at one of his own jokes. We might have laughed too – or told him to cool it with the neighbours. But not anymore. He was liable to go off the handle at anything these days ... and rather than calm him down, those tranquillisers the doctor had given him for his nerves were making him even more ... gatvol. Gatvol with everyone and everything. A total ... pain to live with.

'What's a bladdy Cape coloured doing in the Transvaal? Bladdy coon must bugger off to where he came from, man ... ! [*Spinning round, viciously.*] And you keep your trap shut, Doris – or I send you back to England ... !'

Pause.

I s'pose they were a strange pair – Oom Carel and ou Joseph. But next to the madness of our house, I found them quite ... refreshing.

Pause.

The story went that Oom Carel Fourie hadn't always been a shift boss on the mines. He'd been a fisherman in the Cape, with his own boat. Apparently the boat had sunk in a storm one night and ol' Joseph – a crew member – had saved his life. Oom Carel had brought him along with him when his brother had managed to organise him a job on the collieries. Officially, ol' Joseph was supposed to be the gardener, but he never ever seemed to do any gardening. It was always the boat. The boat – and nothing but the boat.

Pause.

Oom Carel was a ... was a quiet man. I s'pose what you'd call a ... a deep man. You had the feeling when you were around him that he was thinking things that other people never ... thought about.

Pause.

He had a telescope on his back stoep and sometimes at night, I'd crawl through the hole in the hedge and he'd show me the stars or the moon – 'specially when it was full. He always said that when a man worked so much a' the time underground, it was important that he kept in touch with the cosmos. That was the first time I ever heard that word – cosmos. I hear the word cosmos today, and I still think of Oom Carel. Joseph, of course, hated it when Oom Carel got sidetracked from what he saw as Priority Number One.

[OLD JOSEPH] 'Lossit nou, Carel, kom – ek kry swaar met die vertical coupling rods oppie compressor.'

[OOM CAREL] 'Toemaar, Joseph – ek wys virrie seuntjie die maan ... '

'Boggerie maan, man. Ons moet werk oppie boot! Time en Tides Waits for No Man, man ... !'

Sometimes ol' Joseph would go grab his bottle. And when that happened, that put paid to our stargazing good and proper.

[OOM CAREL] 'Now look there, Eddie, look – on the moon – just off centre there – looks like a big fat pimple ... '

'I see it, Oom.'

'Now that – that is the Crater of Copernicus ... '

[OLD JOSEPH] 'Copernicus se moer, man ... !'

'And that huge open plain next to it – that is where man is going to walk one day – you mark my words ...'

'No, Oom ... ?'

'Oh, yes. It's what they call ... the Sea of Tranquillity ... '

'Twak, man. Don' listen to him, man. Dissie die See of Trankwility nie. Dissie eersie See of Serenity nie. Dissie See of Boggerol! Daar's vokol see oppie maan, man ... !'

'Ja, ja – toemaar, Joseph ... '

'Die maan is net 'n klomp beach sand, man ... ! Die maan issa beach ... ! Dissa beach ... ! Daar's g'n see, man ... ! Where you see a see oppie maan, man ... !? Daar's g'n see anywhere, man ... ! [*Weeping – dronkverdriet.*] Ek wil see toe gaan, man ... ! Ek wil see toe gaan ... !'

Pause.

We all knew he'd never see the sea again. Oom Carel knew it, and I think deep, deep down – ol' Joseph must've known it too. They'd never have the money or the means to get their boat outa' that backyard and ... and more and more at night we'd see ol' Joseph on the boat – hear him praying for the flood that would carry them away to his beloved ocean.

[JOSEPH *kneeling and reaching heavenward*] 'Kom, Lord ... ! Kom nou, Lord – ons vra djou in alle yew-mility en prostrations, jong ... ! Don' come like a crab, Lord ... ! Don' trow us a slap jol now, Lord ... ! Allie ennimals is on board ... ! Al my varkies is bymekaa ... ! Stuur virrie reen, Lord! Stuur virrie reen ... ! Stuur 'sablief virrie reen, Lord ... !'

Pause.

Poor Joseph. It seemed hopeless. Until ... one summer, we bad a thunderstorm the likes of which the Transvaal has never seen before or since. It rained and rained. Three days it rained ... almost nonstop. There was so much water everywhere that all the chickens were up on top of their hoks and people were bailing water outa' their kitchens. We were so busy mopping up, we didn't hear Joseph when he collapsed. All we knew is that one minute he was dancing around, thigh-deep in water – and the next ... he was gone.

[*JOSEPH does a wild, celebratory dance.*] 'Woooo! Dankie, Lord ... ! Djy's 'n daring, Lord ... ! ['*Splashing' in water.*] Sples-sples ... ! Djoo shower me wit blessings like confetti, my Lord. I'm going to go to tsurts every Sunday, Lord. I'm never going to dop again! Sples-sples ... ! Wooo ... ! You my bes friend ... ! Oooo-waah – got-allah!' [*He collapses on the ground.*]

Oom Carel was the first to get to him, but it was too late. Joseph hadn't drowned. He'd died of a heart attack. But at least he'd died happy. Happier, maybe, than he'd ever been in his entire life.

Pause.

The rain had come. Ol' Joseph's rain had come. The sea had come to Joseph ...

He returns to the lamppost – cross-fade of lights again. He sips at a beer and reflects on his own life.

All that came to me at that stage a' my life was problems. Problems, problems and more problems. [*Grimly.*] But we don't talk about that, do we? Not then ... not now ... not ever.

He breaks away and gets distracted by the lamppost – begins looking for something on it.

Wait a minute ... it was here. It was somewhere here. I scratched it ... I don't know how many times ... E du P loves L S. [*Laughing.*] Ed u P loves L S. Lydia Swanepoel. The girl next door. [*As he steps off the pavement, the lights cross-fade to story-telling mode.*] She was the first one who got me ... all shook up. In the chemical sense, that is. I didn't know much about chemistry at age fifteen, but – looking back – I know now it definitely musta' been ... chemical. I mean – I was already clocking into Heartbreak Hotel and we hadn't even said hello to each other – never mind goodbye!

Singing.

'We - ell – since my baby left, I found a new place to dwell –' The crazy thing was, you know – she ... she wasn't even really much to write home about. In fact – to tell the truth – she looked more like a ... like a stick-insect than a chick. But what she had was this ... this ponytail that sort of ... did things to your knees. Everytime she moved from one place to another – that ponytail would sorta' – bob-flick – bob-flick – bob-flick – gwa-daannnggg ... ! [*Semi-collapsing, knock-kneed.*] And you were gone. Sort of – hypnotised. Like a zombie.

Pause.

The first sort of – hullo-howzit? – took forever to organise. But it wasn't for lack of trying, boy – that's for sure. I'd spot her coming down the road and then sort of ... cool-casually go out onto the front stoep for some fresh air. Now in theory, this sounds like I shoulda' been A for Away, but – hell, man – to crack it ... ! Every time she got within chaffing range, it was – bob-flick – bob-flick – bob-flick – gwa-daannggg ... ! [*Crumpled, knock-kneed pose.*] And that was that.

Pause.

I did get it right, though. Eventually. She stopped on the pavement one day to scrape some bubble gum off her shoe and kept that ponytail still just long enough for me to jump in quick-stix. 'Howzit, Lydia ... ?'

[A *totally unimpressed girl-next-door.*] 'Hullo.'

It wasn't exactly Over the Moon stuff, but I'm thinking – no problem – I've heard her playing rock 'n roll music on her Teppaz portable gram, and I got the perfect opener.

'So. What d'you think a' that new song by Cliff Richard ... ?'

She gives me this long, cold stare.

'Who wants to listen to Harry Webb?'

Harry Webb? Who the hell was Harry Webb? How was I supposed to know Harry Webb was the oke Cliff Richard used to be, and that Cliff Richard was feeding the world a bullshit name?

'I don't listen to phoneys. I listen to the Real Thing!'

Bob-flick – bob-flick – bob-flick-! [*Cutting short.*]

Dammit. I'd blown it. For the moment, anyhow. But it didn't take me long to find out who the real thing was, though, uh-uh. A few sessions listening at the fence taught me that the only guy for this chick was Elvis Aaron Presley – the King a' Rock 'n Roll Himself. At last, I knew my angle. I'd found the key. Or so I thought.

Miming balancing on a very narrow, very high wall.

Coupla' days later, I'm balancing on the broken wall at the back where it joins the fence – she comes outside to hang up some washing for her ma. Now I'm concentrating on this wall, you see, so I'm not – I'm not watching that ponytail –

'Howzit, Lydia ... ' [*Balancing on the wall.*]

'Ugh. Hullo.'

If I wasn't so thick-skinned, I woulda' picked up that 'ugh!' before the 'hullo' and quitted while I was ahead. But being the total poephol that I was, I really believed that she was gonna be ... you know – blown away by this ... high-flying refugee from Boswell's Circus. I was windgatting it up so much, I even forgot the clever comment I was gonna make about Elvis Presley. But she's watching me now, you see – I gotta say something ... impressive. The moment sort of ... demands it. 'I was born in North America.' [*Breaking off the balancing.*] Don't ask me why I said that. To this day, I don't know why I said that. It was one a' those doosagtige things that comes into your head and you just say it without thinking about it. [*Back onto wall.*]

'I beg you pardon?'

'I was born in North America.'

'Where in North America?'

Buggerit. I wasn't prepared for that.

'Um – um – Glasgow ...' [*Grabbing his face, mega-horrified.*]

Aaaaaagh ... !!? Thank goodness I lost my balance and fell off that wall ... ! It was far less embarrassing! I mean – Geography was never one of my strong points, but – Glasgow ... !!? She's stomping across the back garden now, and I'm grabbing at straws –

'Glasgow in Texas – there's a Glasgow in Texas. Or ... or Arkansas ...sass ... sauce ... siss!'

Bang... ! Her door slams and suddenly I remember what it was I wanted to tell her about Elvis –

'Elvis is planning to make a new flick ... !'

Hell, man – who was I trying to kid? Here was a chick who probably knew what Elvis had had for breakfast that morning!

Dusting himself off, with grim resolve.

Lydia Swanepoel's ponytail was slowly beginning to lose its charm – but now it was becoming a matter of pride. To make any kinda' inroads here, I was gonna have to go the whole hog. Gritting my teeth and taking my courage in both hands, I headed for the bathroom and planted myself firmly in fronta' the mirror. [*Doing just that.*] Ahaaaa-hah ... ! Jislaaik! All I see looking back at me is this moon face fulla' freckles – carrot-coloured hair and bum-fluff for sideburns. I'm about as close to Elvis Presley as a ... as a bladdy bullfrog is to Brigitte Bardot ... ! [*Dropping his head.*] I try the smile. The famous Presley sneer from the record cover of 'Loving You'. [*Elvis's Southern accent.*] 'Hi, Lydia ... hi, howdy ... ' [*Tries it several times and then drops his head.*] This was gonna be hard. Bladdy hard. But now I'm a Man with a Mission, hey. And, besides – listening to Elvis has got me quite liking the oke. He sang a helluva lot better than ... than Harry Webb or Tommy Steele or ... or – jislaaik – Pat Boone ... ! And now began the War of the Airwaves in our household. My ma – with her *From Crystal with Love* on Springbok Radio – and me with David Davies and LM.

Singing, wildly.

'I ain't nothing but a Hound Dog ... a cryin' all the time!'

'Turn that bladdy racket off right now ... !'

'But, Dad – it's Elvis ... !'

'I know bladdy well who it is. They should arrest that bastard for obscenity and stick him in the gas chamber ... !'

I'd never seen the old man so woes.

'What's obscenity, ma?'

'It – er – it comes from obscene, luv.'

'What's obscene?'

'Woof ...'

'Woof ... ? Woof ... !?'

This was something serious. Soon as she was gone, I'm grabbing the dictionary and digging around for 'obscene'. It took me hellout long to find it, but – boy! – when I did, I knew *exactly* what it was that had Lydia Swanepoel and thousands like her, losing their marbles for the Man with the Blue Suede Shoes ... [*Checking the dictionary.*] 'Obscene: filthy, repulsive, loathsome, grossly indecent, lewd'. Shit! All this time, I'd been barking up the wrong tree. I charged around to Stevie Blignaut's place and dived into his record collection. This oke had everything, man – magazines, pin-ups, posters, the works!

Strutting, gyrating about. The whole Elvis vibe, accent and all.

Soon, I was walking like Elvis. Talking like Elvis. Soon all the guys at school started calling me Elvis. Elvis du Pisanie ... ! With my collar sticking up and my kuif hanging down, I was gonna knock Lydia Swanepoel's stockings right off her feet. He was my Hero, man. I was closer to him than to anyone else ... !

He looks heavenward for a moment, almost as if he has heard or sensed something or someone – some presence. He glances up into the light of the lamppost, over his shoulder, down the street. Quietly – after a brief pause – he continues.

I was going to show her, boy. I was gonna show 'em all – and I got my chance a helluva lot sooner than I ever expected. Page three of the *Witbank News* – 'Calling All Elvis Fans!' – a competition to find the local Elvis ... !! Entry rules were a piece a' piss. Two-and-six to sign up and all you had to do was answer three easy questions and then state what song you wanted to sing. Number One – Where was Elvis born? Hah! Tupelo, Mississippi. Number Two – Where does Elvis currently reside? – Graceland, Memphis, Tennessee. Number Three – easiest of the lot – What is Elvis's favourite snack? Fried Peanut Butter and Banana Sandwich. Zip-zap, I was in there. Jeepers – the night arrives. The Blesbok Park Hall – filled to the brim. Every piepie-joller from Delmas to Dullstroom. They even had more okes than they had for Al Debbo! Everywhere you looked there was just Elvises. Even the okes who weren't even going as Elvis were looking like Elvis ... ! The girls were also out in force, hey – in their starched dresses, alice bands and bobby sox. Lydia Swanepoel was there too, of course – and although she didn't say anything, she just had to be impressed that I was at least going for it.

[*Holding up his hands – Cockney announcer (overweight and greasily repulsive)*] 'Ladies and gentlemen ... !' [*Aside.*] Adjudicator – 'Ladies aaaaaand gentlemennn ... !!'

Drrrrrrrrrrrrr – dischhhhhh ... ! [*Drum roll.*]

'The Allister Lacey Trio ... !'

Oh, no! As soon as I saw them, I knew I had to change my song. These okes played every Friday night at the Witbank Prison Officers' Club and I knew straightaway the old farts were far too dof to crack any real rock 'n roll.

'Ladies and gentlemen, boys and girls. Before we begin, a few brief announcements. To the ladies – could you please refrain from screaming. This is after all, a singing competition, and we'd like very much to hear the songs as they're sung. To the gentlemen – if you must chew gum – could you please keep that gum inside your mouths and don't stick it under your seats. Right. On with the Show – and May the Best Elvis Win ... !'

'Waaaaaaaaaaaaa-aaaaah ... !!!' [*Crowd screams.*]

[*Indicating.*] Crowd.

'Waaaaaaaaaaaaa-aaaaah ... !!!'

'Right, right … ! Thank you, thank you … ! [*Waving his arms.*] Our first contestant – from Clydesdale Colliery – to sing for us 'Won't you Wear my Ring Around your Neck?' – Master Errol Kemp … !'

'Waaaaaaaaaaaa-aaaaah … !!!'

Poor Errol. We hardly heard a word he sang. And it wasn't because he was so brilliant, no, no, no … ! It was just that Witbank had been waiting so long to join the 20th century, that as soon as he kicked-off the whole joint went bananas –

'Waaaaaaaaaaaaaaaaaaaa-aaaaah … !!!! Waaaaaaaaa-aaaah … !!!!'

By numbers five and six, I was beginning to feel a heck of a lot more confident – 'specially since the crowd were getting a bit hoarse by now and maybe the judges would have a chance of hearing me sing.

'Cedric du Presanie … ! [*Looking about, louder.*] Cedric du Presanie … !!'

Ooh, shit - that was me … ! [*Hastily grabbing his jacket and putting it on.*] I hated it when guys use my second name … ! Up onstage. Last comb through my black boot-polish hair. Swish-swish … ! Swish-swish … ! [*Combing frantically.*]

'Master du Presanie is going to sing for us – 'Tutti Frutti' … !'

'No, no, no – 'All Shook Up' … !'

'I beg yours?'

'All Shook Up.'

'It says here Tutti Frutti … '

'Ja, I know. I changed my mind.'

A pregnant pause, during which the Cockney does his best to suppress a scowl.

'All right. All right. Off you go, then.'

Eddie puts up his collar loosens his tie, preparing the 'Elvis look'.

I turn to the band. The old vrots are pissed off with me now because I changed my song. But there's no ways I'm going back now – and even if I did, they'd sabotage me, guaranteed.

'All Shook Up. C– flat.'

The band is obviously totally in the dark – they've never heard of the song.

'All Shook Up … uh-hum – uh-hum – uh-hum – uh-hum … you never heard of – uh-hum – uh-hum … ? [*Elvis lip and accent.*] Okay, you follow me … just … follow me … '

Throwing the full Elvis look, stance – the works!

'A-one – a-two – a-one-two-three-four ... '

Singing quietly, intensely, he gets through the first verse of 'All Shook Up', pulling up on 'I'm in Love!'

[*Breaking out of it, losing his 'Elvis' pose*] You gotta understand there were four categories, okay? – Looks, style, singing ability and originality. You got most points for originality because you were gooiing something of yourself in. You weren't depending on Elvis. I decided to gooi in more vibrato, you know – sort of ... trembling in my voice. This was also a pretty smart move in case I forgot my words. Then I could just busk my way through, sorta' ...

Singing, ultra-vibrato, he launches into the second verse of 'All Shook Up' ... jitterbugging his way through the third and fourth verses too, and finally swinging out of it on ... 'I'm All Shook Up ... !'

Pause.

For three or four seconds, there's total silence ... and then ... the joint went tekere. If I coulda' gone on a nation-wide tour right there and then there woulda' been queues round the block. Unbridled adulation is a terrifying sight to behold, and for one brief moment – as they escorted me from that stage – I knew what it was like to be a total ... *total* ... hero.

[*Crowd in raptures.*] 'Waaaaa-waaaaaaaaaaaaah ... !'

There were still three or four okes to go ... I didn't hear them ... but I did hear the crowd, and it wasn't half as loud as for me –

'Right, ladies and gentlemen – Thank you, thank you, thank you ... ! We have a winner ... !'

'Waaaaaaaaa-aaaaaah ... !!!'

'Yes, yes, yes ... ! Our very own Elvis Presley is ... !'

Drrrrrrrrrrrrrrrrrrrrrrrrrrr-disssssssscch ... !!! [*Drum roll.*]

I'm already standing up, hey –

'From Gravelotte in the Far Northern Transvaal – Master Dennis Cruikshank ... !'

Pause.

I was stunned. Speechless. Dennis Cruikshank ... ? Dennis Cruikshank ... !!? The oke yodelled, man ... !! Since when did Elvis yodel ... !!? Elvis woulda' sooner *died* than bladdy yodelled, man ... !!! I mean – this wasn't originality – this was ... this was ... hell, man... this was obscenity ... !!

297

Pause.

I didn't even hear who came second. All I know is that he wore a green tie! Jislaaik, don't these okes know that Elvis would never – but never wear a green tie ... ! [*Breathing deep, shaking his head.*] I realised as I went up to collect my third prize the moment I must've blown it. It was when I changed my song. That's what got them. That's what pissed them off and now they were paying me back.

'Well done, my lad. You had plenty of *elan. Eclat.*'

Eclat ... ! Eclat .. .!! If these okes thought Elvis had 'eclat' – no wonder they couldn't judge a bladdy Elvis Presley Competition! They knew less about Elvis than Allister Lacey and his stupid Trio and what *they* knew was sweet ... bugger all!

Pause.

When I looked around again for my so-called fans, they were gone – even ou Stevie Blignaut. [*He mooches across to the milk crate and sits on it, dejected.*] A coupla' hours later, I'm sitting all on my own behind the hall, clutching my pathetic little pink ... third-prize teddy bear, and suddenly there's this voice –

'Elvis ... '

I turn around – ... it's her!

'Lydia ... ?'

I forgot the smile. I forgot the accent. I forgot everything. But it didn't matter anymore, because she was looking right at me for the first time ever.

'If it makes any difference ... I still think you were the best ...'

Jislaaik. I was glad I was sitting down, hey – my knees would never of held me up. She comes across to me and ... she's holding out her hand. [*Taking Lydia's hand.*] I don't believe it ... I'm actually holding hands with ... with Lydia Swanepoel. If this wasn't heaven, then heaven must be something else, hey. I hand her the teddy bear and she lowers her eyes.

'I can't take that. It's your prize!'

'Think of it ... think of it as a gift from Elvis.'

We walked home – hand in hand – watching the night sky. It was the single most fantastic moment of my entire laaitihood. I may only have been the third best Elvis in the whole a' the South-Eastern Transvaal, but as far as Lydia Swanepoel was concerned – I, was definitely *it* ... !

As the lights go into cross fade, EDDIE backs away to the lamppost. From the heart-warming memory of greatest triumph, he is thrown cruelly back to the harsh present. He leans against the post, wondering what to do next.

He digs into his jacket pocket, fishes out the suicide note he never had the courage to leave behind. He begins reading it – as though it was written by someone else.

> 'My Darling Eunice, when you find this note, I'll be long gone. With any luck, I'll be with the Lord and the rest of my family. I hope you and the kids will be OK. Please try to find it in your heart to forgive me and remember that I'll always, always love you.' Maybe I shoulda' left it on the bookshelf. Maybe I shouldna' gone back for it.

He stares out front – seeking some kind of guidance.

> What do I do now, Eunice? Hey? Do I drive back home – quietly get into bed and ... and pretend that all is well?

Pause.

> Or do I get in the car and keep on driving? Keep on driving until I ... 'til I hit something – something hits me ... ?

Pause. He wrestles with his emotions now, trying to make sense of his life thus far.

> I can't tell you what happened, Eunice. I can't tell you where it all began, because I can't even tell it to myself. I've blocked it out. I've cut it from my mind, as sure as if I'd cut it with a knife. I'm ... I'm scared, man. There are so many ... questions.

Pause.

> How long must a life be to be called a life, hey? A few minutes ... days ... ? Sixteen years?

Pause.

> Sixteen years, three months and two days. That's how old I was – the night it happened. The night I stood here ... under this lamppost. [*He hesitates, fighting his own demons.*] Come on! Come on, Eddie ... !

It is crunch time for EDDIE. Now or never. He slams the pole, turning and pointing across the road at the ex-movie house.

> It was right there. Right across the road. It was a rerun of 'Jailhouse Rock'. Me, Lydia Swanepoel, Stevie Blignaut and all the rest had just seen the flick. I had a guts-ache so I didn't feel like our usual jol to the Boulevard Cafe, so I went home. Stevie and the okes went to play sticks in the Station Hotel.

Pause.

That night, I had a dream. I dreamt of Elvis. This was nothing new. I was always dreaming of Elvis in those days. But this night, in my dream, I see him coming out of the light of the lamppost opposite the Carlton Bioscope ... he's singing 'One Night'. 'One Night with You'. This also wasn't so strange, because this was a song I sang a helluva lot myself at that time ...

Pause.

Normally, I woulda' forgotten about it, but – the next day, at school, Stevie and the guys are telling everyone the story about what happened the night before. They'd been kicked outa' the Station Hotel around midnight, and suddenly they hear this shouting round the front. They charge round, there's this woman pointing across the road ... she's saying, yes – yes – she's seen the man who was in the movie! Now Stevie and the guys are laughing, hey – this crazy woman saying she's seen Elvis in the light of the lamppost. But I go all cold ... I know I gotta talk to her ... ! Straight after school, I charge down to the Carlton ... !

'Which one of you's Delilah ... ?'

They point her out. She's sweeping in the aisle.

'Listen, listen ... did you see Elvis last night ... ?'

She carries on sweeping –

'Look, it's not so strange, man. Elvis can astral-travel. He does it in his sleep. I read it in a magazine ... !'

She carries on sweeping.

'He was singing a song, wasn't he?'

She stops sweeping.

'He was singing 'One Night'? 'One Night with You? That's all I'm dreaming of ... call my name, I'll be there ... '

She looks at me ... and as she looks at me I know it. He's calling me. He's gotta be calling me ... !!

Pause.

That night – I don't sleep, hey ... ! I'm lying in bed with all my clothes ... Twenty to midnight, I slip downtown ... I come here to the lamppost ... !

Looking up at the heavens – heartfelt.

No bullshit anymore, man ... ! Why didn't you call Nigel ... !? Nigel coulda' done something with his life ... ! Nigel coulda' sold underfloor heating ... ! Why me, man – why me ... !!? [*Pacing about, tearing up.*] Come on, Eddie ... ! Come on ... !

He just has to get through this. Driving on.

I waited 'til one o' clock ... but, of course ... [*Looking up at the lamplight.*] He doesn't come ... ! So I go home. But long before I get home, I know something's not right ...

He sees it all before him, like he is seeing it for the first time.

There these cop cars ... ambulances ... and now ... I'm trying to get in ... !

'Wait ... this is my house! I live here ... !'

And then I see them – they carrying these stretchers covered in blankets and there's this cop – he's pulling me back ... !

[*Cop, struggling violently with him*] 'He was a very sick man.'

[EDDIE] 'I know ... !'

'He was sick ... '

'I know ... !!'

'He was a very sick man ... '

'I know ... ! I know ... !! I *know* ... !!!'

EDDIE *is crying now it is all coming out.*

They never told me all the details ... ! They never told me what happened that night. All they told me were these fairy stories, like ... they're sitting at the right hand of Jesus now, or ... or they playing with the angels. But ... but that isn't what happened ... that isn't what happened that night ... ! Come on, Eddie ... what happened ... what ... how was ... !

He slams his fist into the palm of his hand, again and again – until he is still – marshalling all his strength and energy into one last effort at confronting his awful pain.

He snaps. He snaps like he nearly did so many times before. He goes to his bedroom ... he takes the .38 army issue special from on top of the cupboard ... he goes to Tienkie's room. He puts the pillow over her head ...

He slams his fist into the palm of his hand – indicating the first fatal bullet that night.

Then he comes through to our room. Me and Nigel. He would've come to me first, but – I'm not there, of course – I'm ... I'm ... [*Looking up at the lamplight.*] But he can't go back now because Tienkie's gone, so ... so ... [*Miming a pillow over a head.*] – Nigel ... !

Another fist-slam into his palm.

Then he goes through to the bedroom ... [*Really cracking up now – a long mournful cry from the depths of his soul as he sees it happening.*] ... Maa-aaaa ... !

There is no slam of his fist for this bullet that took his mother – just a fading away into pitiful, body-wracking sobs – he is nearly there now.

He goes through to the lounge ... and in fronta' the radiogram ...

He puts a fist to his head and jerks as he re-enacts the final shot into the brain of his father.

He bends forward at the waist, sobbing until he can cry no longer. Slowly he rises, looking down at his hands.

I've said it. I've said it. [*An echo of his mother's North Country accent.*] There. There.

All is quiet. It is as if a huge load has been lifted off his shoulders. For a while, absolutely nothing happens. As he walks beneath the lamppost, looking up into the light, it is as if he is walking on air.

Pause.

He takes the suicide note out of his pocket and slowly rips it to shreds. The pieces flutter to the ground.

Pause.

He pats his pockets and takes out his car keys. He looks across the road, up and down the street, and – one last time – up into the night sky. Smiling now, he wonders where he might be ... The King of Rock 'n Roll, who altered the course of his life ...

He speaks the words quietly.

'One night ... '

As EDDIE *begins to move off to his car, we hear the quiet, haunting strains of an unmistakable voice. It is Elvis – with 'One Night'. The song seems to be coming out of the light of the lamppost and as Eddie reaches up (a kind of 'Space Odyssey/Close Encounters' feel here) there is a ...*

Major sound and light cross-fade – as the instrumental build-up leads into 'Just call my name ... ' The sound is banged up, so that we hear these words (and the rest of the song) as if it is Elvis in concert (crowd screams included). Eddie is bathed in pink light – a mirror ball twirls and splashes points of light across the audience. Elvis is suddenly with us and EDDIE *lets go with wild abandon, miming to the song and gyrating as if he were The King himself.*

After a good few bars, EDDIE *stands centre stage, looking out and smiling. A pin-spot picks up his face and the lights fade ...*

The pin-spot fades to leave EDDIE *smiling, Elvis singing and the crowd roaring ...*

Blackout.

Printed and bound by CPI Group (UK) Ltd, Croydon, CR0 4YY

13/04/2025

14656575-0005